Rockne of Notre Dame

KNE

of

Notre Dame

THE MAKING OF A FOOTBALL LEGEND

Ray Robinson

OXFORD
UNIVERSITY PRESS

OXFORD

UNIVERSITY PRESS

Oxford   New York
Auckland   Bangkok   Buenos Aires
Cape Town   Chennai   Dar es Salaam   Delhi   Hong Kong   Istanbul
Karachi   Kolkata   Kuala Lumpur   Madrid   Melbourne   Mexico City   Mumbai
Nairobi   São Paulo   Shanghai   Singapore   Taipei   Tokyo   Toronto

and an associated company in

Berlin

Copyright © 1999 by Ray Robinson

First published by Oxford University Press, Inc., 1999
198 Madison Avenue, New York, New York 10016
First issued as an Oxford University Press paperback, 2002

Oxford is a registered trademark of Oxford University Press

Library of Congress Cataloging-in-Publication Data
Robinson, Ray, 1920 Dec. 4-
Rockne of Notre Dame : the making of a football legend
/ by Ray Robinson
p. cm.
Includes index.
ISBN 0-19-510549-4 (cloth) ISBN 0-19-515792-3 (pbk.)
1. Rockne, Knute, 1888-1931
2. Football coaches--United States--Biography
3. Notre Dame Fighting Irish (Football team)
I. Title.
GV939.R656 1999
796.332'092--dc21
[B] 99-13712

1 3 5 7 9 10 8 6 4 2
Printed in the United States of America

To Mr. Rockne's fellow Indianans—
Tad, Amy, Tyler, and Avery

THERE were things he stretched, but mainly he told the truth.

Mark Twain, writing about Huckleberry Finn

MUCH has been written about Knute Rockne and like some fisherman's catch much has grown with age.

Ed Probst, who attended Notre Dame with Jack Rockne, Knute's youngest son

Contents

Acknowledgments

IN PUTTING TOGETHER my research and reflections about Knute Rockne many people provided invaluable help. I would like especially to thank the following contributors, in no special order: John Heisler, sports information director of Notre Dame and his assistant, Mike Enright; Bill Bilinski of the *South Bend Tribune*; Harald Hansen of the Norwegian Tourist Bureau; Kurt and Karethe Fromberg of Gyldendal Books, Copenhagen; Robert Lipsyte of the *New York Times*; Michael Anderson of the *New York Times*; Dave Anderson of the *New York Times*; David Kaplan of the *New York Daily News*; Steve Robinson of CNNSI; Tad Robinson; Emil Klosinski; Robert Peterson; Arnold Grobman; Edmund J. Probst; Peter Golenbock; Professor Douglass K. Daniel of Kansas State University; Lawrence Scalia; Chris Jennison; Ed Fitzgerald; Joe Goldstein; Dave Camerer; Darrell D. Henning of the Norwegian-American Museum; Johannes Gjerdaker and Jorgen Rokne of Voss, Norway; Herbert J. Curtis; Dr. Samuel A. Nigro; James S. Pacy; H. Baird Tenney; Jean B. Kelley; Linton E. Simerl; Norm Bobrow; Frank Marto; Emmett Stewart Epley; George Newill; Wayne Coffey of the *New York Daily News*; George Vecsey of the *New York Times*; Nancy Griffin; Valerie Sayers; Angelo Bertelli; Alvin Yudkoff.

I would also like to acknowledge my indebtedness to a number of books and other periodicals, including the following: *The Notre Dame Story*, by Francis Wallace; *The Realm of Sport*, by H. Warren Wind; *Football's Unforgettable Games*, by Harold Claassen; *The Encyclopedia of Football*, by Roger Treat; *The Fighting Irish*, by William Gildea and Chris Jennison; *Football's Greatest Coaches*, by Edwin Pope; *Knute Rockne*, by Francis Wallace; *Shake Down the Thunder*, by Murray Sperber; *Sportsworld: An American Dreamland*, by Robert Lipsyte; *The Glory of Notre Dame*, by Fred Katz; "Knute Rockne," by Coles Phinizy (an article in *Sports Illustrated*); *Book of Sports Legends*, by Joseph J. Vecchione; *The Fireside Book of Football*, edited by Jack Newcombe; *The Aspirin Age*, by Isabel Leighton; *Red*, a biography of Red Smith, by Ira Berkow; *Reagan's America: Innocents at Home*, by Garry Wills; *Dementia Pigskin*, by Francis Wallace; *The Red Smith Reader*, by Dave Anderson; *En-*

cyclopedia of Sports, by Frank Menke; *Sportswriter: Life and Times of Grantland Rice,* by Charles Fountain; *College Football,* edited by Christy Walsh; *The Tumult and the Shouting,* by Grantland Rice; *Rockne of Notre Dame,* by Delos Lovelace; *What a Year,* by Alex Morris; *The Greatest Sports Stories* from the *New York Times,* edited by Allison Danzig and Peter Brandwein; *Brass-Knuckle Crusade,* by Carleton Beals; *The History of American Football,* by Allison Danzig; *Collier's Greatest Sports Stories,* edited by Tom Meany; *Hooded Americanism,* by David Chalmers; *Sport: Mirror of American Life,* by Robert H. Boyle; *Great Men and Moments in Sport,* edited by the editors of *Esquire; Rockne: Idol of American Football,* by Robert Harron; *The Madness in Sports,* by Dr. Arnold Basser; *You Have to Pay the Price,* by Earl Blaik with Tim Cohane; *The Saga of American Football,* by Alexander Weyand; *West Point: America's Power Fraternity,* by K. Bruce Galloway and Robert B. Johnson; *Paddy's Lament,* by Thomas Gallagher; *On This Rockne,* by Ralph McInerny; *The Best of the Athletic Boys,* by Jack Newcombe; *My Favorite Football Stories,* by Red Grange; *The Story of Football,* by Lamont Buchanan; *Farewell to Sport,* by Paul Gallico; *Knute Rockne: Man-Builder,* by Harry Stuhldreher; *The American Irish,* by William Shannon; *Prairyerth,* by William Least-Heat Moon; *Sports Classics,* by Harry Siner; *Fair Enough: The Biography of Westbrook Pegler,* by Finis Farr; *The Great War,* by Jay Winter and Blaine Baggett; *John McGraw,* by Charles C. Alexander; *Dempsey,* by Randy Roberts; *Sports Extra,* by Stanley Frank; *Army vs. Notre Dame: The Big Game,* by Jim Beach and Daniel Moore; *Knute Rockne's Pro Football Roots,* by Emil Klosinski; *Creating the Big Game,* by Wiley Lee Umphlett; *Dempsey,* by Bob Considine and Bill Slocum; *Will Rogers,* by Ben Yagoda; *The Ziegfeld Touch,* by Richard and Paulette Ziegfeld; *The Notre Dame 1997 Football Guide; Huey Long,* by T. Harry Williams.

My appreciation and gratitude to Sheldon Meyer of Oxford University Press, who encouraged me to write about Rockne; to Peter Ginna, Sheldon's successor, for his gentle and conscientious prodding; and to my wife and best friend, Phyllis, who has always been unfailingly supportive and generous with her attention and time. A hearty thanks to Joanne Curtis for scrupulously retyping my manuscript; and last but not least, a pat on the head to Penelope, my canine companion, who was a presence under my desk through every chapter of *Rockne.*

Rockne of Notre Dame

Introduction

IN THE ROARING TWENTIES, when sports icons were as potent as bathtub gin, Knute Rockne of Notre Dame was to college football what Babe Ruth was to baseball, what Jack Dempsey was to boxing, what Bill Tilden was to tennis, and what Bobby Jones was to golf. Rockne was one of the most formidable and dynamic figures of that impressionable era, and his reputation was considerably enhanced through florid and excitable sports page effusions, which regularly celebrated his machinations rather than simply report on them.

To this day Rockne is generally regarded as the foremost football coach of all time. If he wasn't that, he was at least the most colorful, dramatic, and original. As a native of Norway, he was also typical of a number of personalities in the 1920s and 1930s who used sports to surmount their exotic backgrounds and to counter a streak of xenophobia that often lurked in Americans. The two greatest ballplayers of that time, the Babe and Lou Gehrig, were of German descent; Joe Louis, the dominant prizefighter, was a black man; the most successful jockey was an Italian, Eddie Arcaro; the baseball manager who won most often was an Irishman, Joe McCarthy; the most adept wrestler was Jim Londos, a Greek.

Rockne's gridiron strategy, his restless enterprise, and his constant salesmanship of the game and himself captured the imagination of millions in the so-called Golden Age of Sports. He was a personality of such stature that when he was killed in a plane crash in the windswept farm country of Bazaar, in western Kansas, in 1931, the funeral services were broadcast over the world. The mourners included President Herbert Hoover in the White House and King Haakon VII in Norway. In a nontelevision age radio had carried the message of Rockne's sudden death to a disbelieving country while also luring hundreds of ghoulish souvenir-hunters to the site of the accident.

In his daily newspaper column, the entertainer and cracker barrel philosopher Will Rogers eulogized Rockne in this way: "We are becoming so hardened by misfortune and bad luck that it takes a mighty big calamity to shock all this country. But Knute, you did it. We thought it would take a president's death to make a whole nation shake its head in real sorrow and say, 'Ain't it a shame he's gone!' Well, that's what this country did today, Knute, for you. You died one of our national heroes. Notre Dame was your address. But every gridiron in America was your home."

From 1918 through 1930 Rockne held forth at Notre Dame as a head football coach who reigned absolutely over his boys on the squad. During this period he guided a succession of national champions, known everywhere as "The Fighting Irish." It seems that almost everyone, from New York's gritty subway alumni to midwestern chauvinists, to bankers and bartenders, to longshoremen and office workers, delighted in rooting for Rockne's South Bend, Indiana, teams. These varied groups had one thing in common: They loved a winner, a fighting winner. And that's exactly what Rockne was all about. Overall his Notre Dame teams won 105 games, lost only 12, and tied 5 times. In five seasons—1919, 1920, 1924, 1929, and 1930—Notre Dame fought its way to undefeated and untied years.

When Lou Holtz resigned as Notre Dame football coach in November 1996, he hinted that one of the reasons for his decision was that he didn't wish to pass Rockne in victories. Holtz's teams had won 99 games at the time. Accepting that Holtz's rationale sounded somewhat peculiar, there is no denying that the legend of Rockne has relentlessly dogged the heels of many of his successors at South Bend.

Rockne's winning record has placed him among such storied coaches as Pop Warner, Jock Sutherland, Clark Shaughnessy, Bob

Neyland, Percy Haughton, Fritz Crisler, Lou Little, Gil Dobie, Bob Zuppke, Hurry-Up Yost, Amos Alonzo Stagg, Bernie Bierman, Howard Jones, and a host of others. But there was more to Rockne than his accomplishments on the field. He was a complicated, enormously ambitious man who was probably more articulate than any other figure ever produced in the game. Those who had listened to his entreaties, humor, sarcasm, and occasional bullying swore that he could talk the birds out of the magnolias. He was, some insisted, an orator of positively Ciceronian dimensions, although his voice was nasal and metallic.

It was Rockne's sublime talent as salesman and talker that caused some critics to adjudge him to be a cynical, image-concerned opportunist who specialized in tinkering with the truth. The sports columnist Westbrook Pegler described Rockne as "a battered oil can giving off champagne." Pegler went on to say that Rockne was "consistently amazed to find himself a great national celebrity who wants to make all the money he can, lest the public suddenly get next to him." These words did not sit well with the thin-skinned Rockne, though the two men did later manage to effect a rapprochement. As facile a speaker as Rockne happened to be, he still hired the professional ghostwriter Christy Walsh and others to write articles that appeared under his name. Such artifice did not seem to give him any qualms.

In his inevitable brown fedora, with the front rim characteristically turned up, Rockne projected a rather unprepossessing figure of a man. At five-eight he was shorter than anticipated, balder than expected, surprisingly spindly-legged (oddly, Babe Ruth had the same celery-stick legs), obese, and remarkably short-armed for a fellow who had caught passes as a college player. His nose, reported to have been painfully mashed in his childhood by an unruly baseball bat, provided his face with the look of an embattled middleweight prizefighter. By the time he was barely thirty years old, Rockne appeared middle-aged and jowly. He had the weatherbeaten mien of a man who had worked under the sun in too many farm fields—which, of course, he hadn't. He was a first-rate athlete but also cherished books and words and might have spent his life as a chemistry professor.

He possessed one remarkable faculty, above all others: He seemed to have an almost terrifying knowledge of the human heart and was determined to exploit his shrewd perceptions to the limit.

He managed to be rough on himself, too. "The only guy dumber than a dumb Irishman is a smart Norwegian," he said with typical self-deprecating wryness.

Looking at one of his linemen, he said: "The only qualifications for a lineman are to be big and dumb . . . to be a back you only have to be dumb."

Rockne was out to perpetuate the football world as a special preserve for American manhood. He urged his Jazz Age collegians, brought up in an era of hot music, illicit booze, flappers, flagpole sitters, fixed fights, and urban crime, to avoid such time-wasting activities as dancing, socializing, and debating. "Get out there where the going is rough," he exhorted his charges. "This world needs rugged men, not flabby, perfumed ones." The thinly veiled homophobia was not, unfortunately, unusual for that time period.

It seemed he was able to get a little bit more out of his players than might have been expected. He achieved this result by preparation previously unheard of on the football field and by his own brand of inspirational leadership. Before certain games he might ask his team to win the game for him or for some greater glory. It was not unusual for him to tell his players that he might be fired if they failed to win. Feigning an illness, he could plead that the recovery of his health depended on a Notre Dame victory. When he asked his team at halftime against Army in 1928 at Yankee Stadium to go out and "win it for The Gipper," the young men *did* go out and win. George Gipp had been a Notre Dame player of immense talent but also of questionable habits off the field. Nevertheless, this particular pep talk, premised on deathbed remarks supposedly uttered eight years before, gestated into a football legend.

In Rockne's scheme of things the quarterback was always the "vicar on the field," an extension of himself. Thus, in his time at Notre Dame, he taught a number of quick, agile, relatively small, speedy quarterbacks all of his tricks and tactics. This list included Harry Stuhldreher, one of the famed Four Horsemen, and Frank Carideo, of the late 1920s teams. Comparing Stuhldreher with Carideo, Rockne once cracked, is like trying to "compare Caesar with Napoleon."

Rockne was a revolutionary in practically every aspect of football. He was a ceaseless innovator and the first to use "shock troops," or subs, to soften up his opponents. Of course, the fact that he had so many enthusiastic players under his command helped him to implement this strategy. He was the first coach to send his team from coast to coast, certainly to reap profits, but also for "intangible" benefits for his players. Rockne needled one of his stars by saying that "you have the nerve to travel twenty thousand miles from Notre Dame and still flunk geography."

He was the first to have the wisdom to carry local water on trips, one of the first to emphasize spring practice, one of the first to break down his players into small groups, rather than mass drills. He was the first to include inept players on road trips because he believed that kids with spirit and brio would help to boost the morale of his team. He *didn't* invent the forward pass, as many believe, but he *improved* on it and learned to exploit it. He popularized the famous Notre Dame shift—to the quarterback's cadence—that ran out of a single-wing formation. He certainly did *not* write the irrepressible Notre Dame "Victory March," but that stirring fight song became as much a signature for his years at South Bend as any other artifact.

As a Protestant coach at a Catholic institution in a state (Indiana) where perhaps a third of the white males were supporters of the Ku Klux Klan, Rockne stubbornly believed that hard work, guts, determination, and savvy could overcome such blatant bigotry. (In 1925 he converted to Catholicism.)

A host of expressions originated with Rockne. Many have become part of the language. "When Rock opened his kisser the throng became silent as a tomb," said Harry Grayson, a tough-talking sports editor of INS. Rockne loved to excoriate "the downtown quarterbacks" and "the mezzanine hurdlers." The latter were those young men who preferred the quiet charm of the tea dance to the grind and pain of the gridiron. "A minute man" was a player who entered a game only a minute before the other team scored.

To play under Rockne at Notre Dame was, for most, an unforgettable experience. His demanding system became a way of life, a mission, a perpetual "scrum." He was a Teddy Roosevelt transplanted to the football arena. Like Roosevelt, he decried "soft living" and believed that colleges could be incubators of a muscular Christianity. The old Rough Rider Roosevelt had argued, disconcertingly to many, that the country should find more ways to "continue the manliness to which the military mind clings." He preached "the strenuous life," opting for a "moral equivalent of war" in the behavior of young men. Rockne never specifically endorsed such reasoning, but his actions and words often echoed Roosevelt's philosophy.

Rockne had been an excellent student himself and was hardly opposed to academic achievement, yet he felt that a man's character probably benefited more from disciplined effort on the football field. Classroom work may have taken a subordinate place in Rockne's scheme of things, though Rockne constantly denied this was the case.

The writer Carl Sandburg, a fellow Scandinavian Midwesterner, tried to explain the old coach this way: "The pure Norse strain made it inevitable for him to push outward whenever he was conscious of a limit."

However, there has been no limit to the ever-expanding and extravagant Rockne legend. The late sportswriter Francis Wallace, a student at Notre Dame from 1919 to 1923 and one of the most avid and lyrical of Rockne's hagiographers, was on hand to assist Mrs. Bonnie Rockne in the lugubrious task of packing away her husband's possessions after he died in 1931. A battered football that Knute's son, Jackie, had played with and treasured, turned out to be too large to be jammed into a trunk. So Wallace suggested to Bonnie that the pigskin might be deflated in order to fit into the trunk.

Bonnie shook her head sadly. "No, we mustn't do that," she said. "Knute blew that one up himself."

So Rockne's breath lived on for years in that football, even as his legend continued to grow.

1

In the Land of Fjords

IN 1888 NORWAY was a country of some two million people. The hamlet of Voss, forty-three miles east-northeast of Norway's western coast port of Bergen, and always frosty until June, boasted fewer than ten thousand of those people. One of these was Knute Rockne, born on March 4 of that year.

On the Lutheran church ledger in Voss it is noted that "Knut Rokne" was baptized there the following month. Later an "e" was added to Knute and a "c" was injected into the last name, for there is no "ck" conjunction in Norwegian. A middle name of Kenneth was also added in time, thus filling out a signature that would become the most celebrated name ever to emerge from Voss.

In the heart of the scenic fjord country, Voss is a tranquil agricultural region of glaciers, ice-tipped mountains, lakes, hills, orchards, and waterfalls. At the turn of the century Voss was a rapidly expanding village, due to a recently opened railway connection with Bergen. A Norwegian guide book of the time characterized the people of Voss as "powerful, bold, very intelligent, and obstinate." At the beginning of World War II Nazi bombers practically obliterated the area, leaving only the thirteenth-century Lutheran church standing. During the raids, which took place over three frightening days, twenty-six people were killed and many others were forced to flee to the hills. Because the Nazis suspected that Voss housed a

Rockne's father and mother came from tiny Voss, in the fjord country of Norway. Courtesy: Culver Pictures.

contingent of Resistance fighters, they had sought to reduce the town to rubble.

Voss remains to this day a popular tourist station and is considered a healthy place to grow up. But after 1888, Knute Rockne and his family did not remain there very long, for that was a time in which close to one-fourth of the population of Norway immigrated to other parts of the world.

In his autobiography, Rockne says he was descended from Enidride Erlandson, a landowner of consequence in Losna, Norway. The Erlandsons presumably refused to have anything to do with Queen Margaret's merger of the three kingdoms of Sweden, Norway, and Denmark, returning instead to the mountains of Voss.

Earlier generations of the Roknes were farmers, though work always remained scarce. So it is no surprise that Rockne's great-grandfather, demonstrating the enterprise later so typical of Knute himself, began to construct farm vehicles with wheels. His son, in turn, built wagons and buggies with seats. On the side he was also a hardware merchant. Life was never easy for these men, but they persevered.

Knute's father, Lars Knutson Rokne, aspired to be a carriage builder, using his woodworking abilities to advantage. He manufactured two-wheeled vehicles called carryalls (*karjol* in Norwegian) and found himself with at least one excellent customer, the kaiser of Germany, who often visited Voss's hills while on his annual vacation. Lars exhibited his handiwork at England's Liverpool Fair one year, winning a prize. This bit of good fortune encouraged him to look outside of the limited boundaries of Voss for a future life for him and his brood.

In 1893 Lars set off for America alone to show one of his carriages at Chicago's World's Columbian Exposition, where Buffalo Bill's Wild West Show was a headliner. The exposition was commemorating four hundred years of progress since Columbus discovered America.

Although Lars's carriage attracted only minor attention at the

Lars Rockne manufactured two-wheeled vehicles in Norway. The kaiser of Germany was one of his customers.

exposition, he was much taken with the bustling, energetic city of Chicago. To this venturesome Norseman Chicago seemed to be a place where one might obtain decent employment, unlike Voss, where jobs were limited. And, after all, one wouldn't get too homesick living in Chicago, for when the winds came whistling off Lake Michigan, it was easy to be reminded of Voss. At this time, too, the stockyards and the railroads for which Chicago had become famous gave the city its roaring vitality, and the nefarious Al Capone hadn't yet been born in Naples, Italy. The Chicago politicians may have been wretchedly corrupt and street gangs caroused nightly, but to a wide-eyed Norwegian immigrant these were mostly invisible phenomena.

Before sending for his family to join him in Chicago, Lars obtained a job as a machinist and went to night school to get a better grip on the English language. As he prepared to become an American citizen, he learned that a portly fellow named Grover Cleveland was the president of the United States.

When, at last, the three Rockne daughters and Knut joined Lars in America, they came through Castle Gardens. Little more than five years old, Knut's only equipment for his new life was, in his own words, "a Norwegian vocabulary, a fervent memory of home cooking and pleasant recollections of skiing and skating among the Voss mountains." (Curiously, when Rockne became a famous adult he journeyed to Europe twice but never again set foot in Voss. Despite this oversight, in 1959 some of the natives in Voss decided to honor Rockne's memory with a small brass plaque that sits, appropriately, on a granite rock near the railroad station. The plaque was dedicated by the American ambassador, Clifford R. Wharton, and states in English that Rockne was born in Voss.)

"How my mother ever managed that tedious voyage, which I still recall with qualms, how she guided us through the intricacies of entry, knowing nothing of English, and took us into the heart of a new, strangely bewildering country without mishap," Rockne wrote later, "is one of the millions of minor miracles that are the stuff and fabric of America." Martha Rockne's strength—pulling up her roots and going to a strange land—emanated from a strong religious faith, going back to the clergymen in her lineage. She had, from the start, always made a point of praying with her family, usually before meals, and, in addition, shared musical moments with them. Knute learned to play the flute under her guidance.

The family put down its first roots in a two-storied red-brick

home, in Chicago's Logan Square District, where the Irish and the Swedes lived side by side in an atmosphere of acceptance and sullenness. As the youngsters played endless hours of corner lot baseball and football, games that were unheard of in Norway, the police treated them kindly.

There were, of course, occasional incidents of fisticuffs. But a paternal cop named O'Goole acted as an arbiter, exercising only a minimum of bias in favor of the Irish. If the Irish lads pummeled the Swedes (all Scandinavians, including Knute, were known generically as "Swedes"), O'Goole would beam broadly and was not inclined to intervene. However, when the Swedes recruited several Italians to balance things out against the bigger "Irishers," O'Goole was quick to note that "the game is getting too brutal."

In time a large Swedish cop was brought in in an effort to provide a counterbalance to O'Goole. In all of these affairs, Knute was generally able to take good care of himself. Despite his small size, he was shifty with his feet and quite adept with his hands at fighting. Though his father was appalled that in a family of artisans Knute turned out to be "all thumbs," one aspect of his son's personality pleased Lars immensely: Knute was not one who could be bullied or pushed around by anybody.

Life wasn't all street games and fighting for Knute. At school

Rockne signed his name as "Kanute Kenneth." He struck the "a" from his first name shortly after to indicate that it was to be pronounced that way but spelled without the "a."

He attended Sunday school regularly and went, with his parents, to the local Luther Immanuel Church. Lars loved music, playing the cornet with some skill, while Martha and the daughters (two more were born in America) played the piano. Knute settled for the flute, which he played with pleasure for the rest of his life.

Football, as it was played by these urchins, was a game without helmets. The football often looked as if it had been chewed up by mountain lions, there were never enough shin guards for players, and one's ears had to be taped down to prevent them from spreading. Knute's parents regarded the game as a form of "modified massacre," banning him from further participation. Such an edict was hard to enforce, for Knute loved the body contact. His folks, of course, thought he was too small for such combat. To them he was too *kraftig* (stocky in Norwegian).

Whenever his parents weren't around to superintend Knute's behavior, he went out to play. He always did a good deal of fibbing about it, but his physical appearance after a game betrayed him. He played for a dirty-faced group, mostly Irish lads, who called themselves the Barefoot Athletic Club. With Knute's help the Barefooters got into a game for the district championship against the Hamburg Athletic Club. Crowds lined the gridiron, or what passed for it, and a half-dozen gendarmes were called on to keep the spectators at bay. From time to time some of the fans would slip away to recharge their liquid batteries at nearby saloons.

When they returned they became rowdy and partisan, even scrambling onto the field to prevent Knute from running for a touchdown. "Not a Hamburg player was in front of me. But Hamburg rooters came to the rescue. They threw me down and swiped the ball," Rockne recalled. Needless to say, when Knute, in his patched moleskin pants, returned home, his face was bloodied. His spirit, however, was unbowed, until the moment that Lars, for perhaps the tenth time, reminded him that he didn't want him playing this terrible game.

In the summer youngsters in the district switched to baseball. Gloves that barely covered the hand were trotted out, and mushy old horsehides were substituted for pigskins. Now, this was more to the liking of Lars and Knute's mother, who regarded baseball as a game where the objective was not to maim an opponent. This was a more sensible, less physical game, they believed, and for that reason the family heartily approved of it—and Knute's participation in it.

Ironically, in an extra-inning game one afternoon against the Maplewoods, another local team, a hot argument developed, with Knute in the middle of it. Never one to dodge a good, old-fashioned donnybrook, Knute ended up getting his nose mashed by a bat flung by an unidentified miscreant. Would Knute Rockne ever have been as renowned without that famous smashed beak? "I got this from *baseball*," Knute proudly announced to his bewildered parents when he marched home from the scene of battle. Thereafter Lars pronounced baseball as *verboten*, while in the winter Knute, this time with the unlikely permission of his parents, was allowed to play football.

2

Boyhood Heroes

IN THE FIRST DAYS of the new century the Rockne family lived near South Side Park, a damaged sore of a ball yard, where Charles "Old Roman" Comiskey ruled over his Chicago White Sox club. Comiskey had assembled a platoon of good pitchers, including spitballer Ed Walsh, Nick Altrock, and Clark Griffith. They managed to do fairly well, even with limited batting support. Under the circumstances the Sox earned the nickname of the "Hitless Wonders," a tag that did not escape the notice of Knute and his pals.

However, it wasn't any of the White Sox players whom Knute chose for his personal heroes. Instead, he was much taken with Rube Waddell, an eccentric southpaw who hurled for Connie Mack's Philadelphia Athletics and who was known for chasing after fire engines and for his sudden disappearances. On occasion this big, gawky, generous soul would take the mound, wave in his three outfielders, and then proceed to strike out the side. Such colorful antics drove Mr. Mack crazy but tickled the youthful fancy of Knute, who admired this enemy of gloom. The fact that Knute had never been near Philadelphia made little difference in his affection for the heavy-drinking pitcher.

The Chicago Cubs, a perennial powerhouse in the National League and residents of the North Side, featured many formidable players, including Joe Tinker, Johnny Evers, and Frank Chance, who were later immortalized in Franklin P. Adams's famous poem. Knute ignored the facile double-play combination and chose as his icon Mordecai "Three-Finger" Brown, who often dueled with Christy Mathewson, known to be as fine a Christian gentleman as he was a pitcher. The durable Brown, who lost parts of two fingers on his right hand as a result of an accident on a farm when he was seven years old, defeated Matty on a dozen occasions despite his handicap. Such courage and commitment caused Knute to hold him in high regard.

But due to the moratorium on baseball activities imposed by his father, Knute soon developed football heroes to replace his baseball role models. One was the dashing quarterback Walter Eckersall, one of the first—and possibly the greatest—of Coach Amos Alonzo Stagg's All-Americans at the University of Chicago. Eckersall had apprenticed at Hyde Park High School in Chicago, where he'd been an eye-catching performer. Knute saw Eckersall play for the first time for Hyde Park, when he crashed the gate to watch the quarterback lead his team to victory over Brooklyn Prep, the Eastern High School champion. Rockne's remembrance of Eckersall pointed up how the young man was prone to hero worship but also underlined his facile way with words.

"I sat spellbound before the brilliant, heady play of a lad named Walter Eckersall. His keen, handsome face, his sharp, staccato calling of signals, the smooth precision with which he drove and countered and drove again, handling his players with the rhythm of an orchestra leader—all this gave football a new meaning to me," wrote Rockne. "When the game was over and the Western players went cheering from the field, shouting the name of Eckersall like a slogan over the defeated Easterners, I tried to get close to the hero of the day. But two or three thousand other youngsters were trying to do the same thing, so I had to go home without a handshake, yet for the first time in a young and fairly crowded life, I went home with a hero. Dreams of how, someday, I might shine as Eckersall had shone that afternoon were my lonesome luxury. For years they were nothing but dreams."

Twenty years later W. B. Hanna, writing in the *New York Herald Tribune*, said that "Eckersall was the best quarterback I've ever seen," while Grantland Rice, the éminence grise of the sporting pages, was even more effusive about the man who had been Knute's first football hero. "No quarterback has ever shown a greater number of great qualities than Eckersall showed in his all-around play," Rice wrote.

When Knute chose his gridiron idols he chose well. Of course, it was easy to appreciate Eckersall, for his name was a constant presence in the Chicago newspapers, as he guided his team to victories over such well-known schools as Northwestern and Michigan.

At age thirteen, when he was still a scrawny 110 pounds, Knute won a spot on the scrubs of Northwest Division High School, later to be known as Tuley High. It took Knute several years to graduate from a lowly substitute to the first team, but he did.

Even as Knute was increasingly involved with football, he also was fond of other sports, such as boxing and track. The latter activity especially won his attention, for he appreciated that it placed less emphasis on his size and weight than either football or boxing. Rockne tried his hand at pole vaulting, with the aid of an old clothes pole. He employed a unique way of practicing for that event by walking on his hands on the pickets of a wooden fence in the rear of a nearby church. This was designed to strengthen Knute's wrists, so important an element in vaulting. In a few years Knute was able to vault as high as twelve feet, four inches, an impressive figure at that stage of his development.

He enjoyed distance running even more, making the high school track team as a half miler—and competing in as many meets as he could find. Many of the city wide events were organized by Coach Stagg, who was then in the incubating stages of his long career as a football coach. Years later, when Rockne was questioned as to whether he had ever met Stagg in the course of competing in distance events, he refused to invent an anecdote, which he was thoroughly capable of doing. Instead, he offered that it was possible that when he dropped out of distance events, "as I invariably did, I may have met Mr. Stagg under the stands."

As a runner Knute learned many lessons about competition, which no doubt were helpful when he became a player and a coach with an overwhelming desire to win. He came to realize, too, the role that prejudice might play in sports. One official at a meet, who had a distaste for the Irish, especially when they were winning too much, once deprived Rockne of a meet record in the half mile. The official simply and stubbornly refused to recognize "Kelly's" (as he called him derisively) record.

Going from one track meet to another, Knute spent precious little time attacking his high school studies. He carried the colors of Irving Park Athletic Club, the Central YMCA, and the Illinois Athletic Club, running against some old-timers who had more ex-

Chicago's Northwest Division High School, class of 1905, included Knute, last row, second from right.

perience than he did. Yet he managed to win his share of races. At the time Knute had every reason to believe that he'd finish high school and then go on to college. Toward that end he saved money from a summertime job of cleaning windows at his high school. Other youngsters at the school, envious of the exalted position that Knute held, smashed many of the same windows he had cleaned. They also marked crude, sophomoric statements on the doors. Knute was immediately blamed for this villainy and was promptly dismissed from his job.

One day, when his entire team decided to skip school to practice, the authorities reacted by breaking up the group and assigning them to different high schools throughout the city. Rockne ended up going to Jefferson High, where there didn't happen to be a track team. Knute was convinced the new assignment was done on purpose.

The series of incidents soured Lars Rockne on his son's high school education, to the extent that he encouraged Knute to leave school without a diploma and search for a job. At this stage of his life Knute hadn't even heard of the existence of a college named Notre Dame. Even if he had known, he didn't have the high school diploma that one needed to attend that institution.

For more than a year, without any specific objective in mind, Knute drifted in a series of odd jobs that offered a minimal challenge to his intellect. Prodded by his father, Knute took a civil service examination for postal clerk. On the surface that didn't appear to utilize his energy or curiosity, yet the exam required the applicant to write an essay. From all accounts Knute's thumb-sucker, "The Advisability of Our Having a Larger Navy Is Becoming Greater Since Japan Whipped Russia" was deemed enough to win him his job at the post office.

In March 1907, at age nineteen, Knute became a clerk at the pay of six hundred dollars a year. His assignment at the main post office was as a stamper. In three months he was switched to the job of dispatcher, at a salary of eight hundred dollars a year. When he resigned in 1910, the same year that Jack Johnson defeated "White Hope" Jim Jeffries to retain his heavyweight crown and the Philadelphia Athletics mangled Knute's Chicago Cubs in the World Series, he was making a thousand dollars a year, which, to him, was a princely sum.

"My prep school was the sorting room of the post office," recalled Knute.

As a dispatcher in the Illinois territory, Knute had tried to memorize every main-line and branch-line train. He considered it a wonderful investment in mental energy, even if many of his coworkers thought he was an overzealous fool for devoting so much time to his job. However, after a while he learned to shirk work with the best of them—by his own admission—but by that time he had saved up enough money to think about going to college.

Even though Knute had no overwhelming desire to expose himself to higher education, the thought occurred to him that if he ever went to college, the University of Illinois at Champaign might be the place for him to go. However, his sister insisted that he *should* attend, if only to please his family. It would be far better, she said to him, than aimlessly hanging around Chicago's Loop or watching the Cubs or White Sox play on lazy afternoons.

Two friends, Johnny Plant and Johnny Devine, teammates from the Illinois Athletic Club, announced to Knute one day that they were headed for Notre Dame. They shared a love of track with Knute, although he'd never known either one of them to talk much about education of any kind. He told them he'd been thinking about Illinois. They said he should forget that and come along to Notre Dame with them. Knute told them he'd never heard of the place and didn't even know where it was. What's more, he contin-

21

ued, when was the last time they'd ever won a football game? Knute may have had a curious mind, but obviously he hadn't done any research on this subject. The fact was that in 1908 and 1909 Notre Dame, under coaches Joe Lantry and Frank Longman, had beaten Fielding Yost's Michigan team one year and had lost only to Michigan the other year, while playing to a o–o tie with Marquette, in a total of seventeen games. In *all* of the other games, Notre Dame was victorious. True, their schedule, aside from Michigan and Marquette, included a lineup of humpty-dumpty, whistle-stop schools such as Wabash, Hillsdale, Ross Poly, and Michigan Agricultural. But those were the years when the South Benders had difficulty booking the more prestigious teams playing intercollegiate football.

Knute finally decided to join his friends at Notre Dame because he felt he could get by with less money there, with the help of a job. "I went down to South Bend with a suitcase and a thousand dollars, feeling the strangeness of being a lone Norse Protestant invading a Catholic stronghold," Rockne wrote.

It took more than a modicum of courage for Knute to head for the University of Notre Dame du Lac in Indiana. At twenty-two, he was considerably older than most first-year men, looked oddly out of place with his irregular nose and prematurely bald head, and had only the thousand dollars to carry him through what he anticipated would be a four-year educational process.

Without Plant and Devine along with him, to keep him company at a school that was a day's ride from Chicago, he probably never would have left home.

3

Notre Dame

AT THE START OF the twentieth century, Catholic colleges—the first in the United States was Georgetown, founded in 1789—were few and small, rigid and spartan in discipline, and generally not up to the academic standards of most other non-Catholic schools. Isolated, for the most part, from the American mainstream, many Catholic institutions suffered from gnawing inferiority complexes and a dearth of first-rate students. Notre Dame was no exception to this stereotype, for in the last years of the nineteenth century no young man or boy would suffer a turndown at Notre Dame as long as he could find enough money to pay for his tuition and upkeep. Students seemed to come and go at Notre Dame, and entrance requirements seemingly did not exist. Other, non-Catholic, schools, with specific entrance standards and growing endowments, looked askance at places such as Notre Dame, thus creating a sense of paranoia and resentment at South Bend and other Catholic institutions.

Religious orders such as the Christian Brothers, the Vincentians, the Society of Jesus, the Franciscans, the Marist Brothers, the Augustinians, and the Dominicans, had founded the Catholic schools throughout the country. In Notre Dame's case the founding order was the C.S.C. (the Congregatio a Sancta Cruce or the Congregation of the Holy Cross), a small French group begun in 1820.

In 1836 the bishop of Vincennes, Indiana, Simon Bruté, traveled to the seminary in LeMans, France, in a quest for men who might come to America to preach the gospel and educate the Indians and the incoming white pioneers of the diocese. One of those he discovered was Rev. Edward Frederick Sorin, C.S.C., a twenty-two-year-old steeped in French culture and possessing the body of an athlete. Sorin evolved into a person of considerable energy and charm who had more business acumen than one might have expected to find in someone of such comfortable background.

Father Sorin encouraged six brothers of the order to join him in a journey to America, with the objective of starting a college. On this odyssey of faith Sorin and his followers were beset with several harsh difficulties, not the least of which was the shortage of money and an inability to speak the English language. The group was forced to ship out to America in steerage, in a "company of French comedians and German Protestants," so the voyage of six weeks was hardly a pleasure cruise.

Once in America, Father Sorin accompanied his men by boat, horse, cart, and canal to Vincennes, where they built a school in the wilderness. But it was only temporary quarters, for at this stage an additional team of seven brothers, all from Ireland, then joined them, under orders from their religious superior. Their target was a nine-hundred-acre tract of land owned by the order on the northern border of the diocese, at the south bend of the St. Joseph's River. They arrived there in November 1842, just as the seasons were changing.

"Everything was frozen, yet it all appeared so beautiful," Father Sorin wrote. "The lake, particularly with its mantle of snow, resplendently white, was to us a symbol of the purity of Our Lady. . . . Like little children, in spite of the cold, we ran from one end to the other, perfectly enchanted by the beauty of our new home."

It was not easy working through the harsh winter, but the group was able to make bricks from the soft marl beds found near the lakes. Sorin also was able to persuade some local Protestants to join a number of Catholics into cooperating on the building effort. The first structure that was completed—later known as Old College—was near a replica of the Grotto of Our Lady of Lourdes. Father Sorin's quixotic dreams for his college had to be somewhat temporized, for revenue was limited usually to the one hundred dollars tuition paid by the students.

Other structures gradually made their appearance on campus,

including stables, dormitories, farms, a bakery, and a post office. Notre Dame, Indiana, was established as a separate post office, with Father Sorin nominating himself as postmaster.

By January 1844 John Defrees, a state senator and Methodist friend of Father Sorin, obtained a charter for the university, by a special act of the state legislature. That didn't put any money into Notre Dame's coffers, but it did give the school the official recognition that Father Sorin eagerly sought. At one point Father Sorin even commissioned a group of brothers to venture forth to the California Gold Rush of 1848, but this adventurous scheme failed to yield any appreciable dividends. Instead, the effort, in which Sorin's minions joined forty thousand other prospectors, produced only a censure from Father Sorin's superiors in France.

The hundred-dollar fee was guaranteed to feed a young student, wash and mend his clothes, and provide medical attention, as well as cover the complete courses, ranging from spelling to reading to grammar, history, astronomy, and surveying. If parents found themselves short of money, which often was the case, Father Sorin would oblige them by accepting any useful articles they might offer as barter. Often furniture, grain, or hogs were used. If a student chose to pursue an elective subject such as Latin, that might bring an extra-well-fed hog in exchange.

The Notre Dame student body—in the beginning years it was about four hundred—were sons of tough, hardworking people. Francis Wallace, the popularizing historian of the school, described them as "an advance guard of civilization." They could be farmers, storekeepers, trappers, mechanics, day workers, or plainsmen.

In time Notre Dame's enrollment was augmented by the influx of many young peasant emigrants from Ireland, who had departed their mother country, leaving the smell of thousands of graves behind them. These desperate people came to America in the middle of the nineteenth century, traveling on miserable British "coffin ships" as they sought to escape the stress, horror, and widespread famine that swept Ireland in 1846 and 1847. With Ireland's pivotal potato crop poisoned, more than two million had died of hunger from the "bad sickness." Another two million left the country, never to return. Author Thomas Gallagher compared the departing Irish to "Israelites fleeing Egyptian bondage." They were not an educated class, but for those who gravitated toward the Midwest and Notre Dame, Father Sorin offered hope as long as they were willing to work hard from early morning until darkness.

There was also an infusion of additional students during the Civil War, most of whom were housed in a new, five-storied building. But Father Sorin's diligent work soon suffered a serious setback when a great fire enveloped the campus in April 1879, destroying every building except the church. The loss was estimated at more than two hundred thousand dollars, with insurance covering only one-fourth of the damage.

At the time of the disaster Father Sorin, traveling widely as the superior general of the Congregation of the Holy Cross, was in Montréal, preparing for a trip to Europe. When he heard the news, he hurried immediately to the scene of the smoldering ruins. The sight of it would have been enough to destroy the spirit of a lesser man. But Father Sorin was determined that his ambitions would not be smothered by the flames of the fire.

The religious community had assembled at the church under the aegis of Father William Corby, the president of the school. Father Sorin joined them. Father Corby's credentials as a patriot and man of faith had been established during the American Civil War, when, as an Army chaplain at the Battle of Gettysburg, he had given mass absolution to the troops. (His act was later memorialized on the Notre Dame campus by a statue of him, with his right arm raised to the heavens, as he ministered to the Irish Brigade. When football became the school's fighting symbol, students often irreverently suggested that Corby's arm was signaling to the referee. "Fair Catch Corby," they called the statue.)

What Father Sorin told those gathered in the church that day was just what they needed and wanted to hear. First he prayed with them as they desperately sought words of solace. Then Father Sorin, sixty-five years old, spoke resolutely about the future of Notre Dame. "If all were gone, I would not give up," he told them. The pep talk may have been invented that day. Certainly Rockne himself couldn't have delivered it any better.

If it can be said that one man inspirited the South Bend community, Father Sorin was that individual. Within six months Notre Dame was literally rebuilt. When the reconstruction ended, the campus even had a larger administration building, and St. Mary's, a school for girls, was founded. "Our Lady loomed higher in the sky from a wider golden dome," wrote Wallace.

In the ensuing years Father Sorin never failed to win the help of the "synthetic alumni," those Protestants who pitched in when they were needed. Curiously, even in the fading years of his dominance, Father Sorin, a reconstructed Frenchman, spoke critically of the Irish as a "disobedient group." Few Irish at Notre Dame would have fought him on that point. Yet the presidents and faculty he lured to Notre Dame were all Irish—this despite the fact that non-Catholics at the institution numbered close to 20 percent of the student body. It was Father Sorin's strategy—and very much the strategy of Rockne when he became football coach—to welcome Protestants and Jews to South Bend. "Their attendance helped the school financially and built positive relations with these communities," wrote author Murray Sperber.

By the time Father Sorin died of Bright's disease, on October 31, 1893, at age seventy-nine, Notre Dame was still a relatively small school, still not heavily endowed, and still considered to be a school where baseball was preferred over football. In fact, football was played for the first time at Notre Dame as an intercollegiate sport in 1887, in a game against the University of Michigan: Michigan won, 8–0; touchdowns were four points at the time.

It was just a question of time before Notre Dame would take up football in earnest, for in other parts of the country, especially in the East, such prestigious schools as Harvard, Yale, Columbia, Rutgers, and Princeton were already heavily committed to the sport, while playing seven- and eight-game schedules. In the rugged and masculine atmosphere of Notre Dame it was inevitable that football, like all sports, would become an important part of the agenda. However, nobody could have dreamed of its eventual role in promoting the name of the school.

Few college baseball players at the turn of the twentieth century were playing in the professional leagues. But Notre Dame was already represented in those ranks by the celebrated Cap Anson, who had spent a single year at South Bend before turning pro in 1871. Aside from the Chicago White Stockings' Anson, other Irish names, such as John J. McGraw, Cornelius McGillicuddy (Connie Mack), Ed Delahanty, Iron Man Joe McGinnity, and Wee Willie Keeler dotted the rosters of professional baseball teams. In the world of boxing Irish-American pugilists had won great renown. Foremost among them were Boston's strong boy John L. Sullivan, who boasted he could lick any "son of a bitch in the house," and his rival, San Francisco bank clerk James J. Corbett. Boxers such as Sullivan, Corbett, Jake Kilrain, and Paddy Ryan earned the nickname of "Fightin' Irish." In time the footballers of Notre Dame would inherit that cognomen, which gave off echoes of heart and pugnacity.

4

Knute Suits Up

WHEN ROCKNE FIRST set foot on the gracious, gently rolling campus of Notre Dame, the school, with its six student halls, was still struggling and praying for its place in the sun. Set well away from any large, crowded metropolis, Notre Dame, living alone on mattresses of green grass, was an environment of stately Gothic buildings whose spires pointed to the heavens. Ringed by farms, a cemetery and a forest, Notre Dame was embraced by two lakes, St. Mary's and St. Joseph's. Dotting the area were countless sycamores and strategically located religious statuary. Football, mostly of an informal, intramural variety, was played on Cartier Field.

The school's first two coaches, James L. T. Morrison from Michigan and H. G. Hadden, didn't spend much time preparing their charges for competition. It was not until Frank Hering arrived in 1896 to study law that the sport began to be taken seriously on campus. An outstanding student and orator, who many years later, it is said thought up the idea of Mother's Day, Hering had played quarterback at Chicago under Amos Alonzo Stagg. Although he wasn't a full-time coach at Notre Dame, Hering believed in the sport and was instrumental in booking Michigan in 1887. Notre Dame also succumbed in two subsequent encounters against the Michiganders. Michigan was a member of the newly formed Western Conference, an organization that Notre Dame was eager to join.

However, the Irish were informed that they weren't a large enough institution to be admitted to the conference. There was some truth to the fact that Notre Dame didn't match the size of the other schools. But the rejection hurt Notre Dame's pride, for they knew that they were regarded as a "slum college," with loose eligibility rules—just a bunch of low-life Catholics trying to get ahead in the world. As well, there were constant accusations that several of Notre Dame's players had previously competed for other colleges. Forced to lick its wounds from such continued slights, Notre Dame bided its time, waiting to extract suitable revenge on the athletic field.

Hering left Notre Dame in 1898, ten years after the South Benders had registered their first victory in football against the Harvard School of Chicago (no relationship to the Harvards of New England). By the time of Hering's departure, Notre Dame's powers-that-be were convinced that football, as well as other sports, such as baseball, could play a significant part in attracting students to South Bend.

Despite this belief, the position of football coach at Notre Dame remained as impermanent as that of a French cabinet minister. In 1906 Tom Barry, a former player at Brown and a student, like Hering, of the law, was hired. Barry attempted to see to it at once that Notre Dame adhered to all the regulations of the Western Conference. Yet the Irish still weren't invited to the table.

However, Michigan still remained on the Irish schedule. In Barry's first year Michigan was barely able to eke out a 12–6 win over Notre Dame. Considering that Michigan was generally recognized as the champions of the West, this was quite an accomplishment for Notre Dame. The loss was Notre Dame's only defeat of the season and just their second defeat in three years. Even if the school was beating teams such as Olivet, St. Vincent, Hillsdale, Chicago P&S, and Albion, hardly major powers, there was no denying at this stage that Notre Dame was now a threat to be reckoned with by Michigan and other brother teams in the western loop.

By 1909, when Michigan met Notre Dame again, this time at Ann Arbor, the Wolverines were no longer members of the Western Conference—but that was by their own design. Notre Dame still wanted in—but it didn't happen. In eight previous meetings Notre Dame had lost to Michigan each time. Now, under the guidance of Frank "Shorty" Longman, who had played on Fielding Yost's "point a minute" teams at Michigan and had succeeded Barry as the Irish coach, Notre Dame completely outplayed the Michiganders in every phase of the game. Yost, always known as a bombastic orator, had used the Michigan locker room before the game to accuse Notre Dame of a variety of high crimes and misdemeanors. He charged that Notre Dame had "employed" the services of two linemen, George Philbrook and Ralph Dummick, who presumably were not eligible to play. No slouch at pregame dramatics himself, Longman subscribed to the notion that if he threatened to lick every man on his squad, he could maintain absolute control. In this instance he challenged his men to drub the high-and-mighty Wolverines or face the consequences. Having played under Yost, Longman wanted more than anything on earth to upend his old master.

And that's exactly what Longman did. The score was 12–3 in favor of Notre Dame, as fullback Pete Vaughan became the first of Notre Dame's football legends: He smacked into the goalpost with such force that the post left a startling imprint on his back. At least that was the story that a succession of Notre Dame presidents related for years on the banquet circuit, inaugurating a tradition of captivating myths that never ceased to seize the imagination of several generations of Notre Dame supporters.

"The victory places Notre Dame far in the lead for Western honors and with a claim to eastern superiority as well," wrote Leo Cleary in the *Scholastic*, a local publication. In addition, Notre Dame proved it was far from parochial in its outlook, for the team included players from twelve states, most of whom were directly recruited by Shorty Longman.

So when Rockne entered Notre Dame's portals in 1910 as a freshman, he didn't invent football, as some South Benders would have you believe he did. At the time Notre Dame was already installed on the football map, despite the best efforts of the Western Conference and men such as Yost, who grudgingly would have denied them a legitimate place in the gridiron world.

Even the rousing Notre Dame Victory March—"*Cheer, cheer for old Notre Dame, Wake up the echoes cheering her name, Send a volley cheer on high, Shake down the thunder from the sky . . .*"— which has brought millions of Notre Dame partisans to their feet over the past century, was already being chanted by the time Rockne reached South Bend. It was written by brothers Michael and John Shea, both of whom attended Notre Dame before Knute got there. Neither did Rockne get there first with his inimitable pep talks, for Longman's oratory was a precedent for Rockne's verbal gymnastics. (Years later Rockne would make fun of both Longman and himself when he would tell an anecdote about a veteran lineman who listened somnolently to Longman's locker-room exhortation, then turned to a fellow player and mumbled: "Don't you think Shorty wasn't quite as good today as he was last week?")

Thus, the winning tradition, the love of sports, the fight talks were the vogue at Notre Dame even *before* Rockne brought his own fiercely competitive disposition onto the premises.

Rockne's career, from the early boyhood years in Voss, to his days roaming the crowded streets of Chicago, through his undergraduate years at Notre Dame, and then as the most celebrated football coach in America, did not need padding by press agents. Yet, the mythmakers were always hard at work. Take, for example, the words of the Rev. John Cavanaugh, who served as president of Notre Dame during a good part of Knute's days at the school, both as player and as coach.

"He [Rockne] was duly matriculated after severe examination and was assigned to the 'subway' in Sorin Hall. The subway was a group of half subterranean and half superterranean rooms," wrote Father Cavanaugh in an introduction to a Rockne autobiography published in 1930. The good Father Cavanaugh then went on to describe how Knute met his first roommate, Charles "Gus" Dorais, a young man from Wisconsin, at Sorin Hall. In time Dorais would become one-half of Notre Dame's first great passing combination, with Knute winding up on the receiving end of Gus's passes.

Unfortunately, the tale about Knute and Gus was not true. It happens that Knute was first assigned as a freshman to single quarters in Brownson Hall, not to Sorin. Knute was given little more than a claustrophobic cubicle in Brownson, scarcely enough room for his own body, his bed, and his toothbrush. His clothes had to be kept in a community locker room or a study hall desk. Dorais was nowhere on the premises at that time, insists Coles Phinzy, who reported on the matter in *Sports Illustrated* in 1979. However, Dorais, equally as impecunious as Rockne and weighing, soaking wet, about 145 pounds, ultimately did become Knute's roommate in Corby Hall—but that was some time after the two aspiring footballers had become acquainted.

Rockne's own memory about his football days at Notre Dame often was highly selective and served to underline his penchant for the melodramatic. He once wrote that the first time he went out for football, after a varsity player named Joe Collins had recommended him to Coach Longman, he "froze" when he tried to punt.

"Longman immediately yanked me out of the game and sent me back to Brownson Hall. I was a dub, a washout, not even good enough for the scrubs," wrote Rockne. Except it didn't happen that way, even if Knute preferred to tell yarns about himself that made him out to be the laughingstock of his companions. It was a facet of Knute's personality that he often chose to belittle himself, inventing self-disparaging stories that made him appear clownish.

In fact, Knute started the first game of his freshman year, against Olivet College of Michigan. As Notre Dame won, 48–0, the overage "scrub" played fullback and performed quite well, if one can believe the reports in the *South Bend Tribune* and the student-managed *Scholastic*. In its pregame stories the *Tribune* emphasized that "Rockne" (which is how they spelled his name) was hitting the line in "a way that would make a billy goat blush with envy." In the postgame story Rockne was commended for his adept running, although it was pointed out that he did fumble a few times.

In his freshman year Rockne played at fullback and left end, with a measure of success at both positions. Notre Dame lost to the Michigan Aggies and tied Marquette while winning its other games.

By the time 1911 rolled around Jack Marks, formerly of Dartmouth, had been hired as head coach. He utilized Knute's talents mainly at end, appreciating that Rockne's speed and elusiveness, plus his knack at shifting his weight and his body, were priceless assets. Under Marks Notre Dame won six games, tied two, and did some minor experimenting with the forward pass. The following year they played a seven-game schedule, trouncing St. Viator, of Kankakee, Illinois, in the opening game by the track meet score of 116–7. They then went on to win all six of their remaining games. Pitt and Marquette were the foremost victims. The other victories came over teams that didn't usually measure up in fast company. Several Notre Dame players, including Knute and Dorais, were hailed on the South Bend campus as men of certain All-America caliber, but Walter Camp, the old Yalie who handed down *ex cathedra* judgments each year on All-America selections, ignored them. This only served to support the feeling at Notre Dame that they were being discriminated against.

Rockne credited Longman and Marks, especially the latter, with helping to develop certain aspects of his character. Although Rockne felt that Longman was something of a bully, full of bombast and overheated rhetoric, he acknowledged that the coach had instilled in him "the value of perseverance . . . he pursued his players with a ruthless energy that got results."

Marks, on the other hand, was more imaginative than Longman and certainly less strident. Marks made Notre Dame into a cohesive unit and was never reluctant to try new approaches to the game. If he had a weakness it was his penchant for trying to run up the score. At the same time, he was understanding and sympathetic. In his memoir Rockne tells of how Notre Dame, under Marks, found itself playing one afternoon with only ten men on the field. Their big fullback, named Meyers, sat under a blanket on the bench, refusing to take the field, against Butler. Marks inquired what ailed him, and Meyers, shy and embarrassed, complained that he had suffered a bump on his knee. At first angry, Marks smiled quietly at Meyers's response and didn't pursue the issue further. Another coach might have exploded at the young man. It is clear that Rockne learned something from Marks's behavior—that there were times when it was useful not to be tough and unyielding.

If Longman had remained as coach there was a good chance that Rockne might have left football and Notre Dame behind him. So it was his good fortune that Marks arrived to rekindle his enthusiasm for the game. Then, faced with the death of his father in his junior year, Rockne, who had learned doggedness from his parent, again considered leaving school, since he also had the burden of supporting his widowed mother.

"It seemed imperative that I quit Notre Dame," Rockne later wrote, "but my wise sister interposed. 'If you quit,' she warned, 'you may earn a living someday but it will be as a mail dispatcher.'"

All during his playing years at Notre Dame Rockne continued to have serious concerns about money. He worked at all sorts of odd jobs, including one as janitor in the chemistry lab. On one occasion he was accused of stealing a gallon of experimental wine from the laboratory. He ran a risk of expulsion, but the charge was proven to be false. As a result of the incident "my reputation was not glamorous," acknowledged Rockne.

There is good reason to believe that Rockne engaged in any number of boxing matches at neighborhood clubs for small purses. In this endeavor a Notre Dame student, Joe Gargan, often acted as his manager. (Gargan later became a brother-in-law of Joseph P.

Kennedy, ambassador to the Court of St. James and the father of President John F. Kennedy.)

Rockne's need for sources of revenue was always so acute that he devised a plan, according to Edwin Pope, writing in *Football's Greatest Coaches,* to charge a fee to those students who wanted to bring edibles into Sorin Hall after curfew hours. Knute and Dorais were able to do this because their basement room offered the only entrance to the building. Pope said that they imposed a "radiator fee" for freshly matriculating students, who were bamboozled into believing the radiators would be lifted from their rooms unless they coughed up the "service" charge to Rockne-Dorais, Inc. Such tales, of course, were colorful but were hardly designed to improve Knute's reputation. They did underline, however, how enterprising the two students were.

There's little doubt about another aspect of Rockne's four years at Notre Dame. His splendid academic record, as well as the opinions of those who worked with him and knew him, reveal that he was an exemplary student. He worked diligently at his studies and also became involved in a number of extracurricular activities. He was one of the editors of *The Dome,* the school's yearbook, and played the flute ("a vigorous, industrious performer," said Father Cavanaugh) in the school's orchestra, for which he received modest expense money.

From the fall of 1910 until he received his Bachelor of Science degree in pharmacy in June 1914, Rockne posted an overall average of 90.52 percent. Of the thirty-one grades that he received in those years, only five fell below 90, and of those, all were in the 80s, with an 81 in "Poetry and Poets" being the lowest.

He got a 98 in English in 1913, a course that emphasized oration, an early sign that Knute was warming up for his role as one of the most eloquent football coaches of all time. He received another 98 in anatomy in 1914. He topped all of his marks with a 99 in bacteriology in his sophomore year. In that same year he had a 97 in chemistry. Despite a heavy emphasis on science and chemistry, Knute showed his intellectual versatility with a 94 in a senior philosophy course.

Rockne's intense participation in sports, including the captaincy of the football team in his senior year, plus a load of outside jobs and extracurricular activities, failed to deter him from achieving near-perfection as a student, and magna cum laude honors.

Though Knute was basically shy, especially in the presence of girls, he delighted in playing in campus theatricals and often took the role of a clown or of a woman. Francis Wallace tells of how Knute, decked out as a squaw and garnished with a heavy, clumsy wig and long braids, was a convincing female impersonator. Some amateur psychologists might conclude from this that Rockne was pleased to ridicule women. The explanation, more likely, is that it was not uncommon in those years for college productions to feature boys playing girls—and not in the most flattering way. For years many colleges, such as Princeton, Columbia, Penn, and Harvard, staged their annual college shows with male chorus lines full of exaggerated breasts and lipstick-bearing, muscular athletes.

Father Cavanaugh paid an extraordinary tribute to Rockne, saying that Knute was never unprepared in the classroom. "He would sit in a room with three or four intimates discussing football, politics, or some other subject, follow the conversation accurately, participate in it occasionally with sapient remarks, while studying a textbook with seemingly complete concentration . . . in addition to his scientific studies, he was deeply interested in cultural things and read broadly in general literature. His was a case of brain hunger. It remained so until the end of his life," said Father Cavanaugh.

Father Julius A. Nieuwland, a brilliant priest-scientist on the Notre Dame faculty, who discovered the process that made synthetic rubber possible, was much taken with Knute. He declared that Knute was the most remarkable student he ever knew. It was not unusual for Knute to argue vigorously with Father Nieuwland, for Nieuwland was inclined to accept Rockne as an equal, an enormous compliment considering Nieuwland's accomplishments.

Many students at Notre Dame knew *about* Rockne—but didn't know him. He managed to keep to himself, thus causing some to regard him as standoffish, a judgment with little truth. Rockne, in fact, owned few material possessions and chiefly prized a monogram sweater. When it got too cold in South Bend he might borrow an overcoat. "You must remember about Knute," said Dorais, who probably knew him better than anybody else, "that he came to school about four years older than the rest of us. His thoughts tumbled out in such bursts that he was inclined to stammer. This was the reason for his machine-gun oratory of later on—but he had trouble becoming a speaker. He seemed to have more problems than the rest of us."

As a student Rockne remained uncertain about his abilities to express himself properly. When he finally was called upon to address a student pep rally, he did so with great anxiety.

"There were natural hurdles to be jumped in a social sense," Rockne recalled. "As a lone Norwegian, always mistakenly dubbed a Swede, I had difficulties among so many Hibernians. When I was called on at the rally, and having heard somebody call somebody else a dumb Irishman, I had the good fortune to remark, 'There's only one thing dumber than a dumb Irishman.' Before the bricks could fly, I explained: 'a smart Swede.' "

With his agile mind and tongue, Knute was a master, even in his student years, of the quick retort. When he played baseball with a group of Notre Dame footballers against a bunch of seemingly harmless seminarians, his team lost. After being chided about his team's poor performance, Knute explained that "the diamond just wasn't square."

With the last year of his undergraduate playing career coming up in 1913, Rockne had hardly unpacked, after a glorious summer lifeguarding with Dorais at Cedar Point, Ohio, on Lake Erie, when he was greeted by someone he'd never seen before—Jesse Harper. Harper had been hired as the new football coach after a stint at Wabash College, a small Crawfordsville, Indiana, school that invariably gave Notre Dame a stubborn challenge in football. Father Cavanaugh signed Harper, once a substitute for Walter Eckersall at Chicago, for a reported five thousand dollars, an impressive sum in those days. For that kind of money Harper would have to serve as full-time football coach, baseball coach, and athletic director.

Harper's arrival also signaled that Notre Dame was about to confront head-on its continual scheduling difficulties with Western Conference teams. This state of affairs was threatening to diminish Notre Dame's growing role in the football arena. Coming from the University of Chicago, where he'd learned his tactics from Coach Stagg, one of the game's foremost innovators, Harper was expected to get bookings against the powerful teams of the region. This supposedly would assure more prestige as well as more money for Notre Dame. Though Harper was unable to break through the intransigence of the Western Conference, he accomplished something more significant: For the first time in Notre Dame history, he lured Army onto Notre Dame's football schedule.

5

On the Wings of the Forward Pass

IN THE EARLY YEARS of the twentieth century college football had a classic case of split personality. The game's popular image had reached a high peak. Large crowds flocked to see football in the Midwest and East (twenty-five thousand attended a game between the University of Chicago and Michigan in 1905, while in the same year Harvard and Yale played before forty-three thousand fans, the largest crowd ever to watch a football game); Frank Merriwell, the fictional footballer created by writer Gil Patten, cavorted gallantly in the pages of books and magazines. The president of the United States, Teddy Roosevelt, insisted that he would "disinherit a boy if he were to weigh the possibility of broken bones against the glory of playing football for Harvard." Plays such as *The College Widow* and *Brown of Harvard* enjoyed lengthy runs on New York's Broadway stage, and young men who engaged in the sport were regarded as courageous warriors involved in a splendid cause.

On the other hand, from 1880 to 1905 there were more than 325 deaths reported in college football, plus 1,149 serious injuries. In one year, 1904, 21 players were killed and more than 200 injured. The following year 23 deaths were recorded, as well as a shocking number of debilitating injuries.

Clearly something had to be done, and the nabobs who ran the sport addressed the crisis by tinkering with the rules in an effort to reduce the inherent savagery of the sport. Some changes of equipment were introduced by football "intellectuals" such as Pop Warner and John Heisman, to cushion the impact of body contact. But the game continued to resemble legitimized warfare, causing some schools, such as Columbia, Stanford, Northwestern, and California, to drop the sport.

Late in 1905 President Roosevelt, still a staunch defender of physicality in sports, summoned a group of prominent coaches and administrators to the White House. Fix the sport and reform the rules, he warned, or the game had to go. Even with such a caveat, nothing was accomplished, although the see-no-evil coaches promised to get back to the president.

Finally, in the spring of 1906, and over the opposition of the protective Walter Camp, the college chieftains came forth with some substantial rule changes, including reduction of playing time to sixty minutes (from seventy), a striking prohibition against hurdling (leaping in the air to make a tackle) and mass momentum plays, and a requirement that there be six men on the offensive line. However, the most dramatic new rule was the legalization of the forward pass.

Since 1895 Heisman, the Auburn coach, had been agitating to open up the game through the use of the forward pass. "It will scatter the mob," said Heisman. "Speed will supplant bull strength. Lighter, faster men will succeed the beefy giants whose crushing weight maims or kills opponents." By 1903 Heisman, then at Clemson, won over some converts, including Stagg and Navy coach Paul Dashiell. Even before the legalization, two Kansas schools, Washburn and Fairmont, experimented with the pass.

Most teams were skittish at first about utilizing the newly sanctioned pass. But the handwriting was on the wall as several schools began trying the weapon. The most valid claim for the first use of the pass was that of St. Louis University, in a September 1906 game versus Carroll College of Waukesha, Wisconsin. Eddie Cochems, the St. Louis coach, had long been an enthusiast of such strategy. The St. Louis style of forward pass, as implemented by Cochems, was different from the pass being thrown by eastern players. Cochems did not protect his pass receiver by surrounding him with teammates, as was the case in the East.

In October 1906 Wesleyan University completed a pass against Yale for an eighteen-yard gain, and Marietta College of Ohio turned a forty-seven-yard pass into a touchdown against Ohio University the same month. St. Louis made so much progress with the pass that they put together eleven victories in an undefeated season in 1906.

Years later, in commenting on the adoption of the pass, Lou Little, who coached successfully at Georgetown and Columbia, declared that it "revolutionized football." He emphasized that it took almost heaven and earth to move the officials to make the change—but he felt that it saved the game.

Rockne and Dorais, spending the 1913 summer at Cedar Point, where many Notre Dame students found employment, had not been following the debate about the forward pass. They were just too busy, for they held several jobs at the summer resort. When they weren't tending to their lifeguarding, they filled in as night watchmen, room clerks, and restaurant checkers. But more important for Knute, it was during that long, hot summer that he met and wooed Bonnie Skiles, a pretty young woman from Kenton, Ohio, who was a waitress at Cedar Point's Grill Room. Remarkable to say, Knute found himself eating most of his meals there!

Aware of Knute's all-around athleticism, Harper had given him a football, suspecting that there would be some spare time for the team's new captain to play catch with Dorais on Cedar Point's sandy beach. On any number of sweltering summer afternoons the two friends, in their bathing suits, rehearsed a variety of pass patterns. "Go out to the right," Dorais would say to Knute—and Knute would go right. "Go down the middle," and Knute would follow that command. A small man who probably would never have been able to play in the modern game, Dorais possessed a surprisingly strong arm. More than that, he was accurate, throwing short as well as long. Rockne, on the other end of Dorais's tosses, helped to make Dorais look as good as he did. Spectators on the beach were not used to seeing a football thrown in the air. After all, footballs were made for kicking. They marveled at the insanity of these two young fellows exhausting themselves under a broiling sun.

"What Rockne learned was that if there was an art in throwing, there was also an art in receiving," wrote Harry Stuhldreher, who later became one of Notre Dame's cleverest quarterbacks in the early 1920s. "He saw that it wasn't finished work to have the ball bounce against his arms and chest when he caught it. There were too many chances for fumbles that way. It cut your stride and didn't look neat. So Rockne patterned himself after a baseball player and caught it with his fingers. Each day at Cedar Point they worked

By 1913 Knute was a talented, 145-pound end at Notre Dame who had already started to lose his hair. Courtesy: AP/Wide World Photos.

seriously on perfecting their respective jobs. They learned that the pass had infinite possibilities and could be incorporated into a system of play, along with the line buck, end run, or kick. At night they discussed how Army would be bowled over in the fall, with Dorais calling the signals and tossing the ball and Rockne catching it and running."

By the time Rockne and Dorais returned to South Bend in the fall, not only were they in prime physical shape but also they had cemented a symbiotic relationship that would soon make Notre Dame gridiron history.

As he tried to expand Notre Dame's schedule to include more prestigious schools, Harper (who later became a cattle baron in southwestern Kansas) was a straight-from-the-shoulder guy, quick to seize an opportunity. When he first arrived at Notre Dame he had heard that Army, one of the country's powers in football, might have an open date on its 1913 schedule. Yale had apparently dropped its game with Army due to an increasing perception that the West Pointers scoffed at eligibility rules.

If that was the case, Harper wanted to take advantage of the moment. Some colleges nursed similar negative feelings about Notre Dame's standards, but anti-Catholic bias also played a role in such attitudes. As a Protestant, Harper hoped he could dissuade recalcitrant colleges from practicing their biases.

As far as ethics were concerned, Army's continual flouting of the rules was so notorious that Notre Dame looked pristine by comparison. Many talented athletes enrolled at Army to play football, even after they had "prepped" for several years at other colleges. This practice was widely known and criticized, causing Army to be regarded as pariahs in some circles or, at the least, hypocrites.

Harper was familiar with Army's porous "code of ethics"—but that did not discourage him from pursuing a booking with the soldiers on the Hudson. In those days schedules were usually pieced together along about February. "We wanted an eastern game," Harper once recalled in a conversation with columnist Red Smith, "so I wrote a letter to Army's chief athletic officer. They happened to have that open date and they took us. Why did I pick Army? I don't know. It was a good game, and good games weren't easy to get in those days. Maybe it's true, as all those old stories go, that Army was looking for a midwestern opponent that wouldn't be too tough for them, when they got my letter. But as far as I know, my letter was all there was to it."

The final agreement with Army, arranged by Harper, included a guarantee of a thousand dollars—Army originally offered only six hundred dollars—for a game that would be played on the plains of West Point on November 1, 1913. No admission would be charged and there was no money paid for concessions; most spectators brought their own sustenance in that era. On the road the Notre Dame squad traveled light, with each man carrying his own equipment, in either a satchel or a paper bag. Many of the eighteen Notre Dame players didn't even show up with cleats.

With the addition of Army to its schedule, authorities at South Bend were pleased that Harper had put together the toughest group of games in the school's history. Penn State, Texas, and St. Louis University were also listed as opponents, giving Notre Dame the most heterogeneous collection of rivals ever to compete against them in a single season.

However, the inclusion of Army on Notre Dame's schedule wasn't perceived by non–Notre Damers as a watershed mark in American intercollegiate football. In reporting on the event the

New York Times wrote that Notre Dame's players "were coming all the way from South Bend, *Illinois*," a geographical error that underlined the reality that outside of their home base Notre Dame remained faceless and press agentless. On the other hand, when some chroniclers continued to portray Notre Dame as an obscure school, emerging from the wilderness to face the Army behemoth, this was equally misleading.

Notre Dame did not show up in the best shape possible, for in the opening game of the season against Ohio Northern—won by the Irish, 87–0—Knute suffered an injury to his rib that took him out of the game after the first half. He didn't return to action that day, and the injured rib was still annoying him on November 1.

Behind the U.S. Military Academy's fortress on that chilly, cloudy afternoon in 1913 the whitecaps churned up the Hudson River, and Storm King Highway loomed in the distance. Almost five thousand spectators, including the entire gray-clad Corps of Cadets who had paraded in the morning, and General Leonard Wood, the Army's chief of staff and hero of the Spanish-American War, were on hand for the proceedings. The civilians in attendance sat bundled in overcoats in Cullum Hall Field's circus-seat bleachers, and not a few of them raised their voices and their unfamiliar pennants on behalf of the "foreign" visitors. Never again would Notre Dame's football team have so few of their fans present at a Notre Dame–Army spectacle.

Even if some Cadet adherents had regarded this game as little more than a quiet, friendly workout, Army's coach, Charlie Daly, had not taken the game that lightly. Daly had assigned Captain Tom Hammond, a former teammate, to scout the Irish in their game against Alma the week before the Army–Notre Dame contest. Hammond watched Notre Dame roll to an easy 62–0 victory over Alma, a tiny school in central Michigan. Notre Dame's ground attack, led by Dorais's slick quarterbacking and Ray Eichenlaub's ferocious running, must have impressed Hammond, for when he returned to West Point he whispered in Daly's ear that Army had better prepare its defenses for a grinding duel on the ground. Thus the West Pointers preferred to give only scant consideration to Notre Dame's air attack; they agreed with the maxim that when you throw a pass one of three things is bound to happen and two of them are bad.

As the captain of the Notre Dame team, Knute walked to midfield before the game, accompanied by his opposite number, Benny Hoge of Army. They watched the flip of the referee's coin, which would determine who would receive the kickoff. Knute called the flip correctly and chose to receive, something of a surprise in those defense-oriented days. What happened in the four quarters that followed is best recalled in Knute's own words, making the usual allowances for his literary inventiveness:

"For the first part of the first quarter it looked like a workout for Army. The Army line outweighed ours by about fifteen pounds to the man. They pushed us all over the place before we overcame the tingling realization that we were actually playing Army. I recall Merillat (Army's right end) shouting, 'Let's lick those Hoosiers!' So I asked him in a lull if he knew how the word 'Hoosier' originated. We started it at South Bend, I informed him. 'After every game the coach goes over the field, picks up whatever he can find, and asks, 'Whose ear is this?' Hence Hoosier.

"The gag didn't work so well, but something else did. After we had stood terrific pounding by the Army line, and a trio of backs that charged in like locomotives, we held them on downs. Dorais said: 'Let's open up.' It was amusing to see the Army boys huddle after a first, snappy eleven-yard pass had been completed for a first down. Their guards and tackles would come plunging into us to stop line bucks and plunges. Instead, Dorais, stepping neatly back, would flip the ball to an uncovered end or halfback. We marched up the field, gaining three first downs in as many minutes.

"Our attack had been well rehearsed. After one fierce scrimmage I emerged limping, as if hurt. On the next three plays Dorais threw three successful passes in a row to our right halfback, Pliska, for short gains. On each of these three plays I limped down the field acting as if the thing farthest from my mind was to receive a forward pass. After the third play the Army halfback covering me figured I wasn't worth watching. Even as a decoy, he figured I was harmless.

"Finally Dorais called my number, meaning that he was to throw a long forward pass to me as I ran down the field and started out toward the sidelines. I started limping down the field and the Army halfback covering me almost yawned in my face, he was so bored. Suddenly, I put on full speed and left him there, flat-footed. I raced across the Army goal line as Dorais whipped the ball and the grandstand roared at the completion of a forty-yard pass. Everybody seemed astonished. There had been no hurdling, no tackling, no plunging, no crushing of fiber and sinew. Just a long-distance touchdown by rapid transit.

"At the moment I touched the ball, life for me was complete. We proceeded to make it more complete. The Army resisted. They charged with devastating power and drove through us for two touchdowns. The score at the half was Notre Dame 14, Army 13. In the second half Army changed its defense to meet our open game. It didn't work. Dorais, always alert, reversed our tactics. We now reverted to the Army line-plunging game, with Ray Eichenlaub as our spearhead. He ripped the Army line to pieces.

"In the last quarter Army closed up again to stop Eichenlaub. Dorais instantly switched tactics, opening up with a fresh barrage of passes that completely fooled the Cadets.

"Fitzgerald, our guard, took special interest in McEwen, Army's great center. Their contest grew personal as Army lost ground and we gained it. Superheated between scrimmages, wild words flew. Fitzgerald closed in on McEwen. He socked McEwen on the jaw, then instantly yelled, 'Hey, referee!' The referee turned around just in time to see McEwen crash home a right to Fitzgerald's nose. McEwen was promptly ordered from the game. But as captain of our team I had to stop and explain that both boys had been too boisterous and so the referee let them both stay in the game. From then on their decorum was more proper.

"Hard-fought to the end, this Army game with its final score of

Rockne snared one of Gus Dorais's passes and ran for a touchdown in the first Notre Dame–Army game in 1913. Courtesy: Department of Sports Information, University of Notre Dame.

35–13, in our favor, does not quite represent the difference in playing quality between the two teams. Army was much better than the score showed. It was, however, the first signal triumph of the new open game over the old, battering-ram Army game. And Army was quick to learn. Press and football public hailed this new game, and Notre Dame received credit as the originator of a style of play that we had simply systematized. We had demonstrated that the forward pass could be an integral part of offense. Recognizing this, Army, later in the year, went out itself and forward-passed to a victory by 20–9 over one of the strongest Navy teams."

Rockne was aware, and so were Dorais and Coach Harper, that Army could not solve the pass problem within those few moments of the Notre Dame–Army game. The best way to thwart the pass, Rockne always maintained, was to rush the passer—but Army didn't appreciate that fact at the time.

Following the game, in which the "newfangled" forward pass was thrown for distances of up to forty yards by Dorais, a baseball pitcher in the spring, Harper visited with Army's coaches. The West Point people expressed their astonishment about Notre Dame's air efficiency, 13 completions in 17 tries, for 243 yards. The Sunday *New York Times* joined in the praise, with this headline: "NOTRE DAME OPEN PLAY AMAZES ARMY." The accompanying text went on: "Football men marvelled at this startling display of open football, as the Westerners flashed the most sensational football ever seen in the East. . . . Bill Roper, head coach at Princeton, who was one of the officials at the game, said that he always believed that such playing was possible under the new rules, but that he had never seen the forward pass developed to such a state of perfection."

Certainly the game was not the birthplace of the pass, and many teams went on using the ground attack. However, the forward pass now had become a true offensive weapon, and in the years to come football would never be the same again.

"The Dorais-to-Rockne forward passing combination," wrote John Kieran, a columnist of the *New York Times*, "wakened the East to the possibilities of the new open game on the gridiron. Others had used the play before and had used it well but it so happened that this Dorais-to-Rockne tandem was the inspiration and example for a new system and a new spirit in football over a wide territory."

An amusing story made the rounds after the 1913 game. According to this yarn Dorais, Rockne, and Coach Harper remained over at West Point, by request, to teach the soldiers some of the finer nuances of the pass. The story added to the drama of that weekend. But there simply wasn't any truth to it, for late that Saturday afternoon the entire Notre Dame squad hopped a Pullman for Buffalo. The players spent Sunday gazing at the wonders of Niagara Falls, then they took a day coach home to South Bend, where they arrived on Monday. There they were greeted by what appeared to be every citizen in town, accompanied by brass bands, bonfires, speeches, singing, and cheering.

"You would have thought," said Rockne, "that we had repulsed and conquered an attack on the West by the East." He was so pumped up by the histrionics surrounding this contest that he later wrote that "the nationwide discussion of Notre Dame by football followers after the first Army game had tremendous effect on our own varsity spirit . . . everybody in the school, save the older professors, wanted to be a football player. I recall even Cy Williams, the home run slugger with the Philadelphia Nationals, clamoring for football togs. But the baseball coach barred Cy from football, afraid that Cy might get hurt."

This is a nice little story. But there are some things wrong with the narrative. One was that Williams, once an architecture student at Notre Dame, and an outstanding member of the track team, was the Notre Dame baseball coach in 1913, having finished as a student in 1912. In 1910 he actually played on the football team alongside Knute. Williams became one of the National League's better home run hitters after he started his major-league career in 1912 with the Chicago Cubs. He couldn't possibly have been eligible to play football again for Notre Dame in 1913. But such details never stopped Knute's inventiveness.

On June 15, 1914, Rockne graduated from Notre Dame with an academic record as distinguished as his sports achievements. Knute leaned in the direction of medical school at that moment. But it was also clear he couldn't get the football field out of his mind.

6

A Man Must Coach

AT THE END OF Rockne's career as a student-athlete of many parts, he had managed to win recognition outside of the boundaries of the campus—more, perhaps, than any other Notre Damer. He had been chosen on Walter Camp's third All-America team of 1913 at end, thus breaking through Camp's disdain for the South Bend institution. Rockne was also the holder of the Central AAU indoor record of twelve feet, four inches in the pole vault, a remarkable feat considering his size and build. Now he had to decide what to do with the rest of his life.

There was never a time in those early years that he wasn't in need of money. If he was to attend medical school (Notre Dame has never had a medical school), an idea that had been percolating in his mind for several years, he knew he'd also have to hold a coaching job to make ends meet.

One such coaching opportunity appeared to open up at a St. Louis high school, which happened to be near the University of St. Louis Medical School. He pursued the St. Louis connection after Dorais, also eager to begin post–Notre Dame life as a coach, had won a coin toss with him over an open job at St. Joseph's, in Dubuque, Iowa. With Dorais off to take the post at Dubuque, Knute was prepared to begin the St. Louis job when Father Nieuwland intervened. Father Nieuwland told Knute that there might be an opening for him at Notre Dame as a chemistry assistant. Then, if Harper could come through with an assistant coaching position, Knute could remain at Notre Dame, where his heart was. Completing the demanding portfolio at South Bend, Rockne was also named as track coach, thus assuring that he'd have little time for frivolity or for the books and newspapers he loved so dearly.

By the summer of 1914 Rockne had known the dark-haired, petite and piquant twenty-two-year-old Bonnie Gwendoline Skiles for about two years. Father William F. Murphy also had gotten to know Bonnie during that time, and he regarded her "as a pious and devout young lady, without ostentation, modest in her ways and manners," surely a person of womanly qualities of a superior kind. That was quite an endorsement, even allowing for a certain level of hyperbole. But others who had formed her acquaintance agreed. It is even likely that Rockne never had another girl.

At the beginning of July 1914 Bonnie went to see Father Murphy at his Church of Sts. Peter and Paul in Sandusky, Ohio, not far from Cedar Point, where Knute and Bonnie first met. As Father Murphy knew, she had recently converted to Catholicism, and had

Bonnie Rockne with Knute in a 1930 photo. Courtesy: UPI-Corbis-Bettmann.

come to ask him to preside over her forthcoming marriage to Rockne. On July 15, with Dorais as best man and Marie Balzarina, one of Bonnie's friends, as the other witness, Father Murphy pronounced Knute and Bonnie as man and wife in a simple ceremony in the rectory at Sts. Peter and Paul Church. (In the years to come Bonnie would give birth to four children—William, 1915; Knute, Jr., 1918; Mary Jean, 1920; and John Vincent, 1926.) The two then settled down in a white frame house at St. Vincent's Street in South Bend—and there was never a taint of scandal after their marriage. That is remarkable, considering that Rockne lived most of his adult life in a public vortex, where prurient rumors, invented or otherwise, could quickly follow fame.

From the start of his marriage it was Rockne's aim to preserve the privacy of his clan. Never an isolated or unsociable man, Rockne usually specialized in openness, enjoying the company of others and the give-and-take of conversation. However, when it came to his family and to Bonnie he didn't believe that any of them should be part of his public life. He cherished the privacy of his home life, protecting it almost as energetically as he sought an edge on the gridiron.

Making about two thousand dollars a year from all his activities, Rockne found it wasn't enough to support his growing family. So he did what many other athletes at Notre Dame and elsewhere had done: He played professional football. Even in his final year as a player at Notre Dame Rockne managed to pick up extra cash as long as the regular Notre Dame schedule didn't get in the way. True, such professionalism was generally frowned upon, especially in the East, among the older and more established schools. Because of that attitude many players chose to use assumed names when they played for money. However, Knute was generally quite open about it, using his correct name, which was often featured in programs and in newspaper accounts.

Though he was cognizant of the prevailing ethic, Rockne apparently felt there was nothing to hide.

There were a number of catch-as-catch-can professional teams roaming the Midwest. They usually played on Sundays, when college games ordinarily were not scheduled. In those early days, before any such institution as the National Football League existed, these independent clubs eagerly sought local college stars. Naturally, both Rockne and Dorais were pursued. These pro teams came and went, scarcely giving fans a chance to remember their names.

The Rockne home at South Bend, Indiana, wasn't far from Notre Dame's playing fields.

It wasn't unusual for an athlete to play with different clubs on successive Sundays.

The teams boasted names such as the Shelby Blues; the Detroit Indians; the Racine Malted Milkers; the Steubenville Wildcats; the Toronto Tornados; the Dayton Triangles; the Cincinnati Celts; the Muncie Blues; and the Fort Wayne Friars. There were unverified reports that Rockne played for any number of these teams during a single season. But it appears that his professional indoctrination probably took place in 1913 for the Friars, after Notre Dame's regular season had ended with a victory over Texas. Playing for a Michigan team against the Friars, George Greenburg was taking his pregame warmups when he noticed a stocky Friar player performing the same exercises across the field. Convinced that he'd seen the player somewhere before, Greenburg walked over to take a closer look. Sure enough, it turned out to be Rockne.

At the time Rockne was still paying obeisance to the injunction against professionalism, so he asked Greenburg to call him "Jones." Greenburg was willing to oblige, for the relationship between the two men went back to the time they both boxed for an athletic club in South Bend. Boxing was not on the agenda at Notre Dame, so Rockne went out and fought under such pseudonyms as Kid Williams and "Jab" Brown. The purses were meager, as little as five or ten dollars a fight, but such cash always came in handy for Rockne.

Needless to say, moonlighting for the football pros required more than a simple desire to make extra money. In Rockne's case it demanded an enormous amount of energy and adrenaline, for he was already coaching the game on the side.

In 1913 the Muessel Brewing Company of South Bend was seeking to spread the good name of its beer, so it decided to sponsor a football team, much as local businesses were doing around the country with baseball clubs. Muessel was aware of the growing prominence of Rockne, the captain and end at Notre Dame, so they approached him with the proposition to coach the Muessel Brewers for ten to twenty-five dollars per coaching session. With Notre Dame playing several games at home, Rockne would then be in a position Sunday to work his sorcery on the Brewers. In his first year Rockne's beer team went undefeated, though it played one tie, with the South Bend Century Club.

Another Indiana team, the Huebners, then challenged the Brewers for area supremacy. They were so solid a club that the Muessel company went ahead and acquired them, naming them the Silver Edges, after the company's other popular beer. Right on the heels of this purchase, Rockne was asked if he'd like to coach them as well as the Muessels. Never one to turn down a chance to augment his bank account, Rockne signed an agreement to coach *both* teams for three hundred dollars a year, all the while retaining his job as Harper's assistant. Writer Emil Klosinski has described how Rockne dealt with his dual chores, in a mad whirl of activity that could have been integrated into a Marx Brothers movie:

"After finishing practice at Notre Dame, Rockne would hop into his little Overland to conduct practice sessions with both teams. Laurel Street School had a well-lighted playground, as did St. Stephen's School, which was separated from Laurel by two houses in between. One team would practice on one marked and lined field, while the second team would do the same on the other. Rockne took on a Notre Dame sophomore sensation, halfback Stan Cofall, as an assistant, and both of them alternated between the two squads, teaching whatever Rockne had planned for that particular session. Rockne signed a memorandum to the effect that he would receive three hundred dollars for the season and his assistant would get a hundred dollars. An additional fifty dollars in expense money for each made the entire deal worth five hundred dollars.

"Rockne had nothing to do with the game scheduling for his two teams. Kaz Boinski, the manager and captain of the Silver Edges, and Slicie Niezgodski, the Muessel manager, did the scheduling. However, Rockne, as coach, was a spokesman for *both* teams and would usually reveal his game plan after summoning a reporter to watch the practice sessions." (Even at this stage Rockne had a keen instinct for the use of press exposure, and he would work assiduously to manipulate stories to his own advantage.)

When the Silver Edges were preparing for the Fort Wayne Friar game, the *Tribune* covered the story thusly: "Knute Rockne has been giving the Silver Edge squad strenuous workouts this week, including drill in some fancy plays he picked up at Yale . . . the Edges are improving under Rock's tutelage and look like the best independent bet in the state."

Earlier in the year Yale had crushed Notre Dame, 28–0, in a game that was played at New Haven. With Harper booking this new opponent, Notre Dame was granted a small seven-hundred-dollar guarantee by Yale, a sum that the coach was willing to accept to coax the elitist Bulldogs onto the Notre Dame schedule. What Harper and his aide Rockne hadn't bargained for was Yale's tricky use of Canadian-style rugby laterals, which contributed to Notre Dame's first defeat in three seasons. Later that same year Army defeated Notre Dame, gaining revenge for the beating that Rockne, Dorais, and company had inflicted on them in 1913.

Notre Dame's alumni, getting used to being on the winning side, were in a state of rage over the loss to the Yalies. They were especially annoyed at the toothlessness of the Irish attack, which failed to produce a single score. Curiously, there was no outcry at the many roles that their new assistant coach, Rockne, was assuming all over the state. Had Rockne's multiple jobs hurt Notre Dame's preparation? Nobody seemed to think that Knute's outside activities had anything to do with Notre Dame's failure against Yale.

Shortly after the Yale game, responding to his critics, Harper installed a different shift for his team, something he'd latched onto while playing for Stagg.

Rockne himself described how the shift, known thereafter as the "Notre Dame shift," came into being. "After the Yale debacle of

1914 Harper called me into his Pullman drawing room. He announced that we had to break into something new, something different in the way of offense . . . he began drawing marks on a piece of paper, describing a backfield shift similar to what Chicago had used when he was quarterbacking. Harper's variation was that he made the shift cover more than twice as much territory. I added the idea of shifting the ends in and out, with a stationary line. Harper wanted the line to shift also, but after a day or two of experimenting, the line, from tackle to tackle, was left stationary. That was the beginning of what is known as the Notre Dame offense," Rockne explained years later in the *New York World*.

The shift operated out of the single-wing offense, which had been invented by Pop Warner at Carlisle in 1906. The single wing featured four backs, with the fullback and tailback positioned alongside each other, some 4½ yards behind center. Either man was available to receive the ball directly from center. The quarterback would line up behind the strong-side tackle in an unbalanced line, as the wingback lined up on the outside shoulder of the tight end. Under such an alignment there were no wide receivers. The tailback in this whole scheme was the key player, for he did the running and passing. When the center snapped the ball back to him the tailback would run off tackle or around the end, with blocking provided by other backs or linemen. Rockne added the shift to make the offense more deceptive and to provide momentum to the attack. As the ball was snapped from center the backs were already in motion, giving the offense a quick head start. In time, rules changes in 1924 and 1927 forced the shift to come to an absolute halt prior to the snap of the ball.

This new wrinkle wasn't enough to beat Army, but Rockne thought it might be useful for one of his pro teams, so he instructed Cofall to teach it to the Muessels. Meanwhile, Rockne set about preparing his Silver Edges for the state championship tilt against the Friars, a grudge match that had ignited a rash of betting among supporters of each team.

Betting on games, among followers of the independents, as well as the colleges, was rampant. Though there were rarely accusations leveled against players betting *against* their own team, there was little doubt that it must have occurred on occasion. Players on one team often pooled their money before games, with the winner taking all. Being a highly competitive fellow, it is a good guess that

Rockne probably participated in this practice. If not, he certainly had an awareness of how endemic it was among the people who played alongside him.

It was also no secret that professional gamblers and con men flooded the South Bend area. This was only a few years before the infamous Black Sox scandal occurred in major-league baseball during the 1919 World Series that took place between the Chicago White Sox and the Cincinnati Reds. In that series eight Sox players were accused of throwing games, and later were banned from baseball for life. Any number of Notre Dame students hung out at local taverns and pool halls, where they were proud to back up their team with bets.

Such was the atmosphere before the game between the Friars and the Silver Edges. The Edges came out on top, 22–12, setting off an angry protest among Friar supporters, who, having dropped considerable sums betting on the Friars, pointed to "five Notre Dame ringers" in the lineup of the Edges. Several Fort Wayne sportswriters were willing to investigate such charges. Within a short time they turned over five names to Notre Dame's authorities. These men, whose names were never revealed publicly, were suspended.

At the time Notre Dame's officials failed to connect Rockne with the ringer "conspiracy" despite the fact that they were fully aware of his role as the coach of the Edges. South Bend newspapers, which presumably were read by the Notre Dame hierarchy, had reported that quarterback W. Smith was appearing in practice sessions of the Edges, after having played for Notre Dame against Wabash. How did he wind up in the Edges' lineup? By the following year Smith had become Jimmy Phelan, who stayed around Cartier Field long enough to win Notre Dame's captaincy in 1917. Rockne's rationale for using such ringers as Phelan was based on a fact he knew too well: Many of these young athletes had an urgent need for extra money.

Who did Notre Dame's officials think had recruited the five ringers to play against the Friars? A month or so after the investigation by the Fort Wayne journalists, Notre Dame quietly reprimanded Rockne—a slap on the wrist, if ever there was one—by suggesting that he trim down his activities among the pros. Rockne did lay off coaching for a year, but then went right back to his professional activities. He continued to compete for money as a player, also.

In 1915, despite the strenuous evangelizing of the former baseball players, Billy Sunday, who preached against the evils of drink and the sinfulness of Sunday football, the Canton Bulldogs met up with the powerful Massillon Tigers in another edition of their torrid rivalry. On this occasion the Bulldogs were to be augmented by the presence in their lineup of the celebrated Jim Thorpe. Thinking they were not powerful enough, Massillon went out and hired both Rockne and Dorais to play at Massillon's Driving Park against Thorpe, who was making his debut as a pro after a brilliant career at Carlisle. As might be expected, the contest set off an epidemic of betting in the whole state of Ohio.

Because of Thorpe's appearance in Canton's backfield—and perhaps the rumors that Rockne and Dorais would also play for Massillon—the price of tickets went from fifty cents to seventy-five cents. More than six thousand raucous fans bought their way into the park, and they saw Massillon score a surprisingly easy victory by 16–0.

By Thorpe's own account and the eyewitness observation of others, Rockne did not fare well that afternoon against the great Sac and Fox athlete. This is how Thorpe recalled it: "Rockne told so many tales—some of them obvious inventions—that I have been often asked if his story about his meeting with me was actually true. The answer is that it was. Rockne was playing regular left end for Massillon that afternoon. He was a little guy, not a great end, in my opinion, but with lots of fire and determination. All through the first quarter he kept tackling me and I began to get annoyed, much as a beast would against a pesky horsefly. Finally I said to Rockne: 'Let old Jim run. People come to see old Jim carry the ball. Let old Jim run.' This was in the second quarter. Rockne ignored my advice and tackled me the next time I came around his end. I said to him again that people come to see old Jim run. You better let old Jim run. It was a moment later that I went wheeling around Rockne's end again and he made a dive at me. I gave him the hip and the knee. That's all that Rockne remembered the rest of the afternoon. People had come to see old Jim run. When people do that, Jim runs."

Rockne played in another game against Canton that season but with the same results for him. Dorais turned out to be more the star than Rockne was, as Massillon won again, in a game that again provoked frenzied betting by Canton's backers.

In 1916 Rockne was back coaching with the pros, this time for the Jolly Fellows Club, a team that had borrowed talent from both the Muessel and Silver Edges teams. The Jolly Fellows was a collection of football-crazy South Bend businessmen who had pursued Rockne for some time to coach their team. Finally he consented, but he limited his coaching sessions with the team to two per week, seemingly a concession to Notre Dame's priests, who had admonished him for his involvements with outside coaching and playing. Also, Rockne arranged never to travel with the Jolly Fellows, which meant he couldn't be blamed for the rowdy and execrable behavior of some of his players. Before one game in Rockford, Illinois, a group of Jolly Fellows went out and got roaring drunk. As a result, they lost. A disciplinarian such as Rockne never would have tolerated such a drunken spree had he been on hand. Under Rockne that year the Jolly Fellows won eight games and lost two. They duplicated that mark the next year, after America had entered World War I in the spring.

A particular curiosity of Rockne's playing appearances with the pros were those occasions when he would make a deal to play with a certain team, then get somebody else to fill in for him. Few people outside of South Bend, where Rockne's picture often appeared in the newspapers, had the faintest notion of what he actually looked like. So it was relatively easy to carry off such a masquerade. Since Rockne wore the typical football helmet of the era—flat on the top, round at the sides, and perhaps three sizes too big—that didn't make it any easier to identify him.

"The fans wanted Rockne," reported the football publication *The Coffin Corner,* "and, by gosh, in collusion, they gave them Rockne." In reality it was often a former Notre Dame teammate who took his place.

Up to this point, when Rockne was urged to attack the incubating pro game because of the excessive gambling surrounding it and the undesirable element that had become part of its environment, he refused to do so. He couldn't overlook how much he had learned by playing and coaching in the professional ranks; he remained grateful for the extra money he had earned as a pro and felt that he shared a common bond with many of those men who were involved in the sport. He may have been acting badly when he played under an assumed name, or when he got someone to play in his place, but he could carry hypocrisy only so far. He figured he owed a debt to the game. To assail the sport would have smacked of ingratitude, to say the least.

In serving his Notre Dame coaching apprenticeship under Harper, Rockne had the good fortune to deal with a man who was willing to give him a large measure of authority from the start. Harper was keenly aware of Rockne's credentials and knew that Knute possessed outstanding leadership qualities. An early hurdle that Rockne had to confront was that he was giving orders to men who not long before had been his peers on the Notre Dame team. But he managed to handle that problem with firmness. One day, when a lineman rejected Rockne's advice to crouch low and make a quick, balanced charge, Rockne thumbed the young man off the premises. "Get out of here," Rockne said with a growl at the player. "Turn in your suit. We won't be needing you around here anymore."

Harper was quick to back up his assistant in the brouhaha, despite the fact that Rockne hadn't consulted him ahead of time. The lineman was then forced to apologize to Rockne, under explicit orders from Harper. After the apology the player was then permitted to return to the squad, with his tail between his legs.

Rockne always felt that this incident had marked him as a martinet, which wasn't exactly a job qualification he had sought. However, he did feel that it wasn't too harmful to have such a reputation, provided "that the coach doesn't work too hard at it." Any such reprimand, Rockne felt, should always be followed by a friendly relationship off the field.

During his years as an assistant to Harper, Rockne also acted as the team's trainer, for he believed that his background in chemistry and a modest knowledge of anatomy gave him the right to pass judgment on player injuries and other misfortunes. But it didn't always work out too satisfactorily for either the player or Rockne. A lineman named Ducky Holmes complained of an injured leg in a practice scrimmage one day. Rockne examined the limb and applied his own homegrown diagnostic skills.

"If you can wiggle those toes," Rocky told Ducky, "the leg's not broken." Ducky did manage to wiggle his toes, leading Rockne to assure him that he was only suffering from a bad sprain. "Get in there and shower, then I'll tape it up," said Rockne. However, an X ray subsequently revealed that Ducky had actually sustained a fractured shinbone. Despite his error, Rockne remained on the job.

As Harper knew, Rockne was always quick to spot a weakness in an opponent and to know how to exploit it. In November 1915 Notre Dame played a powerful Army team led by Elmer Oliphant, the star of the West Point offense.

For three quarters the game was a grinding o—o tie. Then, as time was running out late in the fourth quarter, Oliphant attempted a fifty-yard field goal with a drop kick. In those days that's how they did it. The ball had the right direction and distance. But it hit the crossbar at dead center, then bounced straight up into the air. As Army's rooters held their breath, the ball tumbled back onto the playing field. The attempt had failed.

Harper's attention was turned to an injured Notre Dame player at this instant, so the inspiration had to come from Rockne. When Army's team lined up on defense for the last moments of the game, Rockne studied Oliphant's face. The great star's disappointment over the flubbed kick was so palpable that Rockne motioned to the speedy little Dutch Bergman to go into the game. At the same time, he sent in another substitute with a play designed to exploit Oliphant's dejection.

"Tell Cofall [Stan Cofall was the halfback] to pass one to Bergman behind Oliphant," instructed Rockne. Cofall faded back to his own forty-five-yard-line, then unleashed a pass to Bergman, who was hurrying down the field to the left. The bullet pass was a bit high, but Bergman speared it. Crossing the Army thirty-yard-line at full speed, Bergman dodged behind Oliphant and proceeded to outrace him to the goal line for the winning touchdown.

"Slip" Madigan, another Notre Dame player, recounted the incident in later years: "Rockne kept saying, 'Look at that Oliphant, he's got his head down, he's asleep at the switch, he's out of the game, he's down at the mouth.' I don't think that Harper realized it before this day, and neither did the boys, but after Rock's brilliant thinking in that clutch, it dawned on us that he was the real brains of the team."

Chet Grant, the quarterback on the 1916 team, said that players looked to Rockne for inspiration and to Harper for tactics. But Rockne proved to be pretty adept as a tactical coach, too, for he dramatically altered the style of his running attack, an improvisation on the backfield shift that Harper had originally introduced. To that Rockne added "the flexing end," which was employed to offset the superior physical power of the opposing tackle, through feinting and quick change of position, as the play evolved. The shift, which got more offensive men to a given spot than the defense could employ to meet them, contrived to place four backs into three possible formations. As developed further by Rockne in his halcyon years, the shift became the cornerstone of his tactical brilliance. But it was also pleasing to watch as it unfolded, for it looked like its movements had been borrowed from the chorus lines of the Ziegfeld Follies. Such choreographic moves didn't happen by mistake, either, for Rockne spent hours drilling his men to improve their cadences and timing.

Another kernel of wisdom that Rockne picked up from Harper had to do with the sin of overconfidence. Rockne became a past master at reducing swelled heads. "Overconfidence is the toughest poison a coach has to face," he said. "It can wreck any team. That's why coaches rarely predict a victory, even when they expect to win hands down. If your team isn't keyed up and the other team is, the other team can easily overcome a handicap of two or three touchdowns. Football is that sort of game. You either put all out or you get out!"

Rockne sternly stuck to his personal credo that football was "60 percent leg drive and 30 percent fight." He was convinced that a team became a fighting team with the help of inspiring lectures and a refusal to become too cocky. On the way to the Army game at West Point in 1916, the players left the train at Cleveland for a breath of fresh air. Joining them was former president Teddy Roosevelt, who had been a passenger in a private car attached to their train. Roosevelt was an adherent of tough, physical competition (he had often boxed at the White House with instructors and suffered the loss of sight in an eye in one such skirmish), so he enjoyed swapping stories with the players. One of the Notre Dame men suggested, in bravado terms, precisely how Army was about to be eviscerated by his team.

"That sounds just bully, Coach," Roosevelt said to Rockne.

"Yes, sir, just plain bull, sir," Rockne replied, choosing to stay low-key about his team's chances. As it turned out, Army walloped Notre Dame, 30–10, for one of the most humiliating losses of the Harper era.

As another antidote against overconfidence Rockne became unrivaled at delivering inspirational pep talks. He could pump up his players with oleaginous sentiment, macho bombast, cutting wit, or homespun horse sense. The multitalented screen star and humorist Will Rogers felt that Rockne could be as funny as any professional comedian. "I would have hated to follow him on any banquet program," Will said. "He told so many stories, and I retold them, and always got a lot of laughs. If there was anyone I owed royalties to it was Rock."

Rockne was a polymath, who, on instant notice, could regale an audience on almost any subject under the sun. He could wend his way through stories about anything from toothpicks to elephants. With Jesse Harper's astute encouragement he was soon to develop into the nonpareil of locker-room orators.

Father John Cavanaugh was another who suspected that Rockne's spellbinding would be turned into an asset, for himself and Notre Dame. The two men often walked through the woods of South Bend as Father Cavanaugh expounded on the secrets of public speaking. Study your audience to know what they want, advised Father Cavanaugh, then exhaust each thought thoroughly without digressing and, by all means, be brief. Rockne never forgot these hints, for in future years he limited all his speeches to forty-five minutes or less, while in the locker room he was a good deal more abbreviated.

Although some Notre Dame admirers would have you believe that Rockne literally invented the pep talk, that is far from the truth. Baseball managers such as John McGraw and Connie Mack delivered such talks and used free-form group psychology long before Knute opened his mouth in a locker room. Mack was adept at giving what might be considered temperance lectures, and Mc-Graw, as foul-mouthed as any man ever to guide a ball club's destinies, loved to harangue his hard-crusted students in the clubhouse. However, until Rockne came along there were few practitioners of the art in college football.

When Harper came down with a heavy chest cold before the Wabash game of 1916, he turned over the reins of the team to Rockne, to nobody's surprise. Wabash was not known then as one of the powers of the country—nor would they ever be—yet Rockne refused to minimize the challenge. Relishing the opportunity to be in complete control; he chose to motivate his players with a dramatic pregame speech. Gathering his men around him in the locker room, Rockne insisted that little Wabash was determined to destroy Notre Dame. That could never happen, he emphasized, if everyone connected with Notre Dame, including the cheerleaders, gave everything they had, every minute, to the high and noble cause of beating Wabash. Further hinting that Wabash was anti-Catholic and had hired a cadre of evil mercenaries (imagine Rockne talking about mercenaries!) to upend Notre Dame, he wound up his locker-room philippic by shrieking, "Now get out there and crucify 'em!"

With Notre Dame pasting Wabash, 60–0, it is not unreasonable to assume that Rockne's demagogic oratory had something to do with the final result of the game. An observer at that time, Cy DeGree, pointed out that because Notre Dame was expected to win by only a couple of touchdowns, the trouncing may have encouraged Knute to further hone his oratorical skill and make that an integral part of his coaching equipment.

Though Harper was aware of Rockne's talents and was not eager to lose him, he made an effort to get Rockne more pay and a coaching spot at Kansas. When that didn't work out, he recommended Knute to Wabash. That also didn't materialize. Harper then succeeded in getting Rockne's salary raised to fifteen hundred dollars, assuring that Rockne would remain at Notre Dame a bit longer. Harper knew that his assistant was very ambitious, for money and position. Having abandoned the chemistry laboratory, with its test tubes and Bunsen burners, Rockne had made a commitment to the coaching world, where a man could use his cunning and enterprise to win—and also to bend the rules.

Few highly competitive coaches of that era, including Rockne, could come into court with totally clean hands. After all, Rockne had his "ringers," his assumed names, and his rumored betting on games. "He learned to swim with sharks and not bleed," author Murray Sperber has written in *Shake Down the Thunder*.

If Rockne's ethics might be challenged, he bore only a minor responsibility for the sleazy cultural atmosphere of the sport. But he managed to thrive in it, survive in it, and ultimately to dominate it.

By 1917 Rockne was offered the head coaching position at Michigan State. It was a tempting proposal, and Rockne might have snapped it up but for the fact that Harper, long desirous of retiring to his family's thirty-thousand-acre ranch in Kansas, resigned in early 1918. Harper had always harbored mixed feelings about spending his life as a football coach, especially with the uncertainties created by the manpower shortages of World War I and financial troubles at Notre Dame. His decision became inevitable due to the sudden death of a close relative who had been running the ranch. His record of thirty-three victories, five losses, and a tie in five seasons was exceptional. So was his constructive scheduling of Army, Nebraska, and Wisconsin, additions that literally put Notre Dame into football's big time.

There was much moaning at the bar when Harper affirmed that he was leaving. Indeed, some were insisting that "the Hoosiers are through, Harper was the system." As highly regarded as Rockne was by many at South Bend, there were others who believed that this young Norwegian, green and inexperienced as he was, was no match for a man of Harper's background and success.

However, it's doubtful that Harper could have been as enterprising as his successor, for, after all, as time went on, Rockne proved to be unique. Harper himself had said that "of all the men I know who can do this job, Rockne is the man best fitted." There was never anybody else whom Harper thought to recommend to Father John Cavanaugh other than Knute. Among those coaches whose teams faced Notre Dame when Rockne had still been Harper's assistant there was a consensus that he was very smart and invaluable to Harper. What they didn't appreciate at that moment was that he possessed qualities that would enable him to handle men under his command with unusual understanding and insight.

One of the men whom Rockne learned how to handle was the athletic gypsy George Gipp, who came to Notre Dame in 1916 from northern Michigan on a baseball scholarship and who remained around long enough to establish himself as a South Bend football legend.

However, before Gipp became Rockne's problem and pride, the new coach had other matters to deal with. The war in Europe, in which America had become involved, had depleted the ranks of potential college football talent, not only for Notre Dame, but for most other schools as well. The fact that Notre Dame had an open admissions policy and a popular-price tuition of $120 per year failed to help recruit football players at this moment. Rockne also was seeking to build on the strong schedule program that Harper had initiated, even though he knew that he was confronted with a strong anti-Catholic bias. By this time Army had become a permanent fixture on the South Bend schedule—but other schools in the East, as well as the Midwest, made a habit of ducking bookings with the South Benders. One year Harvard had responded to Harper's invitation to play a game with a curt: "Such a game is inadvisable." Usually the rationale for a turndown was that Cartier Field was too small and that Notre Dame's guarantees were even smaller.

Although Rockne didn't have any grand plan for strengthening Notre Dame's schedule, he chose to play it on a catch-as-catch-can basis. If each year a new school, with good credentials, could be added, that would satisfy him, as well as the increasingly vocal Notre Dame alumni group. In time Rockne's lineup of foes for each year would become known as "suicide schedules," in tribute to the talent of the schools that were booked. In addition, Notre Dame, starting in 1919, began to play schedules of nine to eleven games each autumn, a grueling agenda for the ambitious coach and his troops. (Previously the team had played six to eight games each year.)

To satisfy government requirements, after American troops were shipping out to places they had never heard of before, Rockne introduced long daily military drills for his players. This was part of the Student Army Training Corps (SATC) regimen that was put in place in many colleges throughout the country. Not all of the men in the SATC (some insisted the acronym really stood for Safe At The College) were football candidates, for many had enrolled in the program as a means of evading war service. However, the SATC propelled Notre Dame's student enrollment over one thousand for the first time in history. Each year thereafter, as Notre Dame's reputation as the capital of intercollegiate football grew, the school's student body grew with it.

Aware that the daily drills were as boring as watching paint dry, Rockne enlivened the sessions by turning them into simulated chorus line routines. To do this he attended theatrical productions that included dancing ensembles. Then he integrated the tempo, precision, rhythm, and gracefulness of such troupes into his drills. He also mapped out frequent breaks in the drills to make them less monotonous. Since Rockne had attacked dancing as an improper outlet for student energies, such flighty tactics were surprising.

"Rockne regarded football as drama and the squad as a cast," Edwin Pope explained, "and, in essence, he tried to make a theater out of both the practice field and the stadium, to keep both spectators and participants entertained at all times."

It wasn't long before Notre Dame players were extolled everywhere for their agility and nimble-footedness. But Rockne had instituted the "dance" program for one paramount reason: to maintain enthusiasm among men who could become easily bored with the sameness of military drills. "He was a builder of spirit," wrote columnist John Kieran, "the finest spirit the gridiron has ever known."

In Rockne's first year at the helm Notre Dame did not fare especially well. The team opened with a victory over Case by 26–6, then administered its usual beating to Wabash. Paddy Driscoll's Great Lakes Naval Training Station, featuring George Halas, who

Rockne's drills sometimes reminded observers of theatrical chorus lines. Courtesy: AP/World Wide Photos.

would become one of the early architects of the professional game, tied Notre Dame, 7–7. Notre Dame then lost to the Michigan Aggies, 13–7, followed by the one bright spot of the season, the first contest with Purdue's Boilermakers since 1905. The Irish walloped the team from nearby Lafayette, Indiana, 26–6. Rockne felt the Purdue engagement was important because Purdue was a natural opponent, coming from the Western Conference. When Purdue was willing to play host to his team, before some seven thousand people, Rockne was pleased. The season ended with a flat-footed 0–0 tie against Nebraska. There was no game against Army in 1918 because of wartime restrictions on travel. (But the series resumed in 1919 versus the West Pointers, with Charlie Daly returning to Army as head coach.) Another game, against Washington and Jefferson in 1918, was canceled because of an outbreak of Spanish flu.

Rockne had some talented players at his disposal in 1918, including Gipp, out with a broken leg for a good part of the season, Heartley "Hunk" Anderson, Charlie Crowley, Curly Lambeau, and Ojay Larson. (All of these men later won head coaching jobs, with Anderson becoming an unpaid assistant to Rockne.) Anderson and Rockne were a congenial pair as they went about their respective tutoring duties. Rockne would give preliminary instructions to the backs and ends, while Hunk warmed up the interior linemen. Finally Rockne would call to Anderson: "Heartley, would you be good enough to bring the behemoths over here?" To which Anderson, a considerable slice of meat himself, would reply: "Hey, Coach, they ain't even bleeding yet!"

Most of Rockne's players at the time were Catholic boys, attracted to this Catholic school, where athletic scholarships represented an enticement they couldn't turn down. Rockne called such arrangements BT—bed and table—in which the players got a "free ride" but invariably took jobs in the dining hall.

An irony of those early days under Rockne was that Notre Dame, a school where non-Catholics represented little more than 20 percent of the student body (although they were always welcomed), rarely played other Catholic schools. They were getting the pick of the country's Catholic athletes, both in football and in baseball, but these young men generally faced a universe of non-Catholics on the gridiron, diamond, and basketball court.

Notre Dame's growing reputation as a hothouse for football players was enhanced by Rockne's presence. His philosophy that speed, brains, and execution were more important than muscle and poundage was now being grudgingly accepted even away from tiny Cartier Field. And his constant evangelizing for the game, in speeches and in print, was winning converts everywhere, in the press and among the fans. He could charm most people with his gifted tongue, but when he said that an integral part of a Notre Dame education was a fighting, winning football team, he meant every word of it. It was sheer myth that every student at Notre Dame was forced to turn out for football practice. But Rockne wouldn't have minded that, for he had already proven that small, skinny men, like himself, could play the game.

However, in 1919, the new president of Notre Dame, Father James Burns, with an eye to proving that the school was more than a football factory, set out to raise the school's feeble endowment and to earn it a niche as "the Yale of the West." He raised enough money to construct a law school, an alumni hall, and a dining hall, and worked to transform the campus into a place aesthetically pleasing to the eye.

Dedicated as he was to the gridiron, Rockne still understood Father Burns's commitment and didn't find himself at odds with such ambitions. Instead, he became part of Father Burns's plan. Rockne was encouraged to travel around the country, speaking to alumni groups and always stressing the value of football and vigorous athletics as an integral part of the Notre Dame spirit. He often suggested to professors, who might grumble about the lack of attention from their students, that if they made their lectures as fascinating as football they might keep the young men awake in the classroom!

So the final efforts of Father Burns, focused, as they were, on upgrading the school's accreditation, and Rockne, intent on leading his team to the peak, dovetailed perfectly.

With the end of World War I Rockne could concentrate on building his gridiron empire as the boys returned to South Bend to complete their interrupted education. Having been exposed to the Spartan discipline of military life, these men now confronted the discipline on Rockne's practice field. The barked, staccato commands they now heard from the voice of Rockne contrasted with the martinet demands of their drill sergeants in the trenches and woods of France. But they had gained a maturity in the Army, as doughboys and officers, that Rockne could mold into a winning combination.

7

The Legend of George Gipp

THE STRANGEST ASPECT of the brief, curious career of George Gipp is that to this day many people believe he was one of Notre Dame's famous Four Horsemen. He was not, of course. But he remains the most durable icon in Notre Dame's crowded pantheon of legends. He was the greatest all-around athlete in the school's history but also its quintessential "tramp athlete," a man who haunted the poker tables and pool halls of Hullie and Mike's and Jimmy and Goat's in South Bend.

The more we learn about a person the more inscrutable that person becomes. That surely is the case with Gipp. Since his untimely death in December 1920, as the Roaring Twenties hoved into view, we have discovered enough things about Gipp to further confuse his image. How did he grow up? How did he come to Notre Dame? How did Rockne first spot him? Did he really make his immortal deathbed utterances to Rockne? What exactly did he say? What were the facts about his conversion to Catholicism?

About the only thing we know, for a certainty, about this gridiron saint is that his name was pronounced with a hard G—as in *get*— the same as the G in Lou Gehrig, another athlete who died too young.

The single quality of Gipp that those who knew him agree on is that he was "superbly indifferent," an attitude that appears to have

"Tramp athlete" George Gipp was Rockne's first great backfield performer. Courtesy: UPI-Corbis-Bettmann.

characterized his whole life. Grantland Rice regarded Gipp as "self-reliant as a wild mustang," perhaps another way of saying he didn't give a damn for anything. If Gipp had had his way he probably would have settled for driving a taxi back in his hometown or dealing cards all night long in one of the seamier venues of South Bend.

He was born in 1895 in Laurium, Michigan, a small mining and industrial hamlet of fewer than two thousand people, near the shores of Lake Superior, in the tough Keweenaw Peninsula. He was the offspring of Matthew Gipp, a stern Congregationalist minister who had fathered seven other children and who apparently experienced scant success in instilling a workable code of ethics into his prodigal son.

At Calumet High School in Laurium Gipp proved to be an exceptionally gifted athlete, although he preferred baseball and basketball to football because he was relatively slight of build. Despite that fact, he played offensive football with skill, while not shying away from body contact as a blocker and a tackler. However, he never made the first string at Calumet.

As a high school basketball player he was quick and sharpshooting. One year, with Gipp in charge, Calumet took twenty-four of twenty-five games as it won a regional championship. In baseball he was a long-ball hitter and a stylish prospect to any big-league scouts who might wander into the area.

While Gipp could seemingly do anything with panache on the field of play, he also had a compulsive hunger for poker, pool, drink, and betting. He would gamble on almost anything, whether wagering on his own performance or somebody else's. Rockne was aware of Gipp's propensity for taking wild chances on the gridiron, so it is unlikely that a person of his insight wouldn't have been aware of Gipp's off-the-field peccadilloes. However, Rockne always maintained that he only had suspicions. "I have often wondered why Gipp, not a rich boy, always had sufficient funds," he once wrote. Just what was Rockne reading in those days? The local South Bend newspapers, on more than a single occasion, detailed Gipp's glories at "hustling" in billiards in the more celebrated hangouts of the town.

A well-circulated story about Gipp offered an idyllic portrait of him. It said that he invariably turned over any winnings at the gambling table to local people who were in need. This sentimental Robin Hood version was unlikely ever to have occurred.

The academic curriculum of Calumet didn't have much appeal for Gipp. He barely managed to get by in his studies. Much of the time he was a truant from the classroom. Outside of it he was involved in at least one spree of vandalism, which cost him a suspension. Sometimes he went to work on the line gang of a telephone company, work that could be as physically challenging as cracking through a line of two-hundred-pounders.

In the hot Michigan summers he played baseball in the industrial leagues that were so popular in the Midwest. In time he won a baseball scholarship to Notre Dame on the recommendation of William Denton "Dolly" Gray, who experienced three losing seasons as a left-handed pitcher for the Washington Senators. Gray came from Houghton, Michigan, not far from Laurium, and had played at Notre Dame.

The circumstances of Gipp's first encounter with Rockne at South Bend are somewhat clouded. "We drugged ourselves with romantic chronicles," explains Paul Gallico, one of the troubadours of sportswriting in the 1920s. "We emerged from a serious war and now wanted no more reality but only escape."

So it was only natural that there was mystery about the first time these two figures came together. One story offered by Clarence

Manion, a former dean of the Notre Dame Law School, was evocative of an early scenario of Bill Stern, a football broadcaster a generation later. Dean Manion declared that one afternoon when Gipp was hitting a few practice baseballs, a stray football came sailing over a nearby fence and landed on his head. Annoyed, Gipp picked up the football and kicked it back over the fence. As luck would have it, the football bounced to earth among a group of players who were working out under Rockne's tutelage on a nearby recreation field.

Amazed at the distance that the football had been kicked, Rockne blurted out, "Who kicked that ball?" When he was informed that it was Gipp, he at once decided to invite the young man to come out for his team.

Rockne's chronic storytelling had previously included some hard-to-prove whoppers. But in this instance he settled for a much simpler version of the first meeting between himself and the future immortal. It happened, said Rockne, on an autumn day in 1916 when he watched a fellow in street clothes and ordinary low shoes booting footballs (dropkicks, of course) for extraordinary distances near Brownson Hall. "Where did you learn to do that?" Rockne asked—and Gipp told him where he came from. In short order Gipp went out for the freshman team, at Rockne's urging.

Soon Gipp was barracked at Brownson Hall, where he became a waiter to pay for his room and board. If he wanted to have additional money, he would "earn" it with his skill at dice, cards, and billiards. It wasn't long before his reputation as a restless, go-for-broke gambler spread around the campus.

When his associates needed money or a loan, Gipp was often there to provide for their needs. It was said that he'd bet fifty dollars or a hundred dollars on the turn of a card and was so adept at hustling that even inveterate sharks tried to avoid his company. "He was an enigma that we never solved," said Father Charles O'Donnell, who later became president of Notre Dame.

Despite his seeming indifference to football, Gipp had little difficulty making the freshman team, and, in short order, making his first headlines. The lean-muscled, 185-pound, six-foot Gipp, now twenty-one years old and full of hell, immediately put his imprint on a contest with Western State Normal of Kalamazoo, Michigan. With the score tied at 7–7 in the last quarter, Notre Dame had several yards to go on fourth down. An orthodox call at that moment would have been a punt. Instead, operating out of punt formation, Gipp unexpectedly unleashed a booming sixty-two yard dropkick for a field goal. Western State's players were flabbergasted to lose a game in such a way. Imagine, that son of a bitch crossing us up like that! Gipp would exhibit that roguish flair in all of his days at South Bend, even as his behavior remained a cause of bewilderment to Rockne and Notre Dame's ruling powers.

After Gipp's freshman year he showed a preference for football, due to pressure put on him by Rockne. However, Gipp played professional baseball during the summer, with a team in Kenosha, Wisconsin. Rockne pursued him there, as relentlessly as Javert (of *Les Miserables* infamy), so he had to be aware that Gipp was toying with his so-called amateur status. Even under such suasion, Gipp took his good time reporting for football in the fall.

This failed to win many admirers on Notre Dame's campus, for robust football players were much in demand. Some of the better athletes had disappeared into the military, while at some other schools the sport had been abandoned, since it was felt that it was improper to cavort on a gridiron while young men were risking their lives overseas.

Gipp managed to miss the first two games with Kalamazoo and Wisconsin, just as he assiduously avoided attending most of his classes. So it wasn't until a 7–0 loss to Nebraska, on a wretched field, and a Notre Dame victory over South Dakota, that he got to play. However, it was in the fifth game of the season, against now-traditional foe Army, that Gipp flashed the talent that ultimately was to set him apart from all Notre Dame mortals. Rockne always had insisted, from the first time he spotted Gipp, that he "was a perfect performer who comes along only once in a generation." Now Gipp began to prove that assertion.

Despite a muddy field and blustering winds at West Point, Gipp ran well, stealing the show from the Cadet star, Oliphant. It was also in this game that Gipp demonstrated his ability to run out of bounds before he would have been tackled, thus avoiding unnecessary injury. But it was on defense that Gipp truly stood out. In the final minutes of the game, with Notre Dame nursing a 7–2 lead, Army drove to the enemy's eight-yard-line. When the West Pointers set up for a placekick, Gipp, a Euclidean genius when it came to calculating dice odds, quickly figured that a successful placekick would still leave Army trailing, 7–5. Thus he surmised that Army was going to fake the kick and throw the ball. As the play got under way he yelled, "Watch out for the pass!" Sure enough, Army's quarterback hurled the ball into the end zone, where the alert Gipp knocked it to the ground. Notre Dame's slim victory had been preserved.

A large contingent of Notre Dame students assembled at the South Bend railroad station to welcome back the triumphant squad. The one player they singled out for acclaim was Gipp, who was mobbed by his admirers. He stayed around briefly, then left the celebration to join some of his downtown cronies. "He had bet some money for them and was bringing home the winnings, part of which was his commission for handling the transactions," wrote author Jim Beach.

Unfortunately, in the next game, against Morningside, at Sioux City, Iowa, Gipp suffered a broken leg when he was rudely flung against an iron post near the sideline during a running play. The Irish won that game and the next two without Gipp's services. He was spending his time, instead, in the infirmary. When he emerged he went home, on crutches, to Laurium to recuperate.

When Gipp returned to Notre Dame the next spring, in what was Rockne's inaugural year in full charge of the football team, he still walked with a limp. That should have been enough to convince his draft board that he wasn't fit for military duty. But when he reported for football in the fall, his induction board presumed he was well enough to face the Huns in Europe. So they ordered him to report for military duty in mid-October 1918. This time Fate was supportive of Gipp.

After fifteen hundred days of fighting, with more than nine million soldiers from many countries giving up their lives and other millions wounded and scarred, the warfare stopped on November 11, 1918. Exhausted and embittered populations on both the Allied and German sides greeted the news of the Armistice with relief. So did Gipp, for his services as a soldier were no longer needed. Now he could devote his time to football and his other nonacademic pursuits.

In 1918 and 1919 Gipp spent more time than usual on the South Bend campus, although he continued to dodge classes in the same way he eluded tacklers. Although he supposedly was a prelaw student, he failed to take his final exams and was seen often at Hullie and Mike's pool hall on Michigan Avenue. After Notre Dame won three of six of its 1918 games (in an informal, abbreviated schedule that did not count against eligibility), he generally ducked out on student pep rallies, because he regarded them as foolishness. His roommate, Dutch Bergman, also a halfback on Notre Dame's squad, was never pleased with Gipp's smoking and whiskey drinking in quarters and often criticized him for it. By Bergman's own account he spent too much time hauling Gipp out of the local poker and billiards emporiums. Gipp did not take kindly to Bergman's attempts at structuring his life. After all, he seemed to reap his greatest pleasure in his solitary excursions to South Bend's joints.

"George was much bigger than I was. I never weighed much more than 145 pounds," remembered Bergman. "When I'd go into one of these places to get him out, he'd threaten to punch me in the nose, especially if I insulted him, which I often did."

When Gipp became incensed at Bergman's supervision, he'd take off after him. Surprisingly, Bergman could run faster than Gipp. "I never had any trouble letting him chase me right back to the campus," Bergman added.

Gipp continued to receive special treatment from Rockne. A lesser player would have had a tongue-lashing administered to him by the coach and probably would have been thrown off the team. Instead, Rockne pampered his star pupil, preferring to sweet-talk him until Gipp reluctantly would abdicate his Peck's Bad Boy role.

Gipp generally failed to show up for practice sessions the first two days of each week. When he did appear by Wednesday or Thursday—even then avoiding any strenuous tackling or blocking chores—Rockne would remain relatively placid. "George, George, where have you been?" he might say, more in a pleading tone than in one of outrage. "Now get over there with the sixth team." Gipp would then trot over to join the sixth team, work out lethargically for a while with them, then wind up in the starting lineup on Saturday.

On those occasions when Rockne might have been harsh with Gipp, the young man would shrug, fail to suit up, and proceed to the nearest poker game. One observer has suggested that Gipp liked the ladies as much as he did cards, but there doesn't seem much support for that notion. "Gipp cared little for female company," Rockne insisted. Supposedly there was a steady girl named Iris in Gipp's life, but it appears that she was already married, although separated from her husband. She had been described as pretty, cultured, and sensitive, but there is no evidence that she played any major role in Gipp's haphazard life.

In 1919 Gipp came into his own as a heralded performer. There was now a public awareness of his dramatic and idiosyncratic style and his reputation leaped beyond the bounds of South Bend. Arch Ward, later to become one of the Midwest's best sports columnists, with the *Chicago Tribune*, said of him: "Gipp is expected to be a prime factor in bringing the championship of Indiana to the Gold and Blue archives. Gipp is a hard man to stop when skirting the ends and as a hurler of the forward pass he has few superiors in the West. His educated toe, however, is his greatest asset. In recent rehearsals Gipp registered several dropkicks from the fifty-three-yard mark . . . his accuracy in hoisting the oval across the bars from all angles of the field may play a prominent part in stiff battles. . . ." In the opening game against Kalamazoo, the first of nine undefeated contests that Rockne presided over in 1919, Gipp was involved in three running plays that would become a permanent part of his coach's banquet circuit repertoire.

On the first play Gipp ran for eighty yards, only to have the play called back because of a penalty. Then he broke away for sixty-eight yards, only to have the play lost due to a whistle by the referee. On a third effort Gipp ran for seventy yards, but again the disruptive whistle canceled it out. In the aftermath of the three nullified plays, Gipp was as insouciant as usual. He meandered over to the referee and said, "Let's get together on this to save time. From now on, give me one whistle to stop and two to keep going!"

What set Gipp apart as a player was his ability to improvise. Against Nebraska in 1919 he decided to help an unsung substitute experience the thrill of scoring a touchdown, so he literally hauled the third-stringer across the goal line. It was an uncommon display of selflessness on Gipp's part and out of character for a man who had always been accused of self-indulgence.

In the same game, with the Irish ahead, 14–9, early in the fourth period, Rockne's troops were tiring badly. The team had suffered some injuries during the game, putting a heavier burden on the subs. Rockne called Gipp aside, according to Francis Wallace, and instructed him to utilize every legal time killer in the book, and some that weren't in the book. This whispered edict was precisely the sort of cunning strategy that Gipp loved. Naturally, he followed through, causing the home crowd (the game was being played on Nebraska turf) to explode in anger. Gipp's delaying tactics proved to be successful, helping the Irish athletes to take a second breath. When the game ended, with Notre Dame winning, the Nebraska coach, Henry F. Schulte, flung a question at Gipp as the latter loped off the field.

"What course do you take at Notre Dame?" Schulte asked bitterly.

"Plumbing," was Gipp's response.

As Gipp prepared to face Army several weeks later, Rockne was on his way to his first unbeaten season. For the first time, too, many non–Notre Damers from New York—popularly known in subsequent years as "the subway alumni"—journeyed up the Hudson to West Point to take in the proceedings. One of the largest crowds ever to jam Cullum Hall Field, some fifteen thousand, were on hand on a magnificent fall day. They were not disappointed in the game, or in the performance of Gipp.

Army surged ahead in the first quarter, under the coaching leadership of Charlie Daly. Daly had expected that West Point's fine end, Earl Blaik, later to become a legendary coach of the West Pointers, would help to contain Gipp and the two Andersons, Hunk and Eddie. But Blaik was ill that day and couldn't play. Despite his absence, Army still appeared to be a formidable team.

But Gipp's right arm soon went into action. He could throw the ball with great accuracy, like a control pitcher, and by the end of the first half he had gotten the Irish down to the one-yard-line. However, time was running out and Gipp knew it. There were no scoreboard clocks used in those days to tick off the remaining seconds; a linesman's watch was employed to perform that function. Gipp noticed that the official was looking down at his watch and that his hand, holding a gun, was preparing to rise, signaling the completion of the first half. Quickly calling for the ball from his center, Gipp grabbed it and plunged over the goal line for a touchdown. There was no line charge by either team, so the play proved to be even more peculiar. However, the ball had been put into play before the gun sounded. Thus the touchdown was legal, though hardly undisputed by the dismayed West Pointers.

Notre Dame still remained behind, 9–6, but the swift action by Gipp had provided his team with an enormous lift. Helped by Gipp's pinpoint passing in the third quarter, Notre Dame scored another touchdown to go ahead, 12–9. That's the way it ended, giving Notre Dame its second straight victory over Army. A few years before, such success over West Point would have been unthinkable.

Gipp's quick-impulse play at the end of the first half remained

for many years as a devious ploy in the minds of strict construc-
tionists. But it was typical of Gipp, a man whom Father O'Donnell
once noted could sit in his English class and get 100 percent:
50 from the student on his left and 50 from the student on his
right.

8

An Athlete Dying Young

By 1920 THE SPORTS culture in America—"the broad folk highway of the nation" was the metaphor used by Walter Camp—was on the verge of producing a legion of stalwarts. There would be Rockne and Red Grange in football, Babe Ruth, Lou Gehrig, Walter Johnson, and Ty Cobb in baseball, Bill Tilden and Helen Wills in tennis, Jack Dempsey and Gene Tunney in boxing, Bobby Jones in golf, and Earl Sande in horse racing. There were some among these icons who were boobs, racists, or scoundrels, full of beer, ignorance, and untamed lusts, but you wouldn't have known it by reading the sports pages of those days.

All of them, with the complicitous help of an adoring and romanticizing press, became exemplars of everything presumed to be worthwhile about America. Whatever flaws these giants may have possessed were glossed over by sports journalists, who literally invented a segment of social history called the Golden Age of Sports.

George Gipp was a charter member of that group of heralded stars, due to his well-documented performances in the last year of his life. Yet he came precariously close that season to never playing another game for Notre Dame.

Gipp's extracurricular activities at South Bend had long been a source of concern to many on the faculty. These priests didn't buy the proposition that his football feats were sufficient reason to permit him to ignore his studies and to skip classes. However, there were some faculty members who were not aware of Gipp's after-dark roamings with the town's more disreputable elements. Had they known, they probably would have chosen to ban Gipp forever from their school.

Whether Rockne was fully aware of Gipp's egregious lifestyle has never been clear. What is clear is that the protective Rockne regarded Gipp as his pet reclamation project and was willing to overlook his imperfections, in return for dividends on the gridiron. In Gipp's defense, Rockne liked to tell the story about how his protégé lived next door to the common shower room in Sorin Hall and thus had to be more moral than any of this teammates, because "cleanliness was next to godliness!"

Some intimates of Rockne have maintained that it was not common knowledge that Gipp gambled and placed fairly sizable bets on football games. "I worked at the hotel where Gipp sometimes lived," Francis Wallace said, "and where he presumably played cards. Yet I never heard that Gipp was a gambler until years later." Others insisted that Gipp would draw the line against ever playing cards with his teammates or other students.

However, there was never disagreement as to whether Gipp paid much attention to his studies. He didn't. He was a student *manqué* in every sense. He never made any pretense that he cared to attend classes or to improve the quality of what was an agile mind. When Gipp did manage to attend a class now and then, he would choose an easy course that didn't require any work.

Shortly before Christmas in 1919 Gipp was elected captain of the Notre Dame team, fair testimony to the fact that he hadn't exploited any of his teammates at the poker table. But within a few months and after repeated warnings from Notre Dame authorities, the hammer came down on Gipp. He was informed that he was expelled in March 1920. To say that Rockne was distraught is an understatement. Here was his All-America captain being removed from the premises, just when it looked like Notre Dame's football future was brighter than ever.

The official version of Gipp's expulsion was that he'd cut too many classes. But author Patrick Chelland has disagreed with such a glib explanation. Instead, Chelland argued that the school had had enough of Gipp's flouting of all regulations. When he was spotted one more time emerging from a particularly sleazy off-limits hangout, the authorities acted.

Cries of protest went up, from students and townspeople alike, for by this time Gipp had become almost everybody's lovable problem child. Even as his supporters rallied to his defense, Gipp showed no signs of repentance. He knew that many other colleges were interested in him, and he courted these offers to play elsewhere. He traveled to the University of Michigan campus at Ann Arbor, where Hurry-Up Yost was the coach. Michigan wanted to entice top footballers from their own state to play for them, and because Gipp was from Laurium, he seemed like a perfect candidate. But, in this case, Gipp wanted no part of Yost. The humorist Ring Lardner once said about Yost that when a friend asked him if he'd ever talked to Hurry-Up, he answered: "No, my father told me never to interrupt." Like Rockne, the voluble Yost was a nonstop talker. Gipp felt he could live without that; he also must have questioned whether Yost would have been as permissive with him as Rockne.

Pop Warner, who had coached at Georgia and Carlisle and who was now at Pittsburgh, also wanted to have Gipp in his backfield. The University of Detroit, a Catholic school, already had lured halfback Pete Bahan away from Notre Dame. They were also eager to add Gipp to their camp. Another supplicant in the race for Gipp was the superintendent of West Point, General Douglas MacArthur. MacArthur felt that the Military Academy's esprit de corps would be enhanced by victorious football teams. In pursuit of that belief a wire was sent to Gipp in Laurium informing him that he had been recommended for appointment to West Point. There is no record that Gipp ever paid any attention to it.

Meanwhile, as Gipp continued to carouse in South Bend, Rockne worked to get the young man back to Notre Dame. The mere idea of Gipp winding up in Army's backfield, or, for that matter, in any other school's backfield, did not sit well with him. When Gipp made his visit to Ann Arbor, Rockne also journeyed there to remind him of the good old days at Notre Dame. Then Rockne set about to pressure the local leaders, who really needed very little persuading, for they were as eager as he was to have Gipp winning football games for Notre Dame. In the long run, however, it was President James Burns who would have to make the final verdict on the readmission of Gipp.

It was to Burns that the prominent businessmen of South Bend made their appeal. They were convinced that a strong football team was necessary for the area's healthy commerce, and Gipp fit in with that desire. For some time expansion plans were afoot for Cartier Field, and it didn't make sense to have this dynamic player adrift. The pressure ultimately became so intense that Father Burns, who did not value football as much as he prized academic excellence, was forced to relent. He reinstated Gipp in late April 1920.

Word spread quickly that Notre Dame was becoming nothing more than a football factory. These stories insisted that Rockne was determined to win at any cost. Gipp's return to good standing was also accompanied by a tale that he had taken a special test, administered by Father Burns himself, and that he had passed with a surprising display of knowledge. It is conceivable that Rockne, with his belief in a permissible lie on behalf of a good cause, was responsible for the dissemination of this yarn. But it appears that such a grueling test never took place, even if Rockne was portrayed in such stories as waiting anxiously outside the room where Gipp was being examined. In *Shake Down the Thunder,* Murray Sperber assesses these stories as total fabrications. He quotes Notre Dame history professor Robert Burns to that effect, putting to rest one of the more durable fables connected to Gipp's history.

Back at school, Gipp participated in a few baseball games that spring, even as some schools, including Army, still felt they could lure him away from Notre Dame. At the time Gipp was also being eyed by the Chicago White Sox, of the American League. The owner of the White Sox, Charles Comiskey, thought that Gipp could restore some of the luster to a team that was on the brink of being depopulated as the result of the Black Sox baseball scandal.

There was no indication that Gipp had been chastened at this date. He took a room at the Oliver Hotel in South Bend, and in spite of the fact that Indiana had long been "dry" country (the Volstead Act was passed in 1919, making provisions for the enforcement of the Eighteenth Amendment), he spent many evenings drinking heavily. Police in the area invariably looked the other way when it came to clamping down on the local speakeasies, so it was simple for Gipp to supply himself with illicit liquor. As the 1920 football season approached, Gipp appeared to be as self-destructive as ever. Considering his poor physical condition, which must have been apparent to Rockne, it's a wonder that he showed up for the first game, against Kalamazoo. But he did, and the Irish won easily, 39–0.

As Notre Dame faced its remaining eight games, it was comforted in the knowledge that not only was Gipp part of the squad but also that once-reluctant schools were besieging them for a future spot on their schedule.

In Notre Dame's third game, against Nebraska, always a tough opponent for Rockne, Gipp looked tired, which shouldn't have surprised anyone. But the Irish won, 16–7. Gipp was known to his teammates as a fellow who would drink after games. Rockne had to pray that he didn't engage his thirst *before* games as well. In truth, it was a forlorn hope, for Gipp had shown scant ability for controlling himself, even under the most compelling circumstances. He believed he could do anything he wanted and still play a dominant game.

Despite his failure to abide by any decent training regimen, Gipp was able to play in several games that year that easily stamped him as an all-American performer. "Have the team line up and pass the ball to Gipp," wrote Ring Lardner in a simple summation of Rockne's strategy.

Before Army played Notre Dame, a sportswriter asked John McEwan, an Army assistant coach, if he had properly scouted Gipp.

"Who the hell is Gipp?" snorted McEwan.

"You'll find out who he is about two o'clock tomorrow afternoon," replied the writer.

McEwan did. Gipp's skills had never been displayed more completely. When the game was over, Grantland Rice sidled over to the distraught McEwan. "How did you like Gipp?" he asked.

"Gipp's no football player, he's a runaway son of a bitch," snarled McEwan.

It was against Army, that Gipp did everything but write Rockne's patented pep talk. Army had gotten its act together as a football unit, following the personnel complications emerging from World War I. Their attack was headed by a plebe named Wally French, a transfer from Rutgers. French was a fullback who possessed some of Gipp's elusive qualities, except he couldn't do as much on the gridiron as Gipp could.

When Army and Notre Dame lined up on West Point's Plains of Abraham on a pleasant October day, the Irish had already thoroughly beaten four teams. Now they promised to add Army to their list of conquests. Before the game began Gipp was encouraged by

Rockne to put on a demonstration of his dropkicking skill. No doubt Rockne believed this would be a subtle way to discourage the West Pointers even before the whistle blew.

"Gipp walked to the midfield stripe and called for four footballs," Jim Beach wrote in *The Big Game*. "From there, with seeming unconcern, he sent two kicks over the crossbar. Turning around, he did the same thing between uprights at the other end of the field—four perfect fifty-yard dropkicks."

At the end of the first half Army led by 17–14, causing Rockne to reach for his weapon of choice: the locker-room pep talk. Unburdening himself of a few uncomplimentary and goading remarks ("You men look like ladies out there, etc."), Rockne noticed Gipp sitting in a corner of the steamy locker room, calmly puffing on a cigarette. If there was one thing that could set off sparks of hostility in the coach, it was an appearance of complacency by one of his players. The fact that it was Gipp, his meal ticket, even angered him more.

"You, Mr. Gipp, I guess you don't care if we win or lose!" Rockne is purported to have said. Gipp supposedly responded that he certainly did care, for he had five hundred dollars bet on the game. Whether Gipp actually put it that way is questionable, for Rockne was not one to stand still for such a put-down.

Chet Grant, who played alongside Gipp and who later became an assistant coach, scoffed at the notion that Gipp would have said such a thing. Yet Grant didn't have any doubt that money was wagered by Gipp and other Irish players. "We all had money on it," recalled Grant. "Students and fans in South Bend sent money along with us to bet with Army's students and players. In those days it wasn't anything unusual to do that. I think that Rockne bet, too. In one game, against Nebraska, he bet that we'd score more points in one period than Nebraska would score in the entire game. That influenced the way he would handle substitutions . . . he would keep the less experienced men out of the lineup under those circumstances."

According to Grant, Chet Wynne, the Notre Dame halfback, didn't have any money, so Gipp went around collecting money from other players to bet on behalf of Wynne. "Gipp hit me up for ten dollars," said Grant. "I gave him the money, even if I didn't like him very much. I didn't want him to think that I was a cheapskate."

In the second half of the Army game Gipp stepped up the pace, on the ground and in the air. By the third quarter Notre Dame reached the Army twenty-yard-line, and Gipp was preparing to take over the game. At the start of the last quarter, he hit tackle, and a number of Army defenders went with him. With the ball close to the Army goal line, Gipp, in a remarkable decoy, handed the pigskin to Johnny Mohardt, who virtually tiptoed over the goal line for a touchdown that put Notre Dame ahead for the first time. Gipp dropkicked the extra point, making the score 21–17. In the last moments of the game Gipp zoomed down the middle of the field for fifty yards, shedding frustrated Cadets, who reached out for the phantom and found nothing there. After Gipp passed for another fifteen yards to put Notre Dame on the West Point twenty-yard-line, Chet Wynne went over for the score on another trick play, with Gipp in the middle of it.

The afternoon had been a glorious one for Gipp, perhaps the most productive one he had ever spent under Rockne. He had passed for 96 yards, run for 124 yards, returned kickoffs for 112 yards, and dropkicked three extra points (the fourth was missed by another player).

Afterward Rockne was moved to remark that "Gipp was the greatest player that Notre Dame ever produced . . . he was Nature's Pet . . . he had the timing of a tiger in pouncing on his prey . . . he was a master of defense . . . not a single forward pass was ever completed in territory that he defended." Allowing for the usual flush of hyperbole so characteristic of the coach, there were few who would take exception to such a description.

There was no letdown for Gipp in the next game, against Purdue. He ran ninety-two yards and eighty yards for touchdowns, as the Irish shut out the Boilermakers, 28–0. But the following week, against Indiana, Gipp's performance may have been more stunning, for prior to that game he was rumored to have put down a bet that he would personally outscore the whole Hoosier team.

Gipp's estimate of his own abilities may have seemed excessive. But he never thought so for a moment. The night before the Indiana game he was so intent on betting on himself that he supposedly haunted the streets of Indianapolis trying to get the money down, even without any odds. At the time Notre Dame was riding a streak of seventeen games without loss (including one tie), but that was only secondary in Gipp's mind to his extraordinary wager. Adding another fillip to this episode was that it was likely that Gipp began this game with a dislocated shoulder and a broken collarbone. How he contracted these wounds is not clear. One historian of Notre Dame sports hinted that his injuries were incurred in the midst of one of his nocturnal prowls.

Whatever the truth, Gipp found himself handily checked during the first half by Coach Jumbo Steihm's Hoosier team. Underestimating his opponent, Gipp started the game with his injuries, but after being thrown heavily in the first quarter he was removed by Rockne, who realized his star was in considerable pain.

When the teams went to their locker rooms at halftime, Indiana led by 10–0. At this juncture Rockne made one of his inspired moves. He sent halfbacks Mohardt and Norm Barry into the game, with Gipp still licking his wounds on the bench.

"All that year there had been a bitter rivalry between these two men for the right-halfback job," wrote Harry Stuhldreher in his book *Rockne: Man-Builder*. "Here, too, Rockne's psychology was exerted to the nth degree. It took delicacy to handle these two boys, both splendid players, and to keep them off each other's toes. The team trembled in anticipation of what would happen. Much to the surprise of Rockne and the team Mohardt and Barry shook hands with each other and said 'Let's forget our past troubles. We've got to win this game for the Gipper who has been saving our faces for a long time now. Boys, it's up to us to win for Gipp and Notre Dame. Let's go.' "

The Stuhldreher account, introducing for the first time the word "Gipper" into Notre Dame's working lexicon, has been contradicted by Barry himself. Barry said later that the brief kaffeeklatsch between Mohardt and himself was devoid of any mention of Gipp, which meant, of course, that the nickname of The Gipper was never used. What was actually said by Barry to Mohardt was something like the following: "Listen, ya big Polack, knock that big end [referring to an Indiana lineman] out of the ball park or I'll knock ya on your ass!"

The two backs then combined to work the ball down the field until they reached Indiana's five-yard-line, as the third quarter ended. At that stage Rockne, ever the improviser, plucked Gipp off the bench and sent him into action in place of Barry. It was all dramatic as hell, but Barry didn't take kindly to the sudden move.

As Gipp ran onto the field, taped from shoulder to wrist like a mummy, the incensed Barry tossed his helmet in the direction of Rockne. Fortunately for Barry, Rockne ducked. Barry didn't stay around to watch Gipp plunge over for a touchdown, then add the extra point to make the score 10–7, still in favor of Indiana. By that time Barry had hailed a cab outside the stadium and was headed for a local hotel. It turned out that he didn't have any money, so he testily informed the driver to see Rockne and get it from him.

With only minutes remaining in the game, Gipp kicked off to Indiana's goal line. When the Hoosiers failed to move the ball up-field, they were forced to kick. It was then that Gipp again donned his heroic garb. Switching to a sidearm motion because of the pain in his shoulder, Gipp passed the Irish down to the Indiana fifteen-yard-line. At that point Jumbo Steihm sensed that Gipp would try for a game-tying field goal, since his toe was usually unerring. That would also preserve the long unbeaten streak.

But Gipp, permitted in this situation to run his own ball game without Rockne's intrusion, figured that Indiana's defense would be suckers for a pass. So he stepped back and flipped a beaut to Eddie Anderson, who made a nice reception on the one-yard-line. Everyone in the park now expected Gipp to jam over for the deci-sive touchdown. With his head down and his arms protecting the pigskin, Gipp rammed forward. But just as he reached the line of scrimmage, he turned the ball over to quarterback Joe Brandy. Without a finger laid on him, Brandy went in for the touchdown. Notre Dame had won a bruising battle, 13–10, with Gipp perform-ing above and beyond the call of duty.

Gipp didn't often conduct his postgame celebrations with his teammates around to join him. After the Indiana game it was no different; he didn't return to South Bend with his pals. Instead, he got off at Chicago, where he met Grover Malone, once on the Notre Dame roster, and a fellow who shared Gipp's fondness for the grape.

Gipp was scheduled to help Malone coach a group of high school footballers. But his good intentions went astray. Instead, the two men went on a drinking binge for several days. By the time Gipp headed back to South Bend he was in shape for very little, least of all for a confrontation with Rockne, for he was suffering from a sore throat and fever and was coughing up considerable phlegm.

Nevertheless, Gipp chose to join the team in Evanston, Illinois, for the next game, against Northwestern. Someone in the Athletic Office had designated the game as George Gipp Day, so it would have been unseemly of him not to show up. Sitting on the bench, Gipp gave the impression of a man who should have been in a hospital bed. Rockne was quick to notice how pale and distraught

Gipp looked, so he informed him he wasn't going to play that afternoon.

Notre Dame took the lead by several touchdowns after three quarters, thanks to some productive running by Barry. Then the crowd started to chant, "We want Gipp! We want Gipp!" There were almost as many Irish alumni and supporters in the Evanston crowd as there were Northwestern loyalists, and the pleading for Gipp grew in intensity. Finally Rockne turned to Gipp and asked if he felt like playing. George said, "Sure, let's go."

It would be Gipp's last stand—and incredibly, he rose to the occasion. Without so much as a good warmup, Gipp stepped back and threw thirty-five yards to Anderson for a touchdown. The next time Notre Dame got the ball, Gipp hoisted one to Barry for fifty-five yards and another touchdown. The passing yardage was an intercollegiate record at the time. These farewell moments were as baffling in their brilliance as anything he had ever accomplished on a football field. Rockne, of course, couldn't have known it, but he had seen Gipp perform for the last time.

The next week, as Notre Dame walloped the Michigan Aggies, 25–0, Gipp's health had taken a turn for the worse, and he was in the hospital. But when Notre Dame's annual football dinner was held at the end of the season in the upstairs ballroom of the Oliver Hotel, Gipp showed up. For a while he sat quietly, listening to the usual boilerplate speeches. Halfway through the festivities he walked over to Chet Grant and asked to borrow a handkerchief. Then he whispered something in Grant's ear and walked out, even as Rockne was getting up to speak. Nobody thought too much about his exit, figuring it was just typical of Gipp. After all, he wasn't scheduled to make a speech, and nobody expected that he would.

But within a few days Gipp was confined to his room with what was said to be tonsillitis. Shortly after that he was taken to St. Joseph's Hospital in South Bend. The official version was that he had contracted pneumonia. In a few hours his name was placed on the critical list as the virulent poison presumably from a streptococcus infection shot through his body. Word had now reached the students that their enigmatic campus hero was dying. Gipp's life was ebbing away just as Walter Camp had nominated him as the first Notre Dame player in history to make his All-America first team.

There was a mixture of gloom and disbelief in the buildings and dorms of Notre Dame, for it was difficult for young men to cope with the notion that such an electric figure could be succumbing to some terrible disease. As Gipp fought to stay alive, hundreds of telegrams and letters arrived, wishing him well. Outside of his hospital room, newspapers ran almost daily reports on his struggle.

It has been said that Gipp, as he pursued his fast life, was a fatalist who nursed a premonition of early death. This may have dated from the time when Gipp and a friend visited a circus grounds in South Bend. There a gypsy told his fortune by a perusal of her playing cards. She cautioned him to be very careful, for what she saw threatened an early death for him. This was the type of dire prediction that clairvoyants have been warned not to make to their customers. Gipp appeared to be much shaken by the prophecy, to such an extent that after he drove over to Goldie Mann's place he just sat and brooded as he sipped from a bottle of liquor. When he was challenged to a game of pool by someone he could easily have beaten, he coldly turned down the offer.

On another occasion he predicted to Hunk Anderson that when his time would come, and that might be soon, he'd probably become a Catholic because they seemed to have an inside track on the road to heaven. Whether that was a declaration of facetiousness, or bespoke his fears, is difficult to ascertain.

There was another time, too, when Gipp and some friends, on their way home for Christmas break, carried a suitcase loaded with whiskey. Gipp had beaten a liquor salesman at pool, and because the salesman had no money, Gipp had been willing to settle for the liquor. On the train Gipp opened the bottle, sharing his good fortune with his companions. As they drank out of paper cups supplied by the railroad, the train passed a large cemetery. For a moment, Gipp put down his cup and stared glumly at the burial grounds.

"Before long, that's where I'll be," he said.

One of the friends tried to put the matter in perspective. "We'll all be there someday, George," he said. But Gipp was insistent. "My time here is short," he responded. "I'll beat all of you."

Father Pat Haggerty, called in to minister to Gipp's spiritual needs, went to see him on a daily basis in the hospital. In his years at Notre Dame, Gipp, not a Catholic, had rarely shown any interest in religion or in conversion to the Catholic faith. Gipp's mother, Mrs. Matthew Gipp, and two sisters, also at his bedside constantly, were zealous, low-church Protestants who were opposed adamantly to any last-minute conversion. Whenever Father Haggerty came to the room, they invariably departed.

However, Gipp appeared to welcome Father Haggerty's words and attention. When Gipp was informed that a sermon had been preached to Notre Dame students by Father John F. O'Hara, Notre Dame's prefect of religion, in which prayers and a novena for him were included, he indicated that he would like them to keep it up.

Further support for the argument that Gipp welcomed a conversion came from the straight-talking Hunk Anderson, who was a Protestant. A frequent visitor to Gipp in those last days, Anderson gave his blood to him in a transfusion process that required him to lay alongside the dying man. In a manner of speaking, he was in a perfect position to hear Gipp's words, which were uttered as he went into and out of consciousness.

"I haven't been an angel," said Gipp, "but I can be one if I put as many aces up my sleeve as I can." To Anderson that meant that Gipp was eager to be converted.

"He was on his way out and he knew it," said Anderson, "and he wanted the odds to be in his favor." Anderson's gambling metaphor would have pleased Gipp.

Gipp's conversion was vigorously denied by his family, but they refrained from making a public ruckus out of it, mainly because they were hesitant to hurt the reputation of Notre Dame. They also felt that George wouldn't have cared whether Notre Dame made it part of his legend or not. However, Father Haggerty, eager to temper the feelings of the Gipp family, announced that Gipp had received "a conditional baptism and absolution, because the conversion was one of interpreted intention as distinguished from concrete expression."

Rockne's role in Gipp's terminal hours has also become a subject of some speculation. There is little doubt that he was present a good deal of the time, since he was deeply affected by Gipp's impending death. But precisely what Gipp may have said to him has always remained debatable. Though Rockne claimed that he was at Gipp's bedside when he died, it is probable that he wasn't alone with him in those early-morning hours of December 14, 1920.

During those agonizing moments, Rockne said he revealed to Gipp that Walter Camp had selected him to be on his team.

"That's jake with me," Gipp is said to have answered.

Then Rockne leaned close to Gipp and said: "It must be tough to go."

With some effort, Gipp, speaking in a hoarse whisper, was said to have responded: "What's so tough about it? I've got to go, Rock. It's all right. I'm not afraid. Sometimes when things are going wrong, when the breaks are beating the boys, tell them to go out and win one for the Gipper. I don't know where I'll be then, Rock, but I'll know about it and I'll be happy."

The fact that Rockne never revealed a syllable of this remarkable valedictory until eight years later, during halftime of the Army game at Yankee Stadium, must cast some doubt about its authenticity. (Jack Newcombe of *Sport* magazine wrote that Rockne "pulled" the Gipper talk in a hotel room before his players went out to beat Indiana, 28–7, in the sixth game of the 1921 season. "There is an awful lot of ham in the old Swede," Rockne is purported to have said at the time. But Newcombe's report has never been corroborated from any other source.) In addition, nobody previously had heard Gipp referred to by the nickname of *The Gipper*. Certainly Gipp never used that nickname himself. Would Gipp, not a particularly sentimental man, have uttered words that sound, in retrospect, like sentimental hogwash? Murray Sperber and others have agreed, that Gipp's words read suspiciously like the artful crafting of one of Rockne's ghostwriters.

However, there are believers, just as there are detractors. Chet Grant admitted that for a long time he felt that the anecdote was artificial, something that Gipp was unlikely ever to have said, even in jest. But Grant later changed his mind. "I wouldn't for a moment reject the possibility that the whole thing was legit," he said. Ronald Reagan, the Hollywood Grade B movie actor who became president of the United States, once admitted to biographer Richard Hubler that Rockne may *not* have actually heard Gipp say what he was supposed to have said. But it was too good a line, too pure, not to be used by the enterprising Rockne, and also, of course, by politician Reagan. (In a commencement address at Notre Dame in 1981, President Reagan's dramatic climax was devoted to Gipp's words.) Others have suggested that Gipp may have expressed some variation of the theme, leaving it to Rockne, that cunning architect of tall tales, to mold it to his liking. It could be said that the coach believed in telling the truth—but didn't care to wallow in it!

At Gipp's funeral, held in a blinding snowstorm in the pre-

Christmas season, more than fifteen hundred Notre Dame students and townspeople marched behind the casket. There were six pallbearers, including the ever-loyal Hunk Anderson, Joe Brandy, and Norman Barry (Rockne was not one of them), and the sermon was preached by Father John O'Hara. O'Hara was aware of Gipp's character flaws, yet he regarded him as a "keen-minded, resourceful young man who, on the afternoon of his death, spoke not of the honors he had received but of his death in the arms of God. . . . Although we do not think of George as a deeply religious man, his inmost thoughts came to the surface as he faced death."

During those lugubrious moments of the funeral it seemed that every form of activity halted in South Bend. Students, priests, shopkeepers, and children had all come together in their grief to pay their respects to this young man. Gipp was going home to northern Michigan by train, with the last few miles of the trip to Laurium being traversed by sled.

Gipp had been Rockne's special problem child. But the coach had handled him with patience and forbearance, so that expert observers for years regarded Gipp as the best back they had ever seen. It had been beneficial to Rockne's interests to treat Gipp with kid gloves, for it had worked out well for Notre Dame football.

A tragic early death always buttresses a legend. That was the case with Gipp. Rockne chose not to damage this growing myth by minimizing Gipp's skills or special magic. Whatever negative feelings Rockne may have had about Gipp, not as a football player but as a wayward son, were kept well hidden. At the end Rockne had nothing but praise for Gipp's grit and, surprisingly, for his deep affection for his mother.

Even after Gipp was buried, controversy lingered about him. In this case the embroilment concerned the hospital bill and then the substantial expenses for the funeral. During Gipp's illness Rockne had reached out to several specialists, because of the gravity of his condition. But it was always, as Rockne said, with the family's approval. The bill was sent to Notre Dame for these medical services, and it was considerable—close to five thousand dollars.

Father Burns thought it was only fair that Gipp's family should pay part of it. When the Gipps balked at that proposal, Father Burns agreed to have the school pay the entire sum, for he was determined to avoid any further ill will between Notre Dame and the Gipps.

More rancorous, perhaps, was the dispute over the funeral bill.

From some anti-Catholic sources, including Fielding Yost at Michigan, word got around that Notre Dame had refused to pay the bill for the funeral and had passed it along to the Gipp family. In truth, the school and many students decided to pay for it. Rockne was unforgiving about the "slander" concerning the payment of the bill. He accused Yost, a devout Methodist and an archrival, of being chiefly responsible for the negative story. To Rockne, Yost, born in West Virginia, was a bigoted hillbilly. In the ensuing years their relationship, always stormy, was never patched up to any degree.

9

The Ku Klux Klan on the March

AFTER THE CIVIL WAR, during the Reconstruction era, an organization named the Ku Klux Klan (KKK) emerged in the South. There, in Tennessee, an ill-educated Confederate cavalry hero, General Nathan Bedford Forrest, assembled this group, the spiritual successors to the xenophobic Know-Nothings and the American Protective Association.

Forrest led his white-robed marauders at night, terrorizing and lynching blacks, carpetbaggers, and scalawags. More than fifty years later, the state of Indiana, which had voted for Abraham Lincoln and which was on the Union side in the Civil War, ironically became a hotbed of Ku Kluxism, with a large share of its white male population professing an emotional and actual link to this paranoid society. The muckraker R. L. Duffies remarked that Indiana was a "sheeted Tammany," a place where the KKK could bully politicians on the state and county levels.

The anti-Catholicism of Indiana was embedded in a rock-hard Protestant theology, rooted in evangelical fundamentalism, and driven by unleashed bigotry. Tales about orgies with nuns and the lechery of Catholic priests, who were said to have large noses and thick lips, connoting their sensuality, were rampant among the true believers. It was not unusual for a KKK Konklave in Kokomo, Indiana, which was south of South Bend, to attract as many as two hundred thousand people. Many of these adherents shared fears of a "foreign papacy," supported Prohibition—which many Irish Americans opposed—and blamed any economic dislocations on the hated "outsiders."

So egregious had the atmosphere become in Indiana by 1920 that one of the most powerful people in the state was David C. Stephenson, a power-mad, hard-drinking zealot who had come from Texas to assume the mantle of grand dragon of the KKK. Ultimately, Stephenson, a preacher of righteousness, was implicated in the death of a young woman. That, plus the indictment of the governor of Indiana, as well as the mayor of Indianapolis, on corruption charges eventually brought about a reduction of KKK activity in the state.

However, when Rockne first assumed his leadership role at South Bend, Indiana's KKK contingent was in full bloom, openly harassing Catholics, the main focus of their hatred, while also expressing their detestation of Jews, foreigners, and the few black people in the state. At the start of Stephenson's tenure he arrogantly tried to purchase Valparaiso College, near South Bend, with the objective of turning it into an educational outlet. On another occasion pressure was brought by Indiana's reactionary senator James Watson, who openly supported KKK causes, to force Notre Dame to schedule a game with the Quantico Marines in Washington, D.C. In trying to bully Rockne into booking such a game, Watson was flexing his political strength. But Notre Dame's priests stood firm, as they instructed Rockne to turn down the request. He did, in no uncertain terms, for he despised Watson.

The KKK attempted to create more mischief at Notre Dame by holding a tumultuous week-long klavern in South Bend, which was obviously designed to provoke the Catholic student body. Their intention was to march on Notre Dame by the thousands.

In openly goading Notre Dame's students, the KKK achieved its design. Many of Notre Dame's young men, angered by the Klan's arrogance, fought the robed Stephenson disciples in the streets, often ripping off their hoods. As these hand-to-hand battles proliferated, some police went to the aid of the Klan. When a rumor swept the campus that a Notre Dame student had been murdered, hundreds of vengeful students flooded the courthouse area. Fearing more injuries or deaths, President Matthew Walsh made it clear to the students that they should return peacefully to the campus.

Rev. Walsh was aided by a sudden downpour that did more to clear the premises than his warning.

Ironically, the KKK sought to make a propaganda victory out of the guerrilla warfare engaged in by Notre Dame's students. They claimed that "the fighting Irish," a term they used disdainfully, were barbarians who had no control over their emotions. These Irish toughs, said the KKK, were architects of crime and violence, assaulting babies and women in the streets. The words "the fighting Irish," which Rockne had welcomed as a fitting nickname for his team, were now being turned against Notre Dame as a hostile phrase. However, try as the KKK did, it was too late for such hypocritical revisionism, for the label already had taken on a positive connotation. The countrywide image of "the fighting Irish" was recognized, for the most part, as a proud boast.

"The two-fisted, freckle-faced, red-headed Irishman, who is twice as brave as anyone else, was passing irretrievably into American folklore," wrote William Shannon in *The American Irish*. The KKK's ill-intentioned theorists could do little about that, although there were some bigots in the state who chose to believe the KKK's stories.

At this time the ugly shadow of the KKK and its cross-burnings hovered over more than the state of Indiana. On America's national political scene, Al Smith, the Irish-Catholic governor of New York—a bighearted, cigar-smoking, street-smart fellow—brought up in the squalor of his city's Lower East Side, tried for the Democratic nomination for the presidency in 1924. But he was bitterly fought by Woodrow Wilson's son-in-law William Gibbs McAdoo, who, perhaps unfairly, became a symbol of racial bigotry and fanaticism on the liquor issue. The nomination ultimately went to Wall Street lawyer John W. Davis, who was as exciting as paint drying in the attic. But Smith had valiantly raised the flag of Irish immigrants in the United States, the same group that was now drawn to the legions of Knute Rockne at Notre Dame.

In 1928, when Smith did run for the Democrats, he was defeated by Republican Herbert C. Hoover, in a contest marked by an ignorant "whispering campaign" and cries of "Keep the pope out of the White House!"

This was the social environment in which Rockne, who was still a Protestant, raised Notre Dame to widespread acceptance. While the priests and students at Notre Dame were slandered by their

KKK neighbors, Rockne's teams still managed to capture the admiration of college football fans everywhere. In strong measure this helped to drown out the venom of the self-appointed moral custodians and priest-baiting nativists, for whom the papacy was the home of the devil.

The more that Rockne was exposed to the prejudice around him, the more he was attracted to the religiosity of his surroundings. He was always impressed when he saw his players rushing off to Mass on the mornings of games; many times he would join them. A number of the non-Catholics on the squad also attended morning services. Rockne came to understand that these services, as well as the praying, were not meant to produce any football miracles but served to give his athletes the will and the strength to produce victory.

Though he battled against the virulent anti-Catholicism in his area, Rockne basically remained outside of the politics of his time. Notre Dame in those years did not admit Negroes, but the policy of the school was inviting to poor youngsters, Jews, and Latinos. Rockne had nothing to do with the school's admissions policy. On the other hand, he is not on record as protesting in any way about the exclusion of Negroes. On one occasion, however, in response to a black newspaperman's query, he emphasized that he didn't harbor any prejudices against any person, regardless of color or religion. On the whole, his behavior simply echoed the ethos of his era, long before anyone heard of such "cures" as affirmative action. In a country that continued to practice discrimination and in which some leveled words of bias against those who presumably had Negroid facial characteristics (Babe Ruth was often assailed as a "nigger" due to his large nostrils and big lips, while the swarthy president Warren G. Harding was suspected of having Negro blood), Rockne was hardly a trailblazer fighting such stereotypes.

It was not unusual for Rockne to relate stories about black people that today would be judged as politically incorrect and disparaging. One yarn that he told at banquets had to do with an eighteen-year-old Negro boy who thought he was in love with Eliza, a neighbor. The boy went to his father for advice and was told he couldn't marry the girl because she was his half sister. "I'm her father," the boy was told. "Whatever you do, don't tell her mother." A few months later, the boy met another girl. The father again said that she was the boy's half sister, so he couldn't marry her. Meeting still another attractive girl, the boy this time defied his dad and went to his mother. She listened to his story, then advised him that he could marry any girl in the town. "Your father," she said, "ain't no relation of yours."

Rockne did not have any reservations about telling such a story. On the contrary, he probably felt that there was no harm in it, just as there was no harm in Mark Twain's use of the word "nigger" in *Huckleberry Finn.* He also went along with unsubtle homophobic sentiments, sometimes expressed in his pep talks and paid speeches. He'd often criticize young men who seemed effeminate in style and manners, and he would regale listeners with a flouncy routine, in which he envisioned a future in which a "sissified" group managed to emasculate football. There would be gaily clad players prancing in purple-mauvette tunics, the hosiery specially designed by Patou and perfume by Houbigant. Plays would end when one was tagged out by a deft tap on the shoulder. The referees would be dressed in a regulation costume of plus fours and crepe de Chine blouses. At half time tea would be served as teams contemplated how they would break a scoreless tie. Notre Dame's star player would bear the name of T. Fitzgerald Murphy, better known to his cronies as "Two-Lump," because he would always request two lumps of sugar in his orange pekoe. (Murphy was indubitably a send-up of the Roaring Twenties' F. Scott Fitzgerald, the literary lion from Princeton and Paris.) The big game would be lost on a freak play, with a running back named M. Bickerdash Pix III pulling up just shy of the end zone when he noticed a run in his stocking. Bickerdash, of course, came from an effete North Shore family.

The subworld of the American athlete had a vigorous, acerb-tongued advocate in Rockne, who never failed to celebrate the timeworn, ancient values of brave, tough masculinity. "Rockne was particularly adept at perpetuating the twentieth-century jock-frontier theory of sports as the preserve of American manhood," author Robert Lipsyte has written. "He urged Jazz Age college boys to spend less time socializing, dancing, and debating and to go out and play football. . . . get out where the going is rough."

America should be a place for rugged men, said Rockne, not "flabby ones." Intelligent as he was, Rockne freely engaged in such stereotypes, even as he denounced untruthful and unpleasant stereotypes circulated about Irish Catholics.

As far as Jewish people were concerned, Rockne could be said to have been "philo-Semitic." He pursued several Jewish football players on the grounds that they must be "smart," a typical stereotype about Jews. However, those players he sought happened also

99

to be fast and quick, exactly the prerequisites that Rockne demanded in any of his players, be they white, Catholic, Jewish, Protestant, or atheist.

Notre Dame had no strictures against Jews, either in its student population or faculty, and thus was far ahead of many so-called prestigious institutions that in those years had quotas imposed on Jews.

Several of the greatest Notre Dame players of the 1920s, including Marty Brill, a transfer student from Penn, and Marchy Schwartz, were favorites of the coach and happened to be Jewish—in Marchy's case, half Jewish.

10

Life After Gipp

AS HIS TEAM FLOURISHED on the field in 1921, Rockne was still forced to confront continual charges that Notre Dame was little more than an organized football factory. Amos Alonzo Stagg and Fielding Yost still railed about it whenever they got the chance; Bob Zuppke of Illinois was equally adamant, even though he was possibly as vulnerable as Rockne was when it came to his players accepting money for professional play. Others insisted that most of Rockne's men were just mercenaries, who played professionally on the side and rarely attended classes.

The list of accused Notre Dame players was long. It included Hunk and Eddie Anderson, center Harry Mehre, end Roger Kiley, fullback Chet Wynne, tackle Buck Shaw, and halfback Bob Phelan. The owner of one professional team in Carlinville, Illinois, said that he had personally hired and paid eight Notre Dame men for a game against Taylorville, Illinois, the previous fall. Each player was reported to have received two hundred dollars plus expenses. There was also reason to believe that sizable amounts of money were wagered by the players themselves and by many residents in each town.

As the attacks on Notre Dame's integrity continued, Rockne's own reputation was subjected to a certain amount of skeptical inquiry. If there was truth to many of these assaults on Rockne's role, oftentimes there were unsupported allegations that spread stories that even the most cynical couldn't accept.

For example, there was a rumor that a player named Virgil Evans was granted a temporary release from the Kansas State Reformatory to participate in a season for Notre Dame. Evans supposedly played through the year, then returned to the penitentiary to complete his sentence. In truth, no such player as Evans ever suited up at Notre Dame. However, the other charges of professionalism remained so rampant that Rockne, who had played for the Massillon pros as recently as 1919, was pressured to issue a stern warning to his players. His announcement went as follows:

> If any Notre Dame man is found guilty of playing professional football or in any way violating the college rules, either in spirit or letter, we shall not be in the least lenient. We cannot, for we have to protect our college, and we must protect college football from the encroachments professional football is trying to make on it.

Such an antipro *pronunciamento* coming from Rockne had to be taken with more than a grain of salt, considering his background. He had made his share of money playing for the pros, sometimes under his own name and at other times under assumed names; he had always been close to his players, giving him a splendid opportunity to know what they were up to; and his acquaintance with local sportswriters, as well as a number of national journalists, put him in a position to have an accurate comprehension of what was going on in the football world. In 1920 he had already met Grantland Rice, who was then regarded as the poet laureate of the gridiron. As well, Rockne had gotten to know Ring Lardner, a keen Notre Dame fan and perceptive sports columnist. He was familiar, too, with some big shots of the South Bend gambling community, making it even harder to accept his protests of innocence. As Rockne knew, football and betting mixed seamlessly. He may have been measured differently by different people, but nobody ever accused Rockne of being a babe in the woods.

In time Rockne did become less tolerant of those youngsters who chose to augment their incomes by playing professionally on weekends. With the full football scholarship initiated at Notre Dame in the early 1920s, it became easier for Rockne to adopt such a censorious position. Following the Taylorville-Carlinville misadventure, there is reason to believe that few, if any, Notre Dame players took cash for playing football for the pros. Rockne's edict must have helped to bring about such a situation. But so did the post–Black Sox scandal atmosphere, which presumably did much to throw the fear of God into any gambling-oriented athletes.

Rockne may have had his troubles fending off the reformers and naysayers, but he was already becoming a sought-after coach at other institutions. It was no secret that some schools, inspired by the growing popularity of college football in the Golden Age of Sports, were interested in luring this *Wunderkind* away from South Bend. Midwestern schools such as Minnesota and Northwestern, playing in a league that generally ignored Notre Dame, would have been delighted to hire its coach.

Assuredly, there were some priests who would have been pleased to lose Rockne and thus deemphasize football. But the majority of the faculty were fervently on his side. This latter group was proud of Notre Dame's success on the field and agreed with Rockne that he was underpaid. (His salary was less than ten thousand dollars.) Whenever pressure mounted on Rockne to take his cerebral show elsewhere, he reiterated his desire to remain at Notre Dame. He would also point out that it was patently unfair to discriminate against "a brawny boy because he is not good at math . . . four years of football are calculated to breed in the average man more of the ingredients of success in life than almost any academic course he takes."

By 1921, with Cartier Field expanded to satisfy the increasing appetite for Notre Dame's brand of football, Rockne built an eleven-game schedule. This was the most games ever played by a Notre Dame team in a season and included games with schools such as Iowa and Indiana, which at one time would not have chosen to share a ball park with the Irish.

The season was inaugurated with two home games at Cartier Field. In the first contest, against Kalamazoo, known to be little more than a friendly punching bag, Notre Dame romped by 56–0 as a noisy crowd of eight thousand looked on. In the second game, DePauw, the Old Gold team from Greencastle, Indiana, was the foe. (In the next decade Greencastle reached another level of fame thanks to the depredations of the notorious bank robber John Dillinger.) Established in 1837, DePauw was a coed school with a student body that was essentially middle- and upper-middle-class, unlike most of Notre Dame's enrollees. Few gave DePauw much of a chance against Notre Dame, for the school generally faced such weak Indiana teams as Butler, Wabash, Centre, and Valparaiso. Nonetheless, Rockne insisted that the contest would be no walk in the park for his charges. He pointed to the secret talents of De-Pauw's coach, Fred Walker, and noted that DePauw was bringing along its own water for the game. Obviously he feared that his team might be suffering from overconfidence as it rolled along on an unbeaten string of twenty-one games, including one tie. One always had to wonder whether Rockne ever believed his own advance flummery. As things turned out, DePauw played a strong first half before succumbing by 57–10. The DePauw publication *Mirage* noted that the Irish "*almost* swamped the Tigers" and insisted that no better DePauw team had ever "gone out to battle."

Next in line to face Notre Dame, at Iowa City, were the Iowa Hawkeyes, a Big Ten Conference team coached by Howard Jones. Like Rockne, Jones was already regarded as one of the game's most astute strategists. Employing a shift with an unbalanced-line single wing, Jones had other important assets in a giant Negro tackle named Duke Slater, who invariably competed without a helmet, and quarterback Aubrey Devine. As Rockne never took any of Notre Dame's rivals lightly, he warned his boys that the Hawkeyes were a tough squad out for blood. He emphasized that most of Iowa's team were native Iowans who were eager to upend the favored Irish. Despite Rockne's caveats and the fact that his men knew how antagonistic he was to the Big Ten, his team never seemed to get up for the game.

"We were riding high and had big heads," said Eddie Anderson, who captained the team from his post at end. Iowa also had a modest four-game winning streak at the time, as it faced a Notre Dame lineup that resembled a coaching convention of the future (Frank Thomas, Eddie Anderson, Chet Wynne, Tom Lieb, Clipper Smith, Harry Mehre, Hunk Anderson). Before Notre Dame knew what was happening to them, Iowa broke loose for a quick touch-down. Within a few more minutes, the Hawkeyes added a long field goal to take a 10–0 lead. When the Irish responded in the second period with a touchdown, the deficit was reduced to 10–7, and Rockne believed his team was ready to roll.

However, Notre Dame insisted on fumbling away its opportu-nities, even as it piled up considerable yardage. "We murdered them in statistics," said Eddie Anderson dolefully. Rockne was more caustic. "You guys should be penalized for abusing the ball," he grumbled at half time, when it was not unusual for him to break loose with a motivational speech.

There was no improvement for Notre Dame in the second half, although the Irish got as close as the one-yard line. At that point Iowa intercepted a pass. When the game ended, at 10–7, and Notre Dame's undefeated run was shattered, Rockne, attempting to stifle his rage, told his team that they were able to run all over the place but had simply forgotten how to score. In the dressing room many of the players were crying. As disconsolate as he was, Rockne reminded them that they had lost to a good team. "Remember, there are no alibis," he said. "This defeat will do us some good and may teach something to our followers, who think we can't be beaten."

If Rockne had sought an alibi, he could have had a good one. Notre Dame's colors were blue and gold, and it wore jerseys that were dark blue. Iowa's jerseys were black. In the gloom and darkness of the final period, played under a heavy cushion of fall clouds, Notre Dame resorted to forward passes. It was then that Iowa came up with its crucial interception. There were some in the Notre Dame camp who blamed the similarity of jerseys for the loss, for they felt that Mohardt had mistakenly thrown into the arms of a Hawkeye defender. Whatever Rockne may have thought about this theory—and he publicly never endorsed it—all of his future teams were decked out in *green* jerseys.

At one o'clock in the morning after the defeat, the train carrying Rockne and his disappointed crew rolled into the South Bend railroad station. The coach literally felt like hiding. But that proved to be impossible, for over a thousand students, slogging three miles into town, greeted the train as it pulled in. Insistent cries went up for Rockne to appear and to say a few words. The coach had tears in his eyes as he gazed at the upturned faces. But he composed himself long enough to blurt out that he couldn't imagine ever leaving Notre Dame after such a reception.

"As long as you want me, I'll be here," he declared. In the coming years there were times when he may have regretted this profession of loyalty.

One of Rockne's favorite themes over the years was to remind his players that they had to possess "mental poise" to win. After the Iowa loss, two Notre Dame players were confronted in their off-campus apartment by the irate janitor of their building.

"What happened to you guys?" he asked. "What beat you?"

"Mental poise," one of the boys responded.

"I always knew that bum couldn't play football," the janitor snapped.

During the week following the Iowa setback, Rockne was in no mood for forgiveness. He put his squad through several days of unyielding practice sessions as the players worked themselves into a lather over the impending game with Purdue's Boilermakers, another hated Big Ten member. Rockne's versions of "tough love" worked admirably. The Irish pounced on their rivals as they took out all of their frustrations on Coach Will Dietz's undermanned team. At halftime Notre Dame was ahead, 30–0 (the final score was 33–0), due mostly to the furious play at guard of Hunk Anderson, who blocked two punts within three minutes. Each time Hunk scored a touchdown. "The team had fever in the blood," remarked a Notre Dame publicist.

Next came Nebraska, in the Homecoming Game played at Cartier Field. By this time enthusiasm had reached a new peak on the campus as students tended to regard Nebraska as something of a sacrificial lamb, substituting for an Iowa team that had rudely upset the Irish applecart. Even at half time, when the Irish held on to a bare lead, there was no need for Rockne to be disappointed, for his team was playing with great intensity. (On many occasions Rockne would sit morosely during the intermission period if his team failed to live up to his expectations. Then, as his boys ran back to the field, he'd bark disparagingly, "All right, girls, let's go!" Throwing up questions about his players' lack of masculinity was standard operating procedure for the coach.) In a display of defensive pugnacity that warmed Rockne's heart, the Irish limited Nebraska to three first downs, and won, 7–0.

Rockne was up to his old tricks again the following week as his team faced Indiana in a downpour at Indianapolis. He was determined to set matters straight with a Big Ten team that he felt had played unfairly with Notre Dame the year before. In a pregame philippic, Rockne reminded his team that the Hoosiers had possibly contributed to Gipp's early death by their unsportsmanlike tactics. However, what was most surprising about the speech was that there was no mention of Gipp's supposed deathbed request and no use of the nickname "the Gipper." Just a year after Gipp's demise, the story should have been fresh in Rockne's mind.

After the Irish emerged victorious against Indiana, by 28–7, Rockne visited the losers' locker room. Once there he congratulated a big lineman whom he thought had played a magnificent game. "I want to shake hands with a sportsman, the greatest football player, and the only clean-playing man on your squad," he said. Even if one young man came away with a coachly benediction, the statement, of course, was meant to chastise the Indiana team. It was rare for Rockne to make disparaging comments about opponents. But he felt compelled to do so in this instance.

Now came an experiment in Notre Dame's expanding gridiron itinerary. Rockne had scheduled three games within eight days, including the now-traditional meeting with Army at West Point. (The two other games that were booked were with Rutgers and Haskell Institute.) The Army game was fast becoming one of the premier productions of the Roaring Twenties, holding its own with other elite sports attractions that kept the American public salivating for more. Each year the game had advanced to the same level as the much-ballyhooed heavyweight championship battles promoted by the legendary Tex Rickard and featuring such warriors as Jack Dempsey, Gene Tunney, Georges Carpentier, and Luis Angel Firpo. Indeed, by the midtwenties, Army–Notre Dame was right up there in appeal with the New York Yankees' baseball dynasty, headed by the home run twins Babe Ruth and Lou Gehrig. In Rockne's wildest dreams he could never have imagined that his little South Bend school would have seized the public's interest to the extent that it did.

When Notre Dame first railroaded East to play Army at West Point, with a guarantee of a picayune one thousand dollars, Rockne was a star player. But by 1921 he was the coach, with Rickardian showmanship qualities. He perceived the Army–Notre Dame annual clash as a wonderful partnership, a rivalry that would reap national exposure. But he was not involved in it solely because he loved competition. Ultimately, he believed, the game would produce large dividends for Notre Dame's exchequer.

As long as the game was played at West Point there was little chance for the latter, as there was no gate admission charged by Army. The demand for these free seats became so high that West Point installed extra wooden stands. Additional trains were also scheduled to enable the fervent supporters from New York City and environs to get to the game. For this eighth contest between the two squads, twenty thousand people were jammed into the stands above the Hudson, the largest assemblage ever for a Cadet game. Intent on maintaining order on these grounds that he always considered sacred, General MacArthur, superintendent of the Military Academy, was forced to call on the Military Police to prevent any overenthusiastic fans from causing trouble.

There was also another controversy prior to the game. Army authorities continued to take exception to Rockne's celebrated backfield shift, which some critics insisted gave the Irish backs illegal momentum before the ball was snapped. It wasn't the first time the issue had been raised by Notre Dame foes, for ever since Rockne had installed the rhythmic system it was said that the Irish players appeared to be beating the ball. This supposedly caused opposing teams to be caught off-balance, thus bringing about innumerable penalties for offside infractions. So insistent were Army's pregame objections to Rockne's well-synchronized troops that the game was actually in some danger of being canceled. However, Rockne, who badly wanted things to go smoothly in this relationship, worked to iron things out so the game could go on.

However, by the time the first half was over, with Notre Dame ahead, 14–0, Army's coach, Charles Daly, raised the issue again. He was shrill enough to draw the attention of Rockne. Cagily diplomatic, Rockne then informed Ed Thorp, the game's chief referee, that for the rest of the game he would instruct his backs not to use the infamous shift. Rockne must have known that it wouldn't make any appreciable difference in the final analysis, and it didn't. Notre Dame added two touchdowns in the second half, running its plays out of a stationary formation, and finished the game with a 28–0 margin. Before the next football season got under way a new rule went into effect designed to minimize the impact of Rockne's original Notre Dame shift. There was to be a total halt in momentum between the completion of the shift and the snap of the pigskin. That didn't rule out the possibility of Rockne's pupils swaying to maintain the cadence of the play. It would take further rulings, in coming years, to put an end to any of Rockne's artful evasions.

The men from South Bend found that West Point was a wonderful place in which to play football. That had as much to do with the game itself as well as the fact that Army was in accessible firing range of New York's Great White Way. Rockne let his players take full advantage of a Broadway education. That included a trip by the squad to the glittering Ziegfeld Follies extravaganza, at the Globe Theatre.

In time Rockne managed to associate with almost all of the sports, political, and entertainment celebrities of his era, among them the Babe; Jack Dempsey; Bobby Jones; Red Grange; Bill Tilden; the sports-loving playboy mayor of New York City, Jimmy Walker; Lou Gehrig; Grantland Rice; Ring Lardner; Westbrook Pegler; and "the man who owned Broadway," George M. Cohan. These people became part of a wide circle of Rockne's acquaintances, although they were not necessarily close friends. When the public viewed Rockne in the black-and-white newsreels together with the Manassa Mauler, Dempsey, or with the pumpkin-faced Ruth, this signified to them that these personalities were all part of a singular, congenial fraternity. Rockne delighted in these casual "palships" with the elite and, doubtlessly, these glamorous figures of the period enjoyed his company, too. But, on occasion, when these friends didn't serve him properly, Rockne's anger would come to the surface. Pegler, who could be as dyspeptic as Granny Rice was softhearted, once described Rockne has having the appearance of "an old punched-up preliminary fighter who becomes a doortender in a speakeasy and sits at a shadowy table in a corner room near the door at night recalling the time he fought Billy Papke for fifty bucks in Peoria." The coach despised this portrait of himself and spoke heatedly to Pegler about it. Though they eventually repaired their relationship, things were never quite the same again between the two men.

Several days after the victory at West Point, Notre Dame faced its brand-new New Jersey opponent, Rutgers. For some time Rockne had been eager to book Notre Dame into a New York stadium, which would fit in perfectly with his design to make the Irish a truly national team. In addition, he was cognizant, as were other Notre Dame authorities, of the enormous constituency that the Irish owned in the big city. Therefore, it was only natural that Rockne should seek out the bathtub-shaped Polo Grounds as the site for the Rutgers clash. The home of feisty John McGraw's New York Giants, a team that had dominated the baseball world for almost two decades, the Polo Grounds was also the playground for the up-and-coming New York Yankees. From 1913 through 1922 the Giants played landlord for the Yankees, as Babe Ruth took aim at the inviting right-field porch while waiting for the Yankees' grand palace, Yankee Stadium, to be built.

The Polo Grounds, situated in the lee of Coogan's Bluff—once called Coogan's Hollow—was on the fringe of Manhattan Island, bordering on the Harlem River at 157th Street and Eighth Avenue. It was probably the only ball park in creation that fans entered by

Super-salesman Rockne (second from left) joined in a hat promotion stunt with New York Yankees home-run sluggers Lou Gehrig (second from right) and Babe Ruth (right). Courtesy: UPI-Corbis-Bettmann.

walking downhill. But Rockne didn't perceive that his move to play Rutgers there in 1921 was in any way a downhill move.

The World Series of 1921, between the Giants and the Yankees, was completed in mid-October at the Polo Grounds, with McGraw's team coming out on top. Since the Yankees were McGraw's tenants, all of the games were played in the Polo Grounds, the first time in Series history that such an odd situation had occurred.

For Rockne to bring his team into such a colorful venue was thought to be a major accomplishment. But the game failed to induce the sports-crazy populace of New York to break down the gates. Fewer than twelve thousand people showed up for Notre

Dame's debut in Manhattan on a perfect football afternoon. Certainly this was a disappointment for Rockne, as the school wound up receiving only five thousand dollars, from which expenses had to be deducted. However, on the field it was nothing less than a famous victory. The Irish battered Rutgers, 48–0, while also succeeding in reaping extensive favorable coverage from New York's dozen or so newspapers. Because the Rutgers coach, Foster Sanford, had little else to crow about, he focused again on the ever-controversial Notre Dame shift.

"I insist that your backs remain rigid after the shift," Sanford said, forlornly, to Rockne. To which Rockne retorted, "Too many of them are already rigid—on their backs in the dressing room."

After the Rutgers game Rockne guided his team to victories over the Haskell Institute Indians, 42–7, at Cartier Field, before a slim home crowd of five thousand. That was followed by a triumph over Marquette at Milwaukee, the third game and victory in little more than a week, possibly the first time that a highly rated team had accomplished such a feat. Rockne was never one to duck a challenge. This one, of course, was of his own making, for nobody had asked him to arrange such a strenuous schedule.

Rockne chose to miss the game against Haskell, for he was off scouting Marquette as they beat North Dakota. He had informed his players that he wanted to bring himself up to date on Coach John Ryan's Marquette squad. This wariness about Marquette was hard to comprehend, for the Milwaukeeans had previously not flashed much of an offense. However, Rockne's advance snooping (another innovation that he strongly favored) might have contributed to the 21–7 victory over Marquette.

One of Marquette's substitute players, Pat O'Brien, became a cinema favorite in the 1930s. After Rockne's death he played the coach in a movie titled *Knute Rockne: All-American*. The popular Warner Brothers film might have caused Rockne to flinch at O'Brien's saintly characterization.

In Notre Dame's final game of the 1921 schedule they defeated the Michigan Aggies, 48–0, on Thanksgiving Day. The noisy crowd of 15,000 at Cartier Field was considered a record assemblage. The team had won ten games, losing only to Iowa, while yielding only five touchdowns in eleven games. Such a performance elevated Rockne to a still higher level among his associates and an admiring press.

"Rockne was the greatest of all in the way of human appeal," wrote Grantland Rice, possibly his most fevered advocate in the press box. "Rockne's personality and rare human touch lifted him to the front. The man had an incisive manner of speech that electrified those around him." Needless to say, all those personality strengths would have meant little if they hadn't been combined with an extraordinary record of achievement on the field.

Now Rockne was also constantly emphasizing the value of college football as a sturdy preparation for life in the real world. He always tried to remain close to his athletes and encouraged them to consult him when they had problems. He had even attempted to make himself available to the unfortunate Gipp, even as Gipp marched to his own drummer.

By this time Rockne had also determined to take an unequivocal stand against professional football. This posture had developed over several years, following a period of ambiguity. Instead of pro football as a career, he advised young men to seek jobs in coaching. Ultimately, a veritable legion of men who had played under him became football coaches, including the early group headed by the two Andersons, Clipper Smith, Frank Thomas, and Dutch Bergman.

From the start of his own coaching career Rockne always put the accent on challenge, perfection, hard work, humor, toughness, and a measure of disparagement. Many of Rockne's most earnest competitors acknowledged him as the paradigmatic figure in his profession and made an effort to emulate him. If Rockne's players failed to play up to his own high standards he could be cuttingly sarcastic and wry. It was not unusual for him to trim a player's sails in a scathing way. Then he'd attempt to build up the besieged player at a later time. A player such as Harvey O'Boyle and some others came to Notre Dame with impressive credentials but were treated so cavalierly by Rockne that they'd threaten to turn in their uniforms. "That's just fine," Rockne would say. "I was just about to ask for it, anyway."

Some of his speeches might have been a paraphrase of the duke of Wellington at Waterloo: "You may not frighten the enemy. But Gad, sir, you frighten me." When Rockne uttered statements similar to that, his players usually accepted it without resentment. Some, of course, may have secretly chafed at such treatment.

Rockne didn't stop coaching when the season ended. Due to his constant need for extra money—and, not the least, because he also loved his chosen profession—he frequently held summer school courses. One of his students was Bentley Glass, who later became a celebrated geneticist. Glass was born in China to missionary parents and came to the United States, where he attended the University of Texas. Planning to become a high school teacher, Glass was interviewed for such a job in a small Texas town. He got the job but only after he was informed that he'd also be expected to coach the football team. Glass knew nothing about the game but was reluctant to reveal that to his interviewer. When he heard about a summer course in football, Glass, who had never even seen a football game, enrolled in it. Much to his surprise, he found that he was much taken with the approach and technique of his instructor—Knute Rockne. That fall Glass's high school team won all but one of its games, in the best season the school had ever experienced.

Rockne constantly sought other means to augment his income. As soon as he became famous outside of South Bend he was approached to put his name on articles about football. He had become particularly facile at dealing with the press, most of whom had happily contributed to the buildup of Notre Dame's gridiron mystique. And now it was the press that was offering him a chance to join up with them. In such a concordat he arranged to become a weekly columnist, often predicting the outcome of games on the national circuit, a practice that many school authorities frowned upon, because it obviously encouraged betting. Not a few of the faculty at Notre Dame were dismayed by Rockne's crystal-balling, but the majority were pleased that he was getting such widespread exposure. In other columns Rockne wrote about certain players or strategies or delivered a spate of anecdotes, true or meretricious.

One odd aspect of Rockne's journalistic efforts was that as amusing and talented as he was at speechmaking, he might have been expected to be equally proficient at drafting a readable column of a few hundred words. However, due to the press of time—he was also the school's athletic director and was involved with every phase of the football program, including recruiting—Rockne was willing to relegate the actual writing of his syndicated pieces to ghostwriters. Christy Walsh, considered to be the first person ever employed as a sports agent, convinced Rockne that he could hire surrogates to do his typing. Walsh already handled other sports personalities, including Babe Ruth, who was never known as a rival to Ernest Hemingway. In taking over Rockne's account, Walsh actually worked at some of the writing himself.

However, Rockne and the Babe were hardly the first sports figures to permit their names to appear over ghostwritten material. The angry baseball genius Ty Cobb had a ghostwriter. So did legendary New York Giants pitcher Christy Mathewson, who used a ghost named John Wheeler, a newspaperman who had once performed this magical chore for the Mexican revolutionary Pancho Villa. Such patent artifice did not appear to give Rockne pause, despite the fact that many readers of his words naively believed that each paragraph was carefully created by the coach. Francis Wallace, sportswriter, novelist, and press agent for Notre Dame causes, also did some ghostwriting for Rockne and, in the later stages of Rockne's career, so did John B. Kennedy of *Collier's* magazine.

All the while, Notre Dame insisted that Rockne continue to maintain his portfolio as track coach. Every one of Notre Dame's fifteen hundred students was obligated to participate in some athletic endeavor, even those who had scant desire to move their legs or dirty their pants. This was designed to fulfill the ancient Greek theory that insisted that a man of sound body and mind would be a more fitting member of society. One such "unfit" person was Walter Wellesley Smith, who arrived at Notre Dame from Green Bay, Wisconsin, with only a modest desire to accelerate his heart rate. However, in conformity with the rules of the school, Smith, known as "Brick" to his school pals, went out for the freshman track team.

For a few weeks Smith trained with the varsity, working out on the cinder track that encircled Cartier Field. It was then that he encountered Rockne for the first time. In his postgraduate days, when he had become known as "Red" Smith, one of the most artful chroniclers of sports doings for papers in Milwaukee, Boston, Philadelphia, and New York, he recalled how Rockne presided over track and football on Cartier Field.

"While the padded gladiators butted heads on the field, Rockne somehow seemed able to watch a half-miler and a left end simultaneously," Smith wrote. "In those days his only assistant was Hunk Anderson, who would finish his job at the Edwards Iron Works in South Bend and hustle out to the campus to serve as unpaid line coach. Most practice sessions would start with Rockne giving preliminary instructions to the backs and ends, while Hunk got the interior linemen warmed up."

It was in such an atmosphere, Ira Berkow has written in a biography of Smith, that the future sports columnist trod the cinders as he prepared for a freshman-varsity handicap meet that started the indoor season. Smith ran ten laps of the twelve-lap mile and never ran track again. "I would have finished sooner or later," wrote Smith, "if Rock hadn't got me confused with a judge at one of the turns, who was also stationary. 'Hey, over there at the turn,' Rockne shouted, 'step aside, will you. We want to start the quarter-mile.'"

So, at a school that put such an emphasis on manliness and physical engagement, Smith was content to remain a spectator. "Football, of course, was an exalted activity on campus. There were pep rallies on Friday nights when a parade of students carrying red flares marched through the campus and roused others from dormitories, leading all to the gymnasium. There, team members would speak," Smith wrote. "Then came the highlight—Coach Rockne. There'd be a wild burst of applause and in a brief speech he'd bring down the house."

Smith never ceased to admire Rockne, who, he maintained, was a great man who could have been successful at anything he tried. That Rockne chose football was football's good fortune, according to Smith.

Rockne's improvising mind never ceased coming up with new ideas, all of which presumably would help to win football games. Before many other schools seized on the notion, Rockne inaugurated the tradition of spring football practice. He felt that in this way he could get an advance line on his talent and perhaps gain some valuable insights into those who would do or die for him the next fall. He also scheduled an annual spring game, in which graduating seniors would play those who would make up the varsity squad the next year. In one of these spectacles Rockne decided, as he approached age thirty-four, to participate with the seniors. Carrying around more than the suspicion of a potbelly, he was hardly in shape to compete with the young men in Notre Dame's future. Assigning himself the role of quarterback, Rockne called his own play, a sneak into the line. He was smeared ruthlessly on this attempt, a case of lèse majesté if ever there was one. On an ensuing play he instructed Mohardt to throw him a short pass. With a look of sheer glee on his round face, Rockne caught the ball, then immediately retired from the premises. There was nothing like coming out ahead, even in a mock game such as this one.

11

The Ride of the Four Horsemen

As THE NEW SEASON approached, Rockne, ever an exemplar of the work ethic, was faced with several immediate challenges. He had to develop a new team out of mostly inexperienced sophomores. The veterans of the late war had gone and only Paul Castner and Frank Thomas remained in the backfield. He had to continue to bolster Notre Dame's winning tradition, which had now placed his team among the nation's best. He had to tackle a ten-game schedule with renewed passion. In addition, he would take a hand in designing a new uniform for his troops. Nothing was too far removed from his purview.

As usual, Army would be the big, traditional game, whereas Georgia Tech was a newcomer to the grinding schedule. Others, such as Purdue and Nebraska, would be back for another shot at his men. It was not uncommon for friends, associates, would-be Notre Dame alumni, vicarious Notre Dame students, Irish rooters, and others to recommend football talent to Rockne. He could have filled a telephone directory with names of potential players that had been passed along to him by admirers. The case of Adam Walsh was typical.

A Los Angeles lawyer, Leo Ward, told his friend Rockne about Walsh, a fine high school athlete. But Walsh's mother was reluctant to have Adam go too far away from home to attend college.

Getting word of such reservations, Rockne wrote to Ward: "Send the boy on. Tell Mrs. Walsh I'll treat him like a father." Apparently such diplomacy worked with the Walsh family—even if Rockne had misspoken. He had meant to say he'd treat Adam like a son. In a few years Walsh became center and captain on a Notre Dame line that was known as the Seven Mules.

Rockne was an inveterate letter-writer, cajoler, and schmoozer. In the course of many casual conversations he obtained leads that enabled him to bring many outstanding players to South Bend. The celebrated Four Horsemen backfield—Harry Stuhldreher, Don Miller, Jim Crowley, and Elmer Layden—that emerged between 1922 and 1924 was a direct result of the energetic networking that characterized Rockne's football program.

It is not true that the reputation of the Four Horsemen was based primarily on excessive sports page idolatry, for these men were, indeed, enormously talented and in sync as a group. But memory tends to improve performance to the heart's desire. Don Miller, in musing about the continuing fame of the quartet thirty years later, said, "Each year the Four Horsemen run faster, block better, and score more touchdowns than ever."

Nevertheless, the pieces of the Horsemen fit together like a well-constructed jigsaw puzzle, as the fans were constantly reminded. Rockne assembled other backfields that may have merited almost as much praise. Gipp, of course, was a one-man backfield, to some observers—and there were backfields to come in the late twenties that were of great quality. But it is clear that the Four Horsemen gestated from a system of enthusiastic and open recruiting at a school that was fortunate to have Rockne as its chief psychologist, ringmaster, and cheerleader.

In trying to explain how he developed the Four Horsemen backfield, Rockne planted his tongue firmly in his cheek. "How it came to pass that four young men were so eminently qualified by temperament, physique, and instinctive pacing to complement one another perfectly and thus produce the best coordinated and most picturesque backfield in the recent history of football—how that came about is one of the inscrutable achievements of coincidence of which I know nothing save that it's a rather satisfying mouthful of words," he said.

Francis Wallace insisted, however, that the Four Horsemen would always remain nonpareil because "they resulted from a series of accidents, involving many creative people, not likely to be repeated."

Rockne knew football talent on the hoof when he saw it. He had a sixth sense about a player's potential. He truly liked the boys who played for him—and he'd do almost anything for them. In their postgraduate years, he'd help get them jobs—often coaching football. They, in turn, would do almost anything for him. That certainly applied to the Four Horsemen. A surrogate father to so many Notre Dame players, Rockne never seemed to have much time left over to minister to his own sons. "Many of us used to go to him with confidences that we would not have mentioned to our own parents," remarked one of the linemen on the 1924 team. Bonnie more or less raised the boys by herself, with only occasional help from Knute. While Rockne preached the values of football, hard work, discipline, and personal responsibility, he often neglected his responsibility toward his own sons. One observer has even gone so far as to suggest that Rockne was reckless in embarking on his final, ill-fated air trip, thus inconsiderately leaving behind a distraught wife and children. Certainly, he couldn't have anticipated such a dreadful accident. However, exempting him from blame in this fatal incident doesn't free him of blame for other neglectful behavior. His boys did not fare well as they grew up in the shadow of such a famous man. The burden was heavy for them. They were never particularly good athletes and, at Notre Dame, they fared poorly in their studies.

The four players who made up the Horsemen all came from veritable hotbeds of football enthusiasm—Wisconsin, Iowa, and Ohio. Not all of them were stars as high school players, but they were sufficiently skilled to attract the attention of Rockne's unofficial scouts in the field. In fact, the Four Horsemen should have been labeled the Four Ponies, for their average weight was about 155 pounds. Elmer Layden, the heaviest of them, weighed only 161 pounds, but he appeared much lighter than that. Harry Stuhldreher, the quarterback, looked like a little boy on the gridiron and weighed 150 pounds. Miller and Jim Crowley were both 157 pounds.

Layden had been the local pride of Davenport High School in Iowa. He had won a measure of fame in the area for his punting. He needed little persuasion to come to Notre Dame, for his father was a confirmed Notre Dame fan who appreciated what Rockne had done for Irish football. Walter Halas, the coach of Layden at

Davenport High, was Rockne's chief scout and head baseball and basketball coach at Notre Dame. Thus there was never any doubt about where Elmer would wind up at school, even if he had originally enrolled at the University of Iowa.

The Millers of Defiance, Ohio, were a remarkable football family. Nobody ever heard of a Miller who didn't go to Notre Dame and play football. "Red" Miller was a brilliant halfback who led Notre Dame to victory over Michigan in 1909. Ray and Walter also played with distinction, the latter being a teammate of Gipp. Now it was Don Miller's turn. Curiously, his other brother, Jerry, was often judged to be a more formidable candidate for Rockne's team than Don.

Jim Crowley played his high school football in Green Bay, Wisconsin, an area that regarded football as a religion long before the taskmaster Vince Lombardi ever put in his appearance there. Crowley was a talented passer, though in other aspects of the game he wasn't rated too highly. Nevertheless, he was approached by Marquette, the University of Wisconsin, and Washington and Jefferson, where Greasy Neale was coach. Notre Dame alumni who lived in Wisconsin encouraged him to attend Notre Dame. Their feeling was that the pass-minded Rockne would be able to exploit Crowley's arm. (As a freshman Crowley, in Rockne's eyes, "looked dull and always resembled a lad about to get out of bed." Thus the nickname of Sleepy Jim was ultimately bestowed on him.) Before arriving at Notre Dame, Crowley had never met Rockne. He turned out, by his own admission, to be the least apt student of the Four Horsemen. In his freshman year at Notre Dame Crowley was billed by the school's treasurer for a few hundred dollars, money he didn't have at the time. A few days later he scored two touchdowns in a frosh contest. Immediately he gave the bill to Rockne, believing it to be a propitious time to do so. Crowley never heard from the treasurer again. "Like Stuhldreher, I was a little lonesome when I first arrived at South Bend," said Crowley, "because I'd never been away from home. But I was always confident that I'd make it. . . . Rock was a giving man, but in the beginning he swore a lot. He raised hell with me once when he accused me of breaking training. I told him I hadn't. I was hurt by what Rock had said but I got over it."

Massillon, Ohio, had always been an incubator of football prodigies, perhaps more of them than any other community in the country. It took its football as seriously as Indiana took its basketball.

The Massillon High School team, under the direction of Jack Snavely, boasted a number of players who were not only bigger than Harry Stuhldreher but also more talented. In addition, Stuhldreher's older brother, Walter, already at Notre Dame, was talking up the place to Harry from the first time that Harry touched a football. For a while there was a snag, for Harry's studies weren't faring too well. He enrolled at Kiski Prep in Pennsylvania, with the object of buckling down in his classwork. There he played under Jack Marks, who had earlier coached at South Bend and who was pushing for Stuhldreher to attend Notre Dame.

When Harry first arrived at Notre Dame he seemed to have misgivings about his choice. "My brother left me to myself. I had counted on him showing me the ropes and introducing me to his friends," Stuhldreher wrote in his autobiography. "I asked him to help me out but his only answer was, 'It's time to learn to be on your own, go out and find things out for yourself like I had to do. That's the way we do things at Notre Dame.'"

Left to fend for himself, Stuhldreher admitted that Notre Dame appeared to be "the most cheerless place in the world." However, by the time that fall football practice got under way, Stuhldreher had made some friends, in particular with Rip Miller, a onetime rival from Canton, Ohio, not a part of the Miller dynasty, but, in time, part of the Seven Mules line. It wasn't long before Stuhldreher felt very much at home, not only in South Bend but also in the Notre Dame backfield. And not long after that Harry became the first-string quarterback and the acknowledged leader of the team.

As freshmen Rockne didn't think that his future Four Horsemen (they didn't win that name until their senior year) were particularly impressive. "I thought that they could be whipped into a combination of average players. Not much more than that at the time. That's all the dream I had of them then," said Rockne.

There were always the little things that Rockne paid close attention to; that applied to his Four Horsemen as well. He valued brains, mental and moral courage, a sense of responsibility and fair play, and the emotional urge that often lifts a man to another level. But, to him, the element of speed was probably as important as any of these other facets of the game.

Because he regarded Layden and Miller as the fastest of his Horsemen, Rockne tried to bring Crowley and Stuhldreher close to them in performance. To try to achieve this result, he provided

Jim and Harry with lighter stockings, thigh guards, and shoes. When this improvisation failed to bring both men up to the quickness level of Layden and Miller, he told them to dispense altogether with their thigh guards.

Rockne had an appreciation of his own skills and mentor talents, yet he was willing to listen to advice, especially when it came from someone he respected. But if he had reservations about the advice donor he could be sardonic. At one summer clinic Stuhldreher was exhibiting the passing technique taught to him by Rockne. A sideline critic objected to the way the receivers were catching Stuhldreher's passes. Rockne told the critic that it might be a good idea for *him* to demonstrate how to receive Harry's tosses. The man immediately accepted the offer, whereupon Stuhldreher unleashed a bullet right at him. The pigskin was squarely on the mark, but the man's outstretched arms failed to smother the ball.

"We've done a lot of passing around here since 1913," said Rockne caustically, "and we've been more or less successful at it. We're always open to new ideas but they have to be good ones."

With a rookie backfield in place in 1922 Notre Dame won the first four games on its schedule, against Kalamazoo, St. Louis, Purdue, and DePauw. Only DePauw pushed a touchdown across against the Irish.

Fifth on the schedule was Georgia Tech, led by Red Barron and coached by Bill Alexander. Playing psychological games, Rockne announced that Alexander "could get more out of nothing than any coach in America." It was a fine way to put Alexander on the spot and, perhaps, to lessen the pressure on himself.

By the time they confronted the Georgians Stuhldreher and Miller had become Rockne's key backs. Don had sufficiently increased his speed by working out his legs in indoor track. Such commitment pleased Rockne no end. Stuhldreher had also shown signs of developing into a fine defensive back, and he was fearless in his blocking, even when he faced much bigger men. That, combined with his pinpoint passing, caused Rockne to push him ahead of the slower quarterback, Frank Thomas.

Pressure on a group of athletes can take many forms. In traveling to Atlanta, in the Deep South, to face Georgia Tech, there was an additional hurdle for Rockne. He was leading a contingent of largely Catholic football players into hostile territory, home to a substantial presence of Ku Klux Klanners. The Georgia demagogue

Thomas Watson, who was the presidential candidate of the Populist Party in 1904 and 1908, spewed anti-Catholicism in almost every public utterance. He railed at the pope as "Jimmy Cheesey, a fat old Dago who lived with voluptuous women." Catholic priests were denounced by Watson as "sensualists and rapists." Watson was so certain that Catholics were out to get him that he surrounded himself with security personnel. The fact also that Tom Watson occupied a seat in the U.S. Senate, affording him a national pulpit for his ravings, didn't help matters for the Notre Dame youngsters.

Not many years before, in 1915, the twenty-nine-year-old superintendent of a pencil factory, Leo Frank, a Jew, had been hanged from an oak tree in Marietta, Georgia, for allegedly beating to death thirteen-year-old Mary Phagan. (Marietta is not far from Atlanta.) There was good reason to believe that Frank was completely innocent of the crime, but the lynch mob, including some of the most respected citizens in the town, refused to back down from its murderous purpose.

Certainly there were many bigots and anti-Catholics back home in Indiana, but Rockne wasn't sure how to prepare his men for the reception they might receive in Georgia. After all, he had been cautioned by many influential people at Notre Dame not to book Georgia Tech for this game, thus risking humiliation for his players.

After considerable thought, Rockne chose not to lecture his team about the KKK roaming the hills of this red clay and biscuits country. Instead, he simply commented on the unsettling Rebel yells they might hear before and during the game. He let it go at that, concluding that it just wasn't the time to deliver a carping lecture about the residual effects of the late Civil War on the Deep South. But he did unleash a pregame spiel that underlined his continued belief in the power of an emotional appeal.

As his invading Midwesterners huddled uncertainly in the locker room only minutes before the start of the game, Rockne let loose in all of his mawkish glory. "We've come a long way down here into the South to play this game. We're meeting a great team in Georgia Tech, the greatest in the South," he began. "We're playing in a climate that is warm and new to us and that may give us trouble. We're a young, green team. But now I want you to show what you're going to do for Notre Dame and for me and for yourselves. And, remember, I don't want you boys to be the kind who are willing only to go out and cheer for Notre Dame. I want you to go out there this afternoon and *live* for Notre Dame. Remember that Georgia Tech will be playing this afternoon not only for Tech but for the honor of southern football."

Rockne hadn't finished, not yet. "You know," he continued, sotto voce, "I could stand the disappointment and criticism that would come from defeat today. I could stand the criticism that would come in the newspapers, from the football writers, from some of the alumni and the people back home in South Bend . . . but this is the sort of thing that makes this game mean a lot to me. This is the reason why I don't want to go back home tomorrow and have to admit that we failed."

Arriving at this climax, Rockne slowly removed a crumpled telegraph from his pocket. In silence he stared at the words on the missive. Then he began to read aloud: "PLEASE WIN THIS GAME FOR MY DADDY. IT'S VERY IMPORTANT TO HIM."

"It's from Billy," Rockne whispered. "He's very ill and is in the hospital."

Billy Rockne, the six-year-old son of the coach, had won a role as the mascot of the Notre Dame team. He loved being around the players, and they loved having him with them. When they heard what Rockne had to tell them about little Billy, some of them began to cry, while others jumped up from their perches and swore they would annihilate Tech just for Billy. Indeed, that's exactly what they proceeded to do. The final score was 13–3 in favor of the Irish, and all of the hollering and whooping and anti-Catholic epithets from the intensely partisan Southerners couldn't stem the tide.

When the victorious Notre Damers returned to South Bend to be greeted by the usual worshipful throng of admirers at the railroad station, who was on hand to welcome them home? Why, Billy Rockne, of course. Jim Crowley, who invariably could see the humor in such situations, remarked, "You never saw a healthier-looking kid in your life. I don't think Billy had been in a hospital since the day he was born."

It wasn't the first or the last time that Rockne would resort to such chicanery. But his players never seemed to resent such subterfuge. They fully understood what made their coach tick, and they appreciated his need to win. For the most part, they shared his desires.

Against Indiana the following week Rockne trotted out a venerable local priest, who reminded the Notre Dame players at halftime that he'd never seen an Irish team lose on its home field. That

Notre Dame won rather handily that afternoon on Cartier Field may have had some connection to the priest's pep talk. Then again, it probably would have wound up a Notre Dame victory even without the wise goading of the priest.

Coming into the Army game on November 11 at West Point's Cullum Field, the Irish remained unbeaten. But so were the Cadets, a postwar group that had been pieced together from a shrinking Corps of Cadets by Coach Daly. Daly had to work hard to assemble his squad, for there weren't too many aspiring footballers who were eager to attend the Point at the conclusion of World War I. Daly had been working under a cloud for some time because Army's superintendent, Douglas MacArthur, continued to gaze longingly at South Bend. It was still no secret that General MacArthur had a yen to hire Rockne. However, Rockne actually had never been approached by MacArthur for the job, and Daly was permitted to remain in place in an effort to revive Army's fortunes. Using the Notre Dame shift and an unbalanced line, Daly depended on his rugged All-America center, Edgar Garbisch, to instill discipline into his team. The combination worked, for Army had played beyond Daly's expectations.

An excursion train again came from New York City to accommodate all of those noisy fans who now regarded this annual game as the highlight of the autumn season. The rivalry had grown since Rockne had teamed up with Gus Dorais to astound the West Pointers with their passing game. But it was decided that the 1922 contest would be the last ever played between the two squads on Cullum Hall Field.

The event simply had gotten too big to be staged again on the intimate field in the Hudson River Valley. There, on the serene, lush site on the west side of the Hudson, rising some two hundred feet from the river's bank, Notre Dame and Army had battled through the early years of their competition. While Notre Dame, under Rockne, had produced its dynamic teams, West Point's military monastery had been the breeding grounds for America's most esteemed combat generals.

Now Cullum Hall Field would be abandoned, while the Irish were scheduled to face Army in 1923 at Brooklyn's historic Ebbets Field, the home of the baseball Dodgers of the National League. (In time Army would replace Cullum with Michie Stadium.)

The 1922 game was fiercely fought, from start to finish. But it was perhaps fitting that the game would end in a 0–0 tie. Rockne had long felt that any Notre Dame team that could hold its foe for three quarters was bound to win it in the fourth quarter. This time it didn't work out that way, much to Rockne's distress. Notre Dame came close to victory—four yards away from it—in the last quarter. But at that critical stage Jim Crowley fumbled, Army recovered, and Notre Dame was lucky to emerge with a stalemate. Army's Garbisch missed a forty-four-yard field goal by a foot, thus producing the first deadlock in the series.

Rockne's disappointment was compounded by the fact that Notre Dame also had to absorb high travel costs. The guarantee from Army, less than five hundred dollars, was scarcely generous. Nevertheless, when the students turned out en masse to cheer their warriors as they returned home, the pain was eased. This ritual, now standard operating procedure, win or lose, reflected the key role that Notre Dame's players had assumed at South Bend. Rockne also strongly believed that such displays were constructive for morale and esprit de corps, both of which he felt were valuable psychological weapons in his team's arsenal. South Bend may have been an undersized, remote little community, but there was no denying that it could organize tumultuous welcome home parties.

After the standoff with Army, Notre Dame walloped Butler, 31–3. An Indianapolis school, Butler had scheduled Notre Dame for the first time. When regular fullback Paul Castner broke his hip in this game, thus ending a career that once promised to be as brilliant as Gipp's, Layden was switched to his position. Thus the Four Horsemen were introduced as a backfield unit for the first time.

The following week the team journeyed to Pittsburgh for the first time to meet Carnegie Tech at Forbes Field, the major-league ball park inhabited by the Pittsburgh Pirates. With more than thirty thousand fans coming out to watch the Irish play—including a large number of Notre Dame rooters—Notre Dame won easily, 19–0. This time Rockne was pleased that his team received nine thousand dollars of take-home money, which served to compensate for the short cash from West Point. Carnegie Tech, with this game, also became a regular opponent on Rockne's schedule. In future years they would not be as placid a foe as they were in 1922.

The season's finale was against a tough Nebraska eleven, reportedly the heaviest in that school's history. Featuring several backs weighing well over two hundred pounds, Nebraska, always difficult to handle for Rockne, stood in the way of another unbeaten campaign for Notre Dame. Having lost only one game, to

Syracuse, the Cornhuskers were never an easy foe on their home grounds at Lincoln. When Notre Dame had come up against Georgia Tech they were prepared to face a hostile crowd, but the intensity of anti-Catholic feeling in Nebraska came as something of a surprise to Rockne.

Sensing the mood of the crowd in Lincoln, Rockne decided to unload another of his psychological surprises. As his team took the field, Rockne, usually a nervous chatterbox, remained quiet. Gathering his athletes around him in a pregame huddle on the sidelines, Rockne removed the usual prop of a telegram from his pocket. A consummate actor, with a mastery of his script, Rockne could bring a tremble to his lips if the occasion demanded it. This was such an occasion.

The telegram shook in Rockne's hand as he began to tell his boys what it said. "The Tournament of Roses Committee, the fellows who select the teams for the Rose Bowl game in Pasadena, California," Rockne said, "are thinking of us as the possible eastern choice for the Rose Bowl this year!" Notre Dame had never gone to the Rose Bowl, the granddaddy of all the postseason gridiron playgrounds. It was Rockne's intention to provide one more overriding goal for his team that day against Nebraska.

But as happened on occasion, Rockne had overreached. His playacting came up short. Nebraska was just too good that afternoon as they whipped the Irish, 14–6. The loss deprived Notre Dame of an unbeaten year. Cod Cotton, a tackle on that Rockne team and a fellow who was known for his witticisms, felt that his coach had badly oversold the Rose Bowl "invitation."

"All I could think of about the Rose Bowl game and our going," Cotton said later, "was red roses, Mary Pickford, Gloria Swanson, and eternal sunshine." Obviously Cotton echoed the sentiments of other members of the squad.

"It was some game," Jim Crowley recalled, "and the strange part was that when it was all over Rockne was actually pleased about how we played, even though we lost. He shook my hand, congratulating me on a tackle that I'd made. Then, when we were back at the hotel, he went around to every room, shaking each player's hand."

Rockne may have qualified as a certified ham, but he knew how to handle men. Even Max Houser, a lineman and one of the team's true comics, didn't resent the remark that Rockne made to him after he'd played only a few minutes in the loss to Nebraska. "I'm saving you for the Junior Prom," Rockne said to Houser, who laughed along with everybody else within hearing distance. This Rockne comment has since passed into the vocabulary of the sport. *Without* Notre Dame in the Rose Bowl, Southern California beat Penn State, 14–3, on New Year's Day.

Rockne was much in the tradition of Huey Long, another iconic figure of the twenties. Although Rockne probably never met the noisy Louisiana demagogue, his speaking talent was on a par with Huey's. As Louisiana's governor, Long had an abiding affection for Louisiana State University's football team and rarely passed up a chance to address LSU's footballers before a contest or at halftime. Long must have been aware of Rockne's evangelical efforts at Notre Dame and sought to emulate him.

The first time that Long campaigned in rural southern Louisiana, a largely Catholic area, he informed his audience that as a boy he would arise at six in the morning on Sundays, hitch his spavined horse to a buggy, and take his Catholic grandparents to Mass. A bemused aide reminded Long that he didn't have any Catholic grandparents, to which Long replied with glee, "Why, we didn't even have a horse!"

Rockne shared the "permissible lie" technique with Long and also with Ronald Reagan. The latter came along after Rockne's death to invent any number of fanciful stories, which, after much repetition, he began to believe. Reagan's tall tales didn't prevent him from winning the White House, any more than Rockne's yarns prevented him from winning football games. After the constant retelling of many of his own trademark stories, Rockne came to believe them, as much as Reagan did his own anecdotes.

12

Charges and Countercharges

As Notre Dame's countrywide reputation for producing outstanding football teams grew, so did the accusations of excessive recruiting, under-the-table payments, professionalism, favoritism, and phony jobs mount against the Rockne regime.

Rockne generally had the support of his school's administrators, although some of the purists may have nursed objections that they managed to keep to themselves. Certainly the student body, proud to root for a winner, were not critical of Rockne's artful manipulations to entice footballers to South Bend. After all, Rockne's successes had put the school on the map, and such successes increased prestige for Notre Dame, as well as money for the treasury.

However, when the heat became too intense, President Matthew Walsh was forced to publicly deny that Notre Dame was systematically paying its football players. "It's a lie," Walsh declared. He also expressed his anger at the fact that the members of the Western Conference continued to deny Notre Dame entry into its group. He agreed with Rockne, for the most part, that the Big Ten conglomerate was hardly as clean as a hound's tooth. But it was difficult for either man to suggest that the schools of the Big Ten engaged in the same excesses as they did. That would amount to an open admission that Notre Dame was guilty of everything it had been charged with. What's more, Walsh was not about to acknowledge that Rockne was probably more skilled than the others at such skulduggery. That Rockne had developed into the master gridiron salesman of his time was unquestioned. But Walsh was not likely to boast about it. Instead, he preferred to accuse Western Conference members of anti-Catholic bias. There was substantial basis for such accusations, but that didn't make Notre Dame's artifices any more palatable. When newspaper stories charged that there were some players at Notre Dame who had put in full seasons on other college squads before enrolling at South Bend, the faculty board that oversaw Notre Dame's athletic department was forced to drop such students from the school.

However, even under these circumstances, Rockne refused to be defensive. "Football isn't commercialized enough because only about twenty-five out of a thousand colleges make any real money out of it," he said, going on the offensive.

Never reluctant to address the criticism and "slurs" directed against him, Rockne used speeches, interviews, and newspaper columns to deflect such attacks. Often his arguments were wry and philosophical—but he rarely discussed such matters as "ringers," no-show jobs for which players received payments, or recruitment of players who would have had a hard time passing grammar school exams.

"Has anyone ever defined 'overemphasis'? They talk about football and its evils, yet they don't offer any clear-cut analysis of their charges. They do it to get publicity," Rockne would say. "You can't blame them very much for that—but let's stop this scramble for the front page and hiding behind the skirts of fighting for football purity."

His verbal onslaught would continue. "I'm inclined to believe that there are just too many reformers. The government should reform the reformers. Their first kick is always against spring practice. They say it takes too much time from a boy's schedule. If a thorough study were made of it, it would be clearly seen that it doesn't take as much time as crew, track, or basketball. If a boy wants to come out for spring football practice, do these reformers want us to stop him?" he'd ask querulously. "I'd like to have some of these 'no-men' and 'viewers with alarm' talk to any of my football men and find out whether or not spring practice is a bore. Thank God for the type of boy at Notre Dame who prefers physical activity to drugstore athletics."

Rockne also confronted the arguments about the so-called evil effects of intersectional games. "Critics contend that these games give football entirely too much importance, that they take too much time from classroom work, and that in order to correct this fault the schedules should be confined to traditional rivals in a college's own section. . . . Centuries ago the countries of the Balkan states competed annually in what are supposed to be the original Olympic Games. Any jingo propaganda concerning one of these competing countries was quickly quelled because their representatives understood one another's ideas and customs. This did more to eliminate warfare among these states than anything in its history."

Rockne went on to state that intersectional games were a wonderful way to educate young people, to exchange ideas, and to meet and make friends from different parts of the country. "If someone should say to them that Californians are narrow-minded, they can stand up and attack such a belief. They can learn that all Southerners are not lazy, that all Northerners are not cold-blooded, and that all Midwesterners are not hicks. Get out of your backyard and get going!"

As far as the big wads of money that football was bringing in, Rockne again was not about to issue any apologies. "Where does that money go? Does the faculty get it, do the football coaches benefit from it, does it get into the hands of alumni? No, it does not," he argued. "Most of it goes into the college treasury to help new facilities, build new dormitories, classroom buildings, and laboratory equipment. This gives the student body a more complete education. Football helps to carry other college sports, as well as the intramural programs. Those big crowds are necessary for that to happen. There's nothing wrong with football, or any phase of it. When people keep criticizing it, it's [a] sure sign that football is doing well. Football is a great game. If there's any harm coming from it, it's coming from the crowds who flock into the stands. Why blame the game? It's like the man with indigestion blaming the food instead of himself for overeating!"

Some commentators, such as Paul Gallico, a percipient observer of the scene for the *New York Daily News*, did not agree with Rockne's stance. "College football is one of the last great strongholds of genuine, old-fashioned American hypocrisy," Gallico wrote. "It is coming into its own as the leader in the field of double-dealing, deception, sham, cant and humbug . . . the thing that is so inexplicable is that there is nothing wrong with what the colleges are doing to promote good football teams for themselves, except their stubborn and dishonest insistence that they are still playing the game under the old standards. . . . By refusing to admit this the colleges have managed to get themselves involved in a dirty and subversive business."

Gallico had great respect for Rockne as a strategist, and he wasn't pointing his angry typewriter solely at him. But he still felt that Rockne was one of the chief practitioners of the hypocrisy he decried.

As such turmoil threatened to disrupt Rockne's ambitious plans for Notre Dame, the coach still pursued his job with brio. He did everything but write his own press releases, and if called on to do that he would have been equally as adept as Francis Wallace. At one stage Rockne helped plan each year's schedule. If need be, he could have cooked and served the meals at the team's training table.

Generally, Rockne was the beneficiary of a positive press. A man with such a magnetic personality, couldn't fail to attract favorable comment. More and more of the big-city writers and press box giants of the time, including Rice, Heywood Broun, Lardner, Pegler, Damon Runyon, Gallico, and W. O. McGeehan paid attention to him, usually in a flattering way. As they provided mythic and often saccharine accounts of the feats of other heroes of the age, they added Rockne to their list. Most of these writers liked Rockne as a man and were on good terms with him. Pegler, who admired people with brains and spirit, should also have been a friend of Rockne. But when he once wrote that Rockne used ghostwriters, the coach found that to be an unbearable insult.

Football players with talent and the right connections kept arriving on South Bend's doorstep. The squad invariably was one hundred strong, giving Rockne plenty of leeway for choosing the best eleven players as starters. Each year the schedule became increasingly difficult and more attractive. There was no dispute that Rockne continued to get the pick of Catholic players from Catholic schools, and many of these youngsters were helped in getting jobs that kept them at the school. The most desirable jobs were in concessions or program sales—but it was more pleasurable to get a job that didn't even require showing up!

By this time the team was constantly moving around the country on its ten-game commitment and using the railroads to such an extent that Stuhldreher was moved to remark that "our backs have gotten so shifty because they're constantly getting in and out of upper berths."

Not only had Rockne put together the backfield of the Four Horsemen, but he had also rounded up a supporting cast that won almost as many plaudits as the more coddled backfield performers. The line, headed by Adam Walsh, the 190-pound center, came to be known as the Seven Mules and included the following men, none of whom was particularly big: Ed Hunsinger and Chuck Collins at the ends; Rip Miller and Joe Bach at the tackles; and Noble Kizer and Johnny Weibel, the guards. There were some among the Seven Mules who felt that they didn't get their due from an adoring press because of the acclaim heaped on Stuhldreher and Company. But, for the most part, Rockne never felt that there was any true animosity between the backs and the linemen. He believed, instead, that the strengths and weaknesses of the Horsemen and the Mules dovetailed perfectly. For a while, however, the Horsemen moved so rapidly that they would be on the tails of the linemen before the latter could make a move. Rockne solved that problem by getting the Horsemen to retreat a foot or two before they shifted.

Rockne reaped much satisfaction out of the exploits of his Four Horsemen. "Each of these Horsemen shone individually in his day," Rockne wrote. "Destined to be immortal in football, they often caused me pain and labor, but mostly they brought great joy, not only to their coach but to spectators." He especially appreciated their esprit de corps and the pleasure they got out of playing together.

It was Rockne's own philosophy that helped to establish this positive outlook of his players. "We often hear of football teams representing large colleges who have successful seasons ruined because of cliques working against one another or fraternity trouble that forces the coach to play certain men, or the fellows on the team who break training because they are disinterested. Whether this is true or not, I do not know," Rockne said. "At Notre Dame we have a wonderful type of boy, who is thoroughly interested and involved in his team's success. We have no fraternities, so there is no trouble from that angle. There is no forcing me to play anybody. I am not more interested in playing one boy than another. The eleven best men, regardless of nationality, creed, social prominence, or financial status, will make up my team. We try to have one big, happy family." Most of the time Rockne seemed to achieve that state of sublimity, so rare in competitive football.

There were times, however, when aggrieved fathers, suspecting that their sons were not receiving proper consideration from their coach, would storm, uninvited, into Rockne's office. But Rockne was a master in placating them, or at least making them "sullen, if not mutinous" (in the words of Herman Hickman, a Yale coach of another generation).

"Sit down," Rockne would say soothingly, "and let's reason this thing out." Then he'd invariably tell the irate father that he understood why he'd come to see him and that he appreciated that he had his boy's best interest at heart. After a brief, mollifying lecture, Rockne would accompany the man to the practice field, where the coach would emphasize how players had to cooperate with each other to make anything work.

"We can't get very far if players fall down on their jobs. For instance, some young men like to do certain things, like running or passing, but they neglect other things that are equally essential to winning. That's the case with your son. We've got to get him to work on it." More often than not, the father would come away convinced that his boy was playing under a sympathetic, patient teacher.

Rockne expected each man to work hard and to do his bit. For example, the Four Horsemen took advantage of every opportunity to practice, even if the military-type drilling could become boringly repetitious. In no other way could they have become so skilled as a unit. He worked to instill confidence in them and tried, as Stuhldreher said, to get them to achieve a "level mental balance." He knew that football could be a punishing, physically demanding game, sometimes even brutal, so he believed it was important to use humor and to poke fun at the appropriate moment. "Humor goes hand in hand with good sportsmanship," Rockne said.

Rockne didn't mind cockiness if it was kept in proper check. Normally a cocky man, Jim Crowley could be restrained by a measure of delicate needling from his coach. In a game against Princeton in 1923 Crowley took the ball and started on one of those circuitous journeys, aided by his hip motion, that had contributed to establishing his credentials as an All-American. But when a Princeton player dashed up the field after him, Crowley made the wrong move and was stopped from behind. Rockne felt that Crowley should have gone for a touchdown, and he reminded him of this at halftime in the dressing room.

"Yeah, I guess I made a mistake," confessed Crowley. "I didn't know the guy was that fast. I should have cut back."

"That wasn't the mistake you made," interjected Rockne.

"Yes, it was," insisted Crowley. "I admit it, it was a mistake."

"No," said Rockne. "This fellow didn't know who you were. If you had shown him all of those New York clippings that you've been saving up, telling all about how good you are, he wouldn't have dared to come near you!"

There was little question that Rockne was a man in complete control of the men who played under him. If necessary, he would chisel his players down to size or build them up, when the situation required it. But he also possessed a remarkable vision outside of the playing field. Before even half of America had brought radios into their living rooms, he was fully aware of something called television.

"Soon not only will people be able to hear an account of this great game but they'll be able to see it by means of television," Rockne prophesied. "There's no doubt, too, that intersectional games will be increased by aviation, bringing more color into college schedules. Some will be content to sit at home and get the account by radio or television. But the real dyed-in-the-wool fan will want to be out there in the throng."

Rockne's view of the two media was entirely optimistic, even before most intelligent people thought much about their possible impact. It would be years before some frightened sports executives understood how radio and television would expand the popularity of football and other sports. But Rockne appreciated its potential impact even in the 1920s.

As 1923 approached, it wasn't too quixotic for Notre Dame fans to expect wonderful things from their football team. After all, the World War I returnees had won twenty-nine games from 1919 to 1921, during two undefeated seasons, while one game was lost by three points. The 1922 squad had posted the one loss, to Nebraska. Ever the realist, Rockne knew that his line was weak in reserves but that whoever had named his starters the Seven Mules had gotten it right. As for the Four Horsemen, they would be back as a unit, even if Red Maher, Dutch Bergman, and Frank Reese were on hand to mount a challenge to them.

Notre Dame started the '23 season with a home game victory over Kalamazoo. The contest was more like a track meet, with the Irish running up a 74–0 margin over a seriously undermanned opponent. There were some football coaches who chose not to scorch the foe too badly for fear that someday they might be hoist by their own petard. Rockne knew there was always such a thing as retribution. But from the opening kickoff, when Notre Dame went for a ninety-five-yard touchdown against Kalamazoo, Rockne couldn't have prevented the rash of scores, even if he had tried. The seventy-four points rolled up by the Irish was the most ever scored by a Notre Dame team in one game under Rockne.

Before Notre Dame could get too overconfident, they won the following Saturday by only 14–0, over Lombard, at South Bend. Rockne knew that his team was looking past Lombard to the annual game with Army, so he was pleased, in a perverse way, that his players did not win in a walkover. Now he could get his charges practicing with more zeal as they prepared for the Cadets. Organized practice usually began each day at three forty-five, but the Horsemen showed up at two-thirty, demonstrating the kind of commitment that Rockne dearly loved.

Notre Dame's players were aware that Army came into this game with no defeats in their last twelve games, although the mark did include two ties, one against the Irish. So the Irish were determined to put on a good show in New York, where Rockne realized Notre Dame's future reputation could be augmented by the sports journalists in that city.

At first the Polo Grounds had been booked for the game. But a World Series between the Giants and the Yankees, to be played at the Polo Grounds and Yankee Stadium, represented a dramatic counterattraction to the Army–Notre Dame clash. It was no small matter trying to compete with the likes of Babe Ruth, who was in his joyful youth as baseball's most extraordinary home run slugger. The Irish would have preferred playing in the Yankees' brand-new palace, Yankee Stadium, which had opened in April of that year, or, of course, at the Polo Grounds. But it was not to be.

Only a month before the Army–Notre Dame game, it still remained uncertain as to which New York ball park would be used. Then Joe Byrne, Jr., a Notre Dame alumnus with important contacts in the business world, held himself out as "the eastern representative of Notre Dame" and made a deal with Dave Driscoll of the Brooklyn Robins (the baseball team's nickname was a tribute to their chubby, popular manager, Wilbert Robinson). There were some back at South Bend who were annoyed at Byrne's intrusion into the matter. But Rockne couldn't have been more gratified, for he yearned for this game in the Big City—even if it had to go to Brooklyn. The agreement negotiated by Byrne guaranteed Notre Dame a one-third share of the net receipts. Byrne also got a go-ahead to sell and distribute more than a thousand tickets, which he had no trouble doing.

Though Notre Dame's image as a football power was no longer limited to the parochial Midwest, New York's papers were surprisingly delinquent in their pregame coverage of the game. There was some excuse for this omission, due to the World Series being fought out at the time between two local ball clubs. But with its large Irish Catholic student body, Notre Dame might have been expected to reap more substantial coverage in the Gotham tabloids.

Nevertheless, on a warm and pleasant October 13 afternoon, the Ebbets Field bandbox was filled to capacity with more than thirty thousand Notre Dame and Army adherents. Another ten thousand or so clamored to gain entrance. Though the Irish were enjoying increasingly good crowds after the war it marked the first time they had ever played before a sold-out house.

Meanwhile, over at the Polo Grounds that same afternoon, the Yankees of Colonel Jacob Ruppert were winning, 8–4, before forty-six thousand fans, thus putting them within hailing distance of their first world championship. (The unkempt ex-Harvard journalist Heywood Broun, who would become a celebrant of Rockne and Notre Dame, was working the baseball beat that day and writing such lyrics as "The Ruth Is Mighty and Shall Prevail.")

Army, under the leadership of John McEwan, fielded an excellent team against the Irish. McEwan knew exactly how difficult Notre Dame would be, for he had played several times against the Irish. But he had a former All-America from Pitt, "Tiny" Hewitt, in his backfield, as well as the renowned Garbisch at center. The latter anchored a line averaging more than two hundred pounds, unusually hefty in those days. Rockne's troops, were considerably lighter, by his own choice, for he preferred fleet linemen to go along with his scatbacks.

In anticipation of a grueling struggle, Rockne made a rather odd proposal to McEwan before the game. "Maybe we ought to play shorter periods," he suggested, feeling that the traditional fifteen-minute quarters might be too much for both sides. McEwan politely laughed that one off, in a riposte that, for a change, got the better of Rockne. "Once a year," he said, "the Notre Dame team gives us a lesson, so we want the full sixty-minute course."

Prior to the game the Corps of Cadets came marching on the field, looking very much like a stiff-backed invading army. Rockne's squad of more than seventy-five men were almost as precise in their drills as the Cadets.

After a scoreless first quarter, Layden, who had one of his best all-around days as punter, runner, and pass receiver, grabbed an aerial from Stuhldreher and went over for a touchdown. Crowley kicked the extra point. Though the Horsemen had played before as a group, this marked the first time they had *started* the game as a unit. Stuhldreher was number 32, Crowley was 18, Miller was 16, and Layden was 5.

At halftime Notre Dame led by 7–0, with so many players banged up in one way or another that Rockne's suggestion to McEwan appeared more than whimsical. The second half, when Notre Dame scored one more time to account for the final score of 13–0, was equally bruising. Crowley, a true disciple of Rockne, used his mouth as well as his legs in helping to produce an Irish victory. Late in the game, when Notre Dame needed a few crucial yards for a first down, Crowley interrupted Stuhldreher as he was barking out signals. He then proceeded to pace out, almost in slow motion, the yardage needed from his position to the line of scrimmage. In a voice loud enough for Army's players to hear, Crowley said, "Why, it's only ten yards . . . a truck horse could run that far!" On the following play Crowley had no difficulty ripping off a large gain that led to Notre Dame's second touchdown. Rockne invariably gave Sleepy Jim due credit for his improvisations; he did this time, too.

Rockne had pointed for Army in 1923, as he did every year. But the pelt that Rockne truly wanted in '23 was Princeton, the rival the week after Army. If Notre Dame could lick Princeton, that would mean two victories on successive Saturdays over two of the best teams in the East.

Under Jesse Harper, Notre Dame had played Yale in 1914 and was badly beaten, 28–0. But when Notre Dame tried to rebook Yale the following fall they were turned down, which left a sour taste at South Bend. Yale had been the only so-called eastern elite college that the Irish had ever tussled with on the gridiron before this Princeton engagement, so Rockne was determined to beat the men from New Jersey. To him, they were the enemy, a bunch of biased Protestant Yankees who owned banks and summered in palatial homes.

Woodrow Wilson, once president of Princeton, said, strangely enough, that colleges were factories of the privileged and their products were not useful to the nation. As if that was not bad enough, F. Scott Fitzgerald said he never got much out of Princeton. Rockne took note of such feelings and happily shared such stereotypes. He got his hackles up at what he perceived to be the phony class-consciousness of Princetonians and scornfully thought that Princeton was an oasis of upper-class aristocrats, a sanctuary for snobs. These refined young men, he believed, spent most of their off-hours tea-dancing at the Plaza.

With such a negative view of the haughty Princetonians, Rockne prepared for the Tigers almost a year in advance. "He began what might be called subliminal coaching," wrote Francis Wallace. "He projected his occasional questions of a tactical nature into a full-fledged game between Notre Dame and Princeton. He knew the Princeton players and all of their idiosyncrasies, the Princeton system and its strong plays. He tried to acquaint his men with the people and conditions they were apt to face at Palmer Stadium on that next October . . . he wanted to have the boys go away with the idea that they could beat Princeton—but only after a terrific struggle, with tremendous concentration on every detail."

Princeton's coach, William W. Roper, had become head man there in 1919 after having played baseball, basketball, and football at Nassau. Although the overwhelming passion of his life was football, he had been active, as a member of Philadelphia's City Council, in trying to repeal Prohibition and modify Pennsylvania's Sunday blue laws. Thus, like Rockne, he was a man of many dimensions and also something of a romantic when it came to the gridiron game.

"Some coaches were remembered for their systems of play," commented writer Allison Danzig, "but the name of Bill Roper meant dramatic dressing room talk and last-minute victories . . . he used his oratorical ability to great effect in his coaching and was an intense figure at football rallies . . . he could make his team play better than it knew how in the crucial game of the year."

Although the contest with Notre Dame was not Princeton's "crucial game" of the year, as the traditional rivalries with Harvard and Yale always remained the focus of Princeton's season, Roper was still in top form before the clash with the Irish. As he set about rousing his players with a typical pregame oration, Roper was unaware that Rockne could hear every word that he uttered, as the Notre Dame dressing room was right next to the Princeton quarters. Instead of unleashing his own pep talk, Rockne remained quiet; the silence was puzzling to all of his stalwarts. Then he winked at each of his Four Horsemen.

"They tell me that this fellow Bill Roper is a terrific orator," said Rockne. "You fellows just lay on the floor and listen to him, while I save my voice. Maybe you'll learn something."

When the Irish players ran onto the field, they were more keyed up by Roper's words than by anything that Rockne might have provided as his own verbal stimulant.

As it turned out, Princeton was hardly prepared for the precision and speed of Notre Dame's attack, and they succumbed quite easily, 25–2.

The turning point of the game arrived when Miller went off tackle for what appeared to be a sizable gain, only to fumble the ball. Quick as a flash, a Princeton back, trained superbly in the opportunism instilled in him by Coach Roper, scooped up the loose ball and headed for the goal line, some seventy yards away. The only barrier between the Princeton runner and his two blockers was Miller himself. Miller raced across the field to cut off the Princeton men, though it seemed impossible that he could overtake them. But, as Rockne recalled it, Miller ran "in front and to one side of the interferers, crowding them toward the sideline . . . he feinted in and out to slow up the Princeton brigade and did this so calculatingly that by the time they were within twenty yards or so of the Notre Dame goal line, our fastest end, Clem Growe, had time to rush up and tackle the ball carrier from behind . . . thus Miller redeemed his fumble by as heady a piece of work as any I have ever seen. . . ."

Again, Notre Dame played before a crowd of more than thirty thousand, most of whom were heartsick by the setback to their home team. Back at South Bend, where many of the students followed the game via the newfangled Gridgraphic (a play-by-play transmission), there was a raucous celebration. Princeton was every bit the *bête noire* to them that it was to Knute Rockne.

Following the victory, Rockne rewarded his players by taking them to New York City to see the Ziegfeld Follies.

Starring in the Follies at the time was the popular, gum-chewing cowboy philosopher Will Rogers, known jocularly along Broadway as "the poet lariat." During the show, which featured platoons of gorgeous young women bedecked in ostrich feathers—and little else—Will issued some laudatory comments about Knute and his team. Then, suddenly, while twirling his educated rope, Rogers threw his lasso over the shining bald pate of Rockne, who was sitting close to the proscenium. Much against his wishes, Rockne was pulled onto the stage as the crowd and the Notre Dame players roared their encouragement.

Rogers had performed this act before with other celebrities in the audience and he was confident that the publicity-savvy Rockne would have no objection. As things turned out, this little piece of show business shtick initiated a friendship between Rockne and Rogers that would last until the day Rockne died.

Following the successes against Army and Princeton, it appeared that again Notre Dame had a chance at an unbeaten season. The team played well against Georgia Tech, smashing out a 35–7 victory. Because the game was at South Bend, before a sympathetic crowd, Notre Dame wasn't forced to undergo the trauma it had experienced previously against Tech, while playing in the South. Purdue also wasn't much of a foe, going down to defeat, 34–7. But in the seventh and next game, against Nebraska, at Lincoln, Notre Dame was again faced with a rampant anti-Catholicism from the stands. However, it would be unwise to suggest that that was the reason for the Irish suffering their first defeat of the year. Rockne, aware of the bigotry that poured out of the mouths of a number of Nebraska fans, knew that his team simply had played badly. It wasn't until the final moments of the game that Notre Dame was able to score a touchdown in the 14–7 loss. It wasn't easy to comprehend how a team that had played with such opportunism in its earlier games could have performed so ineptly against the Cornhuskers.

Rockne wasn't dismissive of the dismal behavior of some segments of the Lincoln crowd, as well as the local newspaper, which had taken to calling his team "THE HORRIBLE HIBERNIANS." But he was eager to keep Nebraska on Notre Dame's schedule. For one thing, Nebraska rated among the Midwest's football powers each year (although in 1923 they had lost to Syracuse and to Illinois, with its celebrated touchdown manufacturer Red Grange, and had played ties with Kansas and Missouri). For another, it was a certainty that Notre Dame would attract large crowds to its clashes with Nebraska, thus bringing much-needed revenue to Notre Dame's program.

Rockne was diplomatic in the extreme in assessing reasons for the defeat at Lincoln. "My team needs no alibi, its record is good enough," he began. But he did believe that Nebraska's new stadium had something to do with it. "They had been unable to grow grass on the gridiron. The field was hard-baked, so to prevent unnecessary bruises to the players, the field had been plowed to make it soft," he explained. "It was probably a well-meant procedure but it applied four-wheel brakes to the Horsemen."

Some years later Rockne was more philosophical about the loss. "Losing that game did my team a lot of good. It was a game they figured to win. They eased up. They thought they could win at any time. In short, they thought they were better than they were. It was a good lesson, a chastening, humiliating lesson. They would never ease up again," he said.

Any way one looked at the performance in Lincoln, it marked only the second game that the Horsemen lost. The first defeat also had occurred in Lincoln. It gave Rockne a persuasive reason to look forward to revenge against the Cornhuskers in 1924.

In the windup games of the '23 campaign, Notre Dame trounced Butler, 34–7, at South Bend. The following week Notre Dame beat Carnegie Tech, 26–0. Then they beat St. Louis, 13–0, at St. Louis. At the time there were some charges that St. Louis, another Catholic institution, was fielding several "ringers"—men who had previously played football at other schools. Again Rockne muted his criticism, for, after all, similar accusations had plagued the early days of his coaching experience.

The St. Louis game, played at Sportsman's Park, in St. Louis, was not very satisfactory to Rockne. He felt that his players hadn't performed well on a muddy turf, under a steady downpour. Rain is generally a great equalizer on the football field and is often the catalyst for upsets. But Rockne was impatient with such a theory, despite the fact that so much mud had gotten into the eyes, ears, noses, and on the uniforms of his players that they were hardly recognizable to each other. At halftime, as the Irish barely led, 7–0, Crowley jogged toward the locker room, with Rockne not far behind him. Despite the slim lead, Crowley was in his usual good humor. Another player, alongside Crowley, reminded Jimmy that Rockne was close to him and might not be pleased with Jimmy's merry demeanor. "Oh, come on," Crowley said, shrugging off the warning, "Rock probably doesn't even know who we are!"

Another negative element relating to this contest were the rumors, spread by St. Louis supporters, that Notre Dame players had broken training the night before the game. When such malicious gossip reached Rockne's ears, he stoutly denied it, but he was deeply hurt. Criticism of this nature seemingly had become part of his daily challenge. He never chose to believe a word of such slurs and pointed to the miserable weather conditions, rather than partying, as the reason for his team's sluggish performance.

After six years as head coach, Rockne had won a reputation that might have made a lesser man into an unvarnished egomaniac. He was no shrinking violet about his intellect and abilities, but he rarely failed to retain the common touch with his players, as well as the millions who professed a loud loyalty to his school. He did not choose to suffer fools gladly, and no one could question his final authority—but he was a good listener to the grievances of his boys. When he was accused of coddling such outstanding talent as Gipp, Crowley, and others, he would respond that he knew how to motivate such men.

"In a showdown, he was a stand-up guy," Francis Wallace said. "But he could be wrong and could be overly cute." He could also be rough: There was the time that he physically threw a dressing-room crasher down a flight of stairs following a vexing 1920 game. He objected to outside kibitzers who might be critical of his coaching techniques. "If you can't keep quiet, get out!" he roared at them. "I don't come into your classroom and laugh at your methods and results. This is my classroom!"

He steadfastly defended the importance of the game of football, not only for those who played on the varsity but also for all members of the undergraduate student body. "Every boy at Notre Dame who cares to kick or throw a football," he said, "should have some place to do it." He enthusiastically endorsed the system of mass athletics over which he presided at South Bend and believed he knew the right kind of youth to be part of his football program.

13

On a Blue-Gray October Afternoon

GUS DORAIS WAS one among many admirers of Rockne who said that Knute's mind traveled faster than his tongue. That accounted for the fact that at the beginning of his tenure as Irish coach Rockne struggled with some difficulties as a public speaker. He was a stammerer.

Called upon to speak at college functions and alumni dinners, Rockne often experienced trouble. This affliction was embarrassing to Rockne, for he didn't care to hesitate when he was on his feet. But conquering small and large problems had always been second nature to Rockne, so he set about rectifying the situation. He took elocution and speech lessons, soon finding himself with a delivery that was usually clear, crisp, and stimulating. He had an inimitable machine-gun staccato style, supplemented by a mnemonic skill that was positively stunning. He had a knack for remembering names, faces, anecdotes, situations, and relationships that fascinated reporters, who found him to be an unending source of "good copy."

Rockne was probably of superior intelligence to most of the major coaching figures of his time. A dedicated overachiever, student, and eclectic reader, he enjoyed the cerebral process and gloried in words.

As the 1924 season approached, with its challenging nine-game schedule, Rockne continued to have difficulties with his Notre

Dame superiors. One of his troubles was that in the work he did, he didn't want any superiors. He fought for full control over all phases of the football program, including recruiting, training, scheduling of games, and jobs for his players.

On the other hand, Father Matthew Walsh was just as resolute. He had strong convictions about everything that went on at South Bend, and that included football. He was aware of the success of Rockne's gridiron program and the impact that the winning teams had on the school's reputation. He appreciated, too, that the increased revenue that had come to Notre Dame through football also helped to pay the salaries of the faculty.

However, what Walsh most resented about Rockne was that the coach unilaterally arranged schedule plans without seeking faculty approbation. One notable instance was a would-be Christmas game that Rockne promised to Notre Dame's Los Angeles alumni. This, charged Walsh, was going too far. An agreement was finally reached with Rockne in which full control of scheduling would be placed in the hands of a faculty board. Rockne was not happy with such a resolution, and to show his displeasure he began to leak word (through his many pals in the press box) that other schools, including the University of Iowa and the University of Southern California, were anxious to hire him.

When alumni and students learned about such a "lapse" in loyalty (although it was really only a tactic in Rockne's never-ending battle for supremacy at Notre Dame), they were annoyed. But they wanted Rockne to remain at South Bend, under any circumstances. The prospect of his moving to a rival school, which might be on Notre Dame's schedule, sent chills up the spines of the loyalists. Thus they implored the authorities to seek a rapprochement with Rockne. This they did.

In March 1924 Rockne, swearing undying fealty to Notre Dame, signed for ten years at ten thousand dollars per year, a considerable stipend in those days. As part of the arrangement Rockne was relieved of most administrative duties and was provided with a business manager. On the face of it, it appeared that Rockne won the battle. Yet, in the years to come there never was a season when there weren't rumors that the coach was either leaving for other ports or was receiving grandiose offers to go elsewhere.

Rockne's team in 1924 boasted its Four Horsemen backfield (still not called that at the time) and such stalwarts on the line as Adam

Walsh, captain and center; Charles Collins at end; Noble Kizer, a holdover at guard; John Weibel, guard; and Joe Bach at tackle.

One of Rockne's major innovations was his use of as many men on his squad as he could possibly get into the game. Such a plan could be adopted because he had so many capable players to call on, which was not always the case with his rivals. As he pointed for two "breathers" against Lombard and Wabash, both schools without any appreciable football programs, Rockne leaned more and more on the two-team strategy.

Sometimes he would start a second team in minor games, such as against Lombard. He also might opt for a second-string backfield and a first-string line to open a game. At this time the two-platoon system of modern-day football was still years away, but its later introduction owes much to Rockne. Rockne constantly experimented, always on the search for a psychological or a physical edge. He reasoned that if a second team could hold a foe down, then a fresh infusion of first-string talent might be counted on to smother the opposition. Rockne's defensive starters soon won the cognomen of "shock troops." He even had a third team waiting in the wings. Such a group would generally be employed late in a game when, presumably, Notre Dame would be well in the lead. In that way a third platoon could gain excellent battle experience without risking the loss of the game. Invariably Rockne's first team was composed of seniors, while the shock troops were usually all juniors.

After easy victories over Lombard and Wabash, the time came again to face Army, on October 18. Finally Rockne realized his wish: The Irish were about to play in a sports arena—the Polo Grounds in New York City—that could hold more than sixty-thousand people. (John McGraw's Giants had beaten the Washington Senators there on October 8, in the fifth game of the World Series that the Giants would lose in seven games.) The contest at the smaller Ebbets Field in 1923 hadn't fully satisfied Rockne's quest for larger audiences and thus more celebrants for his players. At this stage, any Notre Dame–Army clash promised to be a full-scale drama. So promising was this spectacle that it became the first clash in this rivalry to be broadcast on radio. Two outstanding voices of the 1920s, Graham MacNamee of WEAF and Ted Husing of WJZ, delivered the details over their respective stations.

With his knack for pregame histrionics, Rockne could have qualified for the role of theatrical producer had he not become a football coach. Generally he would begin his act by downgrading his own team's chances before the game. In this instance he confided to reporters that his team lacked the all-around ability to beat West Point. He emphasized how good Army's backs were compared to his own men. True, "Light Horse" Harry Wilson, a transfer All-American from Penn State, was a superbly talented halfback for Army. But he conveniently overlooked his own four backfield performers. The fact also that Army hadn't licked Notre Dame since 1916 was never alluded to by Rockne as he played his psychological game with Coach McEwan's charges.

Notre Dame entered the game as a six-to-five favorite despite the fact that the Cadets badly outweighed the men from South Bend. On the other hand, the Irish backs as a unit could have qualified for any track team in the land; each one of them—Stuhldreher, Crowley, Miller, and Layden—could run a hundred yards in little more than ten seconds, in full football regalia.

As a prelude to this twelfth meeting between Army and Notre Dame, Rockne trotted out his entire squad—six full teams—onto a gridiron that was bathed in the shadows of an overcast fall afternoon. Then, with a precision that characterized all Rockne-trained teams, the sixty-six players ran the length of the field, practicing formations. The punters boomed their punts down the field, and pass receivers crisscrossed under long aerials. All the while, Rockne, under his brown fedora, kneeled on the sidelines, pointing, exhorting, shouting. For those who had never seen a full-scale Rockne production before, it was a sight to see—and Rockne knew it. Even the fourteen hundred Cadets, marching in style, straight, and gray-clad, fifteen minutes before the start of the game, couldn't compare with the display of Notre Dame might.

Up in the crowded press box, hanging high over the Polo Grounds, all of the press royalty of the twenties, the greats and near-greats of sports journalism, had gathered. In a splendidly ragged row, they were: Gallico, Columbia's former crew captain, now a weaver of tough, insightful tabloid stories for the *New York Daily News;* Broun, an "unmade bed" of a man, with strong socialistic instincts; Runyon, coming from Manhattan, Kansas, to Manhattan, New York, to write colorful yarns about gamblers, panhandlers, pimps, and crooked politicians; Gene Fowler, future biographer of W. C. Fields, Jimmy Walker, and John Barrymore; Lardner, betrayed by his beloved White Sox but lured back to the sports desk by the prospect of an Army–Notre Dame clash.

But foremost among the press pack was Rice, covering that afternoon for the *New York Herald Tribune* and the *Tribune* Syndicate. For years Rice had been unleashing volleys of his sweet-tempered effusions about sports events and the athletes who played in them. Born in Murfreesboro, Tennessee, in 1880, Rice was an unabashed enthusiast of the fun and games of the 1920s and a charter member of the "gee whiz" fraternity of sports journalists. Through his worshipful writing he had helped to canonize many of the heroes of the Golden Age of Sports. Having played football and baseball during his college days at Vanderbilt, Rice had a commanding presence and, at two hundred pounds, boasted an athlete's physique. He was popular among his peers partly because he never lost his innocent zeal for the sports scene.

In 1908 Rice wrote a few lines of poetry for the *Tennesseean* that became imperishable, especially for those who believed in the innate purity of sports.

"For when the one Great Scorer comes to write against your name, He marks—not that you won or lost—but how you played the game," is how Rice's poem went. And, until this October day in 1924 at the Polo Grounds, nothing Rice had written, before or since, created quite the impact on a sports-loving public as those few words.

In his time Rice got to know almost every sports personality, entertainer, sportswriter, politician, even a gangster or two—and if he didn't know them, they wanted to know him. But he always remained a Tennesseean to the core, even as he traveled far afield. "He never lost the simple values of small-town America that he had acquired during his youth and had come to hold as fervently as a true believer holds his belief in God," wrote Charles Fountain in a biography of Rice.

As Rice gazed down on the field before the Army–Notre Dame game, he was as excited as any cub reporter might be. For, having known Rockne since 1920, as both friend and interviewee, he appreciated just what this game meant to the Irish coach. When Army's captain, Ed Garbisch, joined Notre Dame's counterpart, Adam Walsh, at the midfield stripe for a pregame handshake, Rice made note of the fact that the two men shook hands left-handed. It was just a little matter of Walsh's right hand, which was broken and in a cast. But, of course, Walsh would play anyway, for Rockne had said of him that he was one tough hombre. "All Notre Damers are game," said Rockne, "but Adam is the gamest." (Before the contest was over, Walsh would have *two* broken hands—and he was knocked unconscious several times—moving Rockne to remark that he didn't think "Adam would last ten minutes, but he lasted the whole sixty!")

Rockne's pregame insistence that Army would be difficult to beat was underscored by what transpired in the first moments of the game. Before the crowd could get settled in their seats, the Cadets had reeled off three first downs. As the Cadets advanced into Irish territory, Rockne sent the Horsemen into the game for the first time. At the end of the first period, after Army failed to score, Notre Dame launched a sustained drive from its own twenty-yard-line. It was then that Rockne's backfield, mixing up quick-starting running plays with an occasional short pass, marched down the field resolutely. Not a single one of the Horsemen dominated the action; it was a group effort.

Only once did Army stop Layden for no gain. Otherwise nothing could halt the Irish as they went eighty yards in eight plays, demonstrating such immaculate syncopation that even the most hardened sportswriters blinked at the artistry of the attack.

Rice reveled in it, too, and was pleased as Layden jammed over for a touchdown to make the score 6–0. Press box residents have always been officially nonpartisan. But many of them were and are secret rooters; Rice privately cheered for Rockne. Crowley failed on the extra-point try, but such a minor indiscretion didn't seem to matter.

Led by the indomitable Walsh, Notre Dame's defense also seemed impenetrable. The Irish appeared to be anticipating "Light Horse Harry" Wilson's every move. But that was more than luck, for Walsh had been helped out by Rockne. In a previous game Rockne had observed that Wilson became red-faced each time he was prepared to carry the ball. This bit of intelligence was passed along to Walsh, who yelled to his fellow players when he thought that Wilson's play had been called. Intuition is important in a football game—but Rockne lent a hand, too. In the press box Rice uttered a sound appraisal: "Wilson can't run through a broken field until he gets there." That afternoon, he never got there.

Always an astute play-caller, Stuhldreher was particularly brilliant that afternoon. Rockne eagerly attested to that fact. "Stuhldreher called two plays that were broken up by Army, but Harry couldn't see just who was doing the damage," said Rockne, "so he actually called the same play again. Each time, Harry never left his position. He merely waited and watched. He saw one of the crack Army backs spoil the play again. Although it was fourth down, Harry again called the same play. But this time he took out that Army back with a terrific block—and we picked up fourteen yards. Now, that's my idea of smart football."

In the third quarter the Horsemen continued to ramble but Army resisted, helped by the interception of one of Stuhldreher's rare stray passes. Then, after Layden retaliated by picking off an Army pass, the Irish moved to Army's forty-eight-yard line. From there Crowley ran for fifteen yards, then Miller plunged for seven. Taking his turn, Crowley went to the Army eighteen, as the Irish rooters set up a din that could wake up the echoes back at South Bend. On the next play, with Stuhldreher, Miller, and Layden blocking fiercely, Crowley smashed through for Notre Dame's second touchdown of the day. "The convoy was so sure in its work and precision that Sleepy Jim was able to trot into the end zone," wrote Spike Claassen of the Associated Press. Crowley then kicked the extra point.

With Notre Dame ahead, 13–0, Army was finally able to unleash Wilson for some substantial gains, culminating in a touchdown by Neil Harding in the fourth quarter. With the score now 13–7, the game evolved into a desperate defensive struggle. One Cadet drive ended in the broken hands of Walsh, who made a key interception late in the game. In the fading moments of the contest the Irish maintained possession and were no longer threatened by Army.

There is little doubt that this 1924 game was hard fought between two dominant teams—both of whom went unbeaten the rest of the year. But that it would ascend to mythical dimensions and that the iconic ghosts of Stuhldreher, Miller, Layden, and Crowley would thereafter be hailed as the finest backfield foursome ever to play the game could hardly have been predicted. (Ironically, that same afternoon "Red" Grange exploded for five touchdowns at Urbana, Illinois, as Illinois walloped Michigan, 39–14. Yet it was the Army–Notre Dame game that became more memorable, thanks to the typewriter of Grantland Rice.)

As soon as the game ended, Rice set about pecking out his description of the proceedings. Within fewer than thirty minutes of deadline time, surrounded by the cacophony and tumult of a press box crowded with the indomitable word-slingers of his generation, Rice completed his task. Working quickly and professionally at his trade, Rice carved out the lines that would inevitably wind up in

Bartlett's *Familiar Quotations* and that would immortalize a quartet of Notre Dame backs.

Whether the four young men were worthy of Rice's Saturday afternoon hyperbole will always remain a moot point. However, it is now apparent that the stage was set for his words a year before, when Army had played the Irish at Ebbets Field. At that game Rice, with a sideline pass, watched from the rim of the playing field with his friend "Brink" Thorne, Yale's football captain in 1895. On a wild end run the Horsemen came sweeping around Army's left end. Leading the way, at high speed, was Crowley, who had to hurdle both Rice and Thorne to keep from trampling them underfoot.

When Rice got up unsteadily, he remarked to Thorne, "It's worse than a cavalry charge . . . they're like a wild horse stampede." So when Rice hyperventilated over his lead for the 1924 game, his horsey precedent had already been established the previous fall.

Rice's Sunday, October 19 story appeared on page one, column one, on the left-hand corner of the *Herald Tribune*. Under the headline NOTRE DAME'S CYCLONE BEATS ARMY, 13–7, here is what Rice wrote:

> Outlined against a blue-gray October sky, the Four Horsemen rode again. In dramatic lore they are known as Famine, Pestilence, Destruction and Death. These are only aliases. Their real names are Stuhldreher, Miller, Crowley and Layden. They formed the crest of the South Bend cyclone before which another fighting Army football team was swept over the precipice at the Polo Grounds yesterday afternoon, as 55,000 spectators peered down on the bewildering panorama spread on the green plain below.
>
> A cyclone can't be snared. It may be surrounded, but somewhere it breaks through to keep on going. When the cyclone starts from South Bend, where the candle lights still gleam through the Indiana sycamores, those in the way must take to storm shelters at top speed. Yesterday the cyclone struck again, as Notre Dame beat the Army, 13–7, with a set of backfield stars that ripped and crashed through a strong Army defense with more speed and power than the warring cadets could meet.
>
> Notre Dame won its ninth game in twelve Army starts through the driving power of one of the greatest backfields that ever churned up the turf of any gridiron in any football

age. Brilliant backfields may come and go, but in Stuhldreher, Miller, Crowley and Layden, covered by a fast and charging line, Notre Dame can take its place in front of the field. Coach McEwan sent one of his finest teams into action, an aggressive organization that fought to the last play around the first rim of darkness, but when Rockne rushed his Four Horsemen to the track they rode down everything in sight. It was in vain that 1,400 gray-clad cadets pleaded for the Army line to hold. The Army line was giving it all it had, but when a tank spears it with the speed of a motorcycle, what chance has flesh and blood to hold?

If Rice felt that his reaction to the 1923 game had inspired his florid lead of 1924, others were not so certain. For example, George Strickler, a Notre Dame publicity assistant and later publicity director for the National Football League, posited the theory that *he* had planted the literary seed in old Granny's head. Having just seen the popular movie idol of the twenties Rudolph Valentino playing Julio in Vicente Blasco Ibáñez's hit film *The Four Horsemen of the Apocalypse* on the South Bend campus, Strickler found himself chatting at halftime of the 1924 game with Rice and several other writers. As the writers marveled at the swiftness and rhythm of the Notre Dame backfield, Strickler volunteered that it "was just like the Four Horsemen!"

Other writers may not have been familiar with the reference to Blasco Ibáñez's 1916 novel *The Four Horsemen of the Apocalypse*, on which the film was based, but Rice was. He also was aware that Blasco Ibáñez, a Spanish novelist-in-exile who vigorously opposed the Spanish monarchy, had gotten his idea about the Horsemen from the Revelation of St. John the Divine. When Rice wrote his football lead he had no idea that it would win the durability of other, alliterative nicknames that he had previously bestowed, on heavyweight champion Dempsey and on Red Grange. To Rice Dempsey was the "Manassa Mauler," while Grange was the "Galloping Ghost." The American public took to these nicknames, just as they immediately adopted the "Four Horsemen."

Once Rice's poetic name tag was out of the stable, it didn't take long for Strickler, enterprising press agent that he was, to implement another plan to ensure that the Horsemen would be forever joined with Rockne and Gipp in Notre Dame mythology. As he read Rice's story on Sunday morning, Strickler immediately envisioned the possibility of a photograph that would feature the four back-fielders on horses.

Others said that Bill Fox, sports editor of the *Indianapolis News,* initiated the idea for such a photo, but Strickler never confirmed that story. Strickler quickly enlisted his father, an employee of No-tre Dame, to round up several saddle horses from South Bend's riding academy. The horses, none of whom had ever won a race, were then brought to Cartier Field on Monday afternoon, when the Irish would be holding their daily practice session. Rockne's men were already preparing for the following week's game, against Princeton.

In this instance, Rockne viewed Strickler's stunt with some mis-givings. Suppose, Rockne thought, one of his stars fell off the horse's back. In addition, none of the men had had much experi-ence with horses, except, perhaps, betting on one. Before the Army game Stuhldreher was having pain in his throwing arm, for which Rockne prescribed one of his favorite liniments—a placebo. So Rockne felt that a horse's back was the last place for Stuhldreher to be.

Nevertheless, Strickler was persuasive with Rockne. With the coach's permission, the four men got into uniform and, somewhat apprehensively, parked themselves on top of the benign animals. Each one of the players was given a football to hold. From left to right, they posed—Miller, Layden, Crowley, Stuhldreher. Nary a smile creased their faces. Strickler slyly hinted that Crowley ap-peared uncomfortable on the horse because he was nursing a pesky boil on his derriere.

While all this was going on, the "Seven Mules" stood around, making disparaging wisecracks. Bill Spaulding, then the coach at Minnesota, happened to be a guest of Rockne that day and kept muttering his mild disapproval. "How do you get away with it?" he asked Rockne. "If we put on a stunt like this at Minnesota, they'd say we weren't taking the game seriously enough."

That day the picture was sent out all over the country, with newspapers everywhere snapping it up. Even without the presence of television, the word spread rapidly about the Four Horsemen. In a few days football fans by the millions picked up the refrain. (Iron-ically, nobody has ever been certain where the "Seven Mules" nick-name came from. So much for linemen!)

Don Miller, later a lawyer in Cleveland, mused about the instant fame he'd won as one-fourth of the Horsemen. "Rock put us to-

The Four Horsemen backfield—Don Miller, Elmer Layden, Jim Crowley, and Harry Stuhldreher—won popularity in 1924, thanks to this famous "photo opportunity." Courtesy: Department of Sports Information, University of Notre Dame.

gether in the same backfield," he said. "But the day Grantland Rice wrote about us as the Four Horsemen he conferred an immortality on us that money couldn't buy. Let's face it, we were good, sure. But we'd have been just as dead two years after graduation as any other backfield if Rice hadn't painted that name on us. In business, being the Four Horsemen has meant more to us in associations, warmth, friendship, and revenue than anyone you'll ever know."

In his autobiography, Stuhldreher said he was proud of the role the Horsemen had played in gaining undisputed championship honors for Notre Dame. But he insisted that the Seven Mules "never did get their share of the glory . . . it was easy for me to pull a signal out of the bag when I knew that the heavy burden of the work would be done by the Mules. Without the Seven Mules to kick up the dust for them the backfield would have stayed put. It was only through their work that the four of us did anything worth remembering."

Still a student at Notre Dame in 1924, Red Smith, later to be-

155

come a cherished friend of Rice (even though he had reservations about Rice's excessive employment of biblical and poetic allusions) read the Four Horsemen lead for the first time in the *Brooklyn Eagle*. With typical irony, Smith mildly questioned how Rice could have seen the backfield "outlined against the sky." According to Smith, Rice "would have had to have been lying on the field, perhaps in the middle of it." However, Smith was much impressed, wrote Ira Berkow, with "the magic of Rice's catchwords, which had transformed a gifted, excitingly wonderful coordinated pony backfield into a quartet of immortals."

All of the Four Horsemen were incredulous at the impact of both Rice's elegant prose and the group photograph that followed. Rice himself was dumbfounded by the widespread reaction, including the sale of hundreds of prints of the Horsemen at one dollar each. The best proof of Rice's blasé attitude was that in the week after the victory over Army he chose to view Columbia beating Williams at Baker Field, in New York City, rather than watch the newly canonized Horsemen cavort against Princeton in New Jersey.

What attracted Rice to Baker Field was the presence on the Columbia bench of Percy Haughton, one of the great disciplinarian coaches, who had arrived from Harvard in 1923 in an attempt to lead Columbia out of the wilderness. (Haughton was no less a locker-room Churchill than Rockne. According to legend, Haughton once exhorted his Harvard players before the traditional game with Yale by hauling a bulldog, Yale's symbol, into the locker room and strangling the pop-eyed animal in front of his astonished team. But Harvard man and author George Plimpton assures us that this never happened because, after all, a bulldog has no neck!) An uninhibited admirer of Haughton, Rice once described the coach as "the builder-up of the down-trodden."

At Columbia Haughton's team won four of five games in 1924, after a .500 year in '23. A few days before Columbia's traditional game against Cornell in late October, Haughton, only forty-eight years old, collapsed and died after a practice session. With Haughton gone so suddenly, Columbia searched briefly for a successor and found one in Charlie Crowley, who had played under Rockne at Notre Dame after World War I. But the one man Columbia truly desired for its coach was Knute Rockne himself.

14

The Smell of Roses

AFTER ALL OF the hoopla about the Four Horsemen, the next game, against Princeton, was anticlimactic by any measure. The Irish won handily, although the final score of 12–0 was scarcely an indication of how well Rockne's boys played. While running for 250 yards, Crowley scored both touchdowns. Miller also scored a touchdown, but it was called back for a rules infraction.

Following the game Charlie Caldwell, who had played on the famous Princeton "Team of Destiny" in 1922 and who alternated at center and fullback against Notre Dame, analyzed the manner in which the Irish had won. (Caldwell later became Princeton's coach, but his early claim to fame was based on his having beaned New York Yankee first baseman Wally Pipp when Caldwell tried out for the Yankees as a pitcher. Thus, inadvertently, Caldwell was responsible for the start of Lou Gehrig's famous consecutive-game streak in 1925, as Gehrig then took over for Pipp.)

"We were better than an average team in 1925," said Caldwell, "yet I felt as if we were being toyed with by Notre Dame. I was backing up the line and I don't think that I made a clean tackle all day. I would get set to drop the ball carrier in his tracks and someone would give me a nudge, just enough to throw me off-balance, just enough pressure to make me miss. There was no getting around it, I was sold hook, line, and sinker on Rockne football."

Already aspiring to a career as a coach, Caldwell believed that Rockne offered a blend of science with creativity, to go along with the element of desire that was present in all of his teams. In his own perceptive way, Caldwell summed up how the daring Rockne system worked, with its emphasis on speed, guile, and imagination. "Rockne blends the traditional with the unorthodox," added Caldwell.

On the sidelines during the Princeton game, Walsh, nursing his two bandaged hands, fervently rooted his teammates on to victory, almost as a second coach to Rockne. After this second straight beating administered to Princeton by Notre Dame, it should have been clear to the "elitists" in New Jersey that they had met their match in Rockne's midwestern Catholics. There is reason to believe that such successive triumphs added immeasurably to the self-esteem that Notre Damers felt about themselves and their school. The students also felt proud about their coach, Rock, who was given the major share of credit for the team's accomplishments and for increasing the size of Cartier Field to more than twenty-two thousand seats.

Georgia Tech came visiting Cartier Field for Notre Dame's fifth game of the season. Playing the Southerners at South Bend presented the Irish with a formidable advantage, for here they would not be subjected to those anti-Catholic epithets that met their ears when they played Tech down South. Notre Dame had no trouble pounding sense into the Georgians, walking off with an easy 34–3 victory before a packed house of admiring fans. The Four Horsemen were so unstoppable—and unflappable—again that it was necessary for Rockne to tell his stars, especially the swaggering Crowley, that the Seven Mules up front were as important to the team's welfare as the Horsemen were. On occasion Rockne would substitute other backs for one or two of the Horsemen, and, almost according to plan, they ran wild. "See," Rockne would then remind the Four Horsemen, "with that line in front of you doing the work, *anyone* can do anything!"

Wisconsin came next for the Irish. For this game the Irish traveled to Madison, where a number of Notre Dame fans from all parts of the Midwest congregated to root for Rockne's men. The game turned out to be almost a duplicate of the Georgia Tech triumph. The Irish won, 38–3, enhancing their reputation among those Big Ten schools who might have continued to regard Notre Dame as pariahs. This runaway victory also was celebrated in other areas of the country, with the help of that squadron of journalists, including Rice, Gallico, Broun, Hype Igoe, of the New York *Hurricane* and Joe Vila, of the New York *Sun*, as well as the enterprising South Bend staff of football press agents, headed by Wallace.

It didn't take long for the Notre Dame message to reach the Rose Bowl administrators, basking in the sun in California, who began to give serious consideration to the Irish as a possible January 1 invitee. Such general acceptance of the Notre Dame team melted the hearts of the policymakers at Notre Dame, who, under ordinary circumstances, might have been expected to be antagonistic to a postseason bowl game.

Rockne, meanwhile, tried his best to push all of these developments to the back of his mind. He now looked ahead to Nebraska, a school that had caused so much heartache for him in the past. It seemed that there was nothing Rockne couldn't accomplish, except, as one comic observer said, grow more hair on his head. Rockne knew that Nebraska could be tough enough to destroy Notre Dame's dream of another unbeaten season, and perhaps the Rose Bowl bid. If the Horsemen had failed in two previous efforts to upend Nebraska, was it likely that they would lose their last chance to defeat the Cornhuskers?

Convinced that his team was better than Nebraska, Rockne wasn't taking any chances. If there was a psychological edge to be won, he would grab for it. Such a situation arose due to the fact that Nebraska had an open date when the Irish played Wisconsin. That gave several Cornhusker players an opportunity to watch the Irish play. When Rockne heard about the presence of the Nebraska men in the stands, he sent word to them that if they liked, they could mingle with his boys after the game was over. He was convinced that the Nebraskans would project a cocksureness that might encourage resentment among his own players. Sure enough, the Nebraskans fell for the bait. They told the Notre Dame boys that Wisconsin wasn't a very good team and that that accounted for the Irish victory. "Wait till you get on the field with us," they crowed. "We're going to beat up on you." Rockne couldn't have delivered a better pep talk.

With the largest Cartier Field crowd in history on hand, screaming its lungs out from start to finish, Rockne's boys were ready for their "get even" afternoon. When his full squad went through its pregame workout, one of the Nebraska coaches inquired which one was Rockne's first team.

"Any one of 'em," Rockne answered.

Somewhat superstitious, Rockne insisted that his players walk on the field backward before the game. Then, with his usual audacity, Rockne put in his shock troops in the opening period.

That didn't work as well as Rockne expected, for Nebraska scored a quick touchdown. Rockne then substituted his first team, including the Four Horsemen. What took place from that moment on was nothing short of mind-boggling. The Horsemen never played better, living up to all their overheated press notices. It may well have been the best game they ever played as a unit. Miller and Crowley zoomed around the ends; Layden, hardly more muscular than Mahatma Gandhi, plunged up the middle; Stuhldreher directed his men with uncanny virtuosity. Once the line opened up a hole through which Crowley scampered eighty yards, virtually untouched, for a touchdown. The Irish line played fearlessly, against a Nebraska team that was much heavier from end to end.

When the whistle blew at the game's end, Notre Dame had amassed thirty-four points, while Nebraska was held to the six points it had scored in the first period. Until this game Rockne felt that the most satisfying game he'd ever been involved with was the afternoon he and Gus Dorais blew West Point out of the ball park little more than a decade before. But this was better. "The most pleasant thing that's happened to me in years," an exultant Rockne chirped after the game.

Drinking the bitter tea of defeat, Nebraska coach Fred Dawson expressed admiration for the "near-dainty" demonstration of the Four Horsemen. "I guess we were lucky to have beaten them the other two years," he said.

After the buildup for the Nebraska game it was no easy matter for Rockne to prevent a letdown for the forthcoming Northwestern game. Chicago's lakefront Soldier Field, which seemed big enough to hold America's entire standing army, was to be the site of the clash against Northwestern. In addition, Notre Dame would be participating in the dedication of the stadium. Playing there for the first time before fifty thousand people, Notre Dame would confront an institution that had had a tendency to look down its Methodist nose at the Irish. But to Rockne it was just another tough football game, though he was wise enough to be aware that there was an unpleasant subtext to these contests.

The Irish had been subjected, after seven winning games, to considerable physical punishment. Most of the team was battle-weary. It had also rained most of the week in Chicago, assuring that the field would be muddy and treacherous. Under such conditions there would be no fast track for Rockne's speedsters, thus preventing any kind of Irish runaway. Already beaten by Purdue, Michigan, and Chicago, the inferior Northwestern team was convinced it had a fine chance to lick the Irish. They were determined to administer a lesson to Notre Dame and to take advantage of Irish overconfidence.

Thanks to two dropkick field goals by "Moon" Baker, Northwestern stayed in contention through most of the game. With Notre Dame ahead by only 7–6, Rockne went into his disparagement routine at halftime, in an effort to arouse his charges.

"You fellows should dig up your press notices," Rockne said with a growl, "then show 'em to these Northwestern guys. Then they'll know who you are and fold up."

However, there was no fold-up in the Northwestern team. Only a brilliant interception and runback by Layden at midfield, which the little fellow ran down the sidelines for a touchdown, enabled the Irish to squeak out a 13–6 victory and thus prolong their winning streak. Northwestern heatedly protested that Layden had stepped out of bounds along the way, but the officials failed to rule on it.

As Notre Dame concluded its season against Carnegie Tech in Pittsburgh, much was riding on a game that promised to be easy for the Irish. It didn't turn out that way, for at halftime the score was 13–13, and Rockne had to outdo himself in the locker room. There was good reason for Notre Dame's subpar performance in the first half, since Layden was forced out of the game with an injury. With their ground game stalled, the Irish unleashed their air artillery in the second half. Stuhldreher took command, completing fifteen of nineteen passes as the Irish came back to win, 40–19. The unbeaten season was saved, Stuhldreher's exhibition of passing won praise as one of the finest ever displayed by a major college team, while Notre Dame received near unanimous acclaim as the finest football machine in the land. No official mechanism or poll made such excathedra pronouncements, but most of the press seemed to agree that Rockne's team was the best.

Whether the Four Horsemen deserved the bulk of the credit for the team's high rating was a subject of controversy, even among the Notre Dame players. Stuhldreher himself stated that "anyone with common sense would know that you couldn't have had the record we attained without complete harmony. We continued to hear that the line hated the backfield. So we took a vote as to which was more important—the line or the backfield. The line won, by seven votes to four! There never would have been a national championship team had it not been for the two-team idea and the help we got from the shock troops."

Under the circumstances, Rockne was more sought after than ever before. He knew it and played a diplomatic game with the Notre Dame authorities. His heart was firmly in the Notre Dame camp—but it was hard not to hear the praise, as incessant as it was. In December 1924 General MacArthur, no longer the superintendent at West Point but perhaps wishing he was, wrote from Manila to his friend Earl Blaik. Blaik was a graduate of West Point and later its coach. The gist of MacArthur's letter was that Army sorely needed aggressive leadership on the gridiron. "Had I stayed at West Point," MacArthur wrote, "I intended introducing new blood into our coaching staff and Rockne was the man I had in mind."

But the other question now facing Notre Dame, was whether they would be invited to play in their first Rose Bowl game. The possibility that Notre Dame might be ignored because it was a Catholic school was less important than the fact that Stanford, the dominant team in the Pacific Coast Conference and undefeated against eight teams, strongly objected to the Irish, as a second-rate institution. Stanford also set up a din about Notre Dame's failure to play by the rules in its recruiting practices.

Annoyed by Stanford's hauteur, Rockne would have preferred to meet the University of Southern California, rather than engage a school that was so patently hypocritical. It was widely known, for example, that Stanford's coach, Glenn Scobey "Pop" Warner, a highly respected gridiron mentor (he had coached previously at Georgia, Cornell, Carlisle, and Pitt), was as adept as any man at recruiting. If anyone bothered to look into it, Stanford was as guilty as any school when it came to subsidization of athletes.

After a persistent lobbying effort pursued by Notre Dame's Far West alumni pried loose an invitation to the Irish, Stanford changed its mind about being the opposition. The reason for Stanford's change of heart was a financial arrangement that called for the two teams equally to split 60 percent of the net gate. Because Notre Dame was the prime gate attraction in such a meeting, many Notre Dame backers and alumni voiced their outrage at such a deal. However, the criticism was muted because Notre Dame was pleased to be in the Rose Bowl. As far as Rockne was concerned, the inequity of the contract only ensured that his men would have an additional incentive for boxing Stanford's ears.

Ever the showman, Rockne arranged an arduous tour across the country to Pasadena. Aware of the enormous interest of the Irish graduates, as well as of thousands of non-Catholics who had never been near South Bend, he made sure that his team would be seen, first in New Orleans, where there was a large and vocal Catholic population. New Orleans hardly was on a straight line to the West Coast, but it was on the way to the Southwest, where Rockne took his men to Houston, and then to Arizona. A local school in Houston proposed that Notre Dame play an exhibition game, even guaranteeing a large crowd. But the Notre Dame faculty, aware that they were already under attack for "overemphasizing football," canceled the idea. In Tucson, Arizona, Rockne put his men through four days of practice. More important, a former Notre Dame player, Slip Madigan, journeyed from St. Mary's College, in California, where he was coach, to tell Rockne a few things about Pop Warner's offense. Madigan's scouting notes included the revelation about a special play utilizing the talents of Stanford's brilliant fullback, Ernie Nevers, on a well-camouflaged screen pass. Rockne dutifully thanked Madigan, an old teammate of Gipp, then rolled his team into Los Angeles. There Notre Dame's players were greeted by hordes of enthusiastic Californians, many of whom represented the West Coast version of the eastern subway alumni.

Rockne wisely ruled out all parties for his team before the Rose Bowl game, counting on celebrating *after* the event. The long trip, the first by the Irish to the West Coast, also served another purpose. Rockne had designed it in a gradual way to accustom his players to dramatic weather changes, as they went from the bitter winter cold of the Midwest to the semitropical breezes of Southern California. (Nine years later, when Coach Lou Little shepherded his Columbia team to the Rose Bowl, also against Stanford, he was inspired by Rockne's travel itinerary, and also stopped off at Tucson. Little brought along his own water for the players, something that Rockne didn't think was necessary at the time.)

Before the game it wasn't certain whether Nevers would play, since he had missed part of the season because of a pair of broken ankles. But Nevers told Warner he wanted to be in there, so he was in the starting lineup. When the game began more than fifty-three thousand fans, straw-hatted and sweaty, were in the stands at Pasadena on a broiling afternoon. In the distance were the "Graham McNamee Mountains," as Rockne delighted in calling them. Close to two hundred thousand dollars were paid in at the gate, the most money Notre Dame had ever enticed to a football game.

Rockne didn't depart from his usual strategy: He opened with his shock troops. But when Stanford recovered an Irish fumble on the fifteen-yard line and then kicked a field goal, Rockne immediately deployed his first-stringers. Before long the Four Horsemen were making life miserable for Stanford. In the second quarter, after tackle Joe Bach, always one of Rockne's favorites, had to come out of the game because of damaged ribs (to be replaced by Joe Boland, who played the rest of the game in more than ninety-degree heat and dropped fifteen pounds), Layden scored Notre Dame's first touchdown. That made the score 13–3 at halftime.

As the second half began Layden, one of the best punters ever developed at Notre Dame, got off a booming kick that was fumbled on the Stanford twenty-yard-line. Ed Huntsinger pounced on the vagrant ball and ran it in for Notre Dame's third touchdown. With a lead of 20–3 it appeared that Rockne had a winner. But the unremitting heat began to take a toll on the Irish players. Despite all of Rockne's advance preparations, the Notre Damers were finding the weather unbearable. More acclimated to the heat, Nevers refused to give up. Violating Rockne's admonitions about throwing passes when his team had what seemed a safe lead, Stuhldreher unwisely threw a pass that landed in the hands of Nevers. A few plays later, Stanford rolled in for a score, making the count 20–10.

The fourth quarter then evolved into fifteen minutes of a defensive struggle, with the Seven Mules holding up magnificently. At one stage Stanford marched to the two-yard line, with four downs to navigate the sparse yardage. If Stanford had scored here, the game's outcome would have been much in doubt. However, Notre Dame put on a goal-line stand that could have been used for a training film. "One of the peaks in Notre Dame football history," insisted Francis Wallace. It had to be, for Nevers was the main attacker of the Irish defenses. After the Notre Dame line held for two downs, Rockne rushed John McMullen, a third-team tackle, into the fray. Since McMullen was obligated to obey the rule that prevented a sub from talking in the huddle on the first play, it wasn't clear what the coach's purpose was. In any event, McMullen stopped Nevers dead on third down. Before Stanford put the ball in play on fourth down, Stuhldreher asked McMullen to reveal what message Rockne had for them in such a desperate situation. "Rock said to hold 'em," whispered McMullen.

Such advice was hardly profound. Yet there was a reason Rockne had directed his words at McMullen. The coach knew that McMullen was a quiet fellow, but capable of rising to the moment. When Nevers threw himself at the line on fourth down, it was McMullen who stopped him cold, just inches away from a touchdown.

With his back against the wall, Layden punted out. But Stanford once again stormed toward the goal. Nevers had already carried the ball 34 times for 114 yards. But at Notre Dame's forty-yard line Warner elected to pass. Ed Walker stepped back and hurled a pass into the flat, where the ever-vigilant Layden popped up to intercept it. Layden had made an art out of breaking opponents' hearts with well-timed interceptions. This time he ran it back for sixty yards and Notre Dame's fourth touchdown.

As soon as the out-of-breath Layden completed his key play, Rockne yanked him out of the game. In seconds tears rolled down Layden's cheeks, and Rockne was quick to notice it.

"Why are you crying?" Rockne asked Layden. "You just put the game on ice."

"I know why you're taking me out," sobbed Layden. "You saw it, you saw it!"

"Saw what?" asked the puzzled Rockne. "Have you gone nutty?"

"I thought you saw me carry the ball in the *wrong* arm on that play," Layden explained.

Notre Dame backs were tutored by Rockne to do things in a certain way. He was a stickler for details—and Layden knew it, even at such a moment.

The Rose Bowl victory reaped large rewards for Rockne and his men, not the least being the enormous popular acceptance of this Catholic school. Previously there had been a grudging admiration for Rockne. Now he won high marks for his handling of men, his vision, his strategy, his preparation, even for his commercial agility. The Four Horsemen, with the help of a manipulative press, were regarded as a backfield without equal. Even though Red Grange had spent the year racking up untold miles of yardage, it was Notre Dame that seized the imagination of the sports-crazy public.

Rockne, a complex and driven figure, had become the Babe Ruth, Jack Dempsey, and Bobby Jones of football, and few would deny him his place in the sun. Even in those purlieus where Notre Dame's team was once greeted with hostility, there was an admission that this coach had gone everywhere and challenged everyone to play his team—and had won.

The Notre Dame squad made a joyous post–Rose Bowl tour of Los Angeles. Then they went on to California's Bay Area, and to the Pacific Northwest. At last they headed home through Wyoming and Colorado, as hundreds turned out to applaud them and to smother them with affection. Now the support for this team extended to many non–Notre Dame white-collar and blue-collar people—mostly men—who found the Irish irresistible.

The whole country, it seemed, had become an extension of the subway alumni of New York City. It didn't matter whether one was Protestant, Catholic, or Jewish, you could still root unashamedly for the Irish. As the New York Yankees were becoming baseball's "national" team, so had Notre Dame become the "national" football team. This was truly a remarkable phenomenon, considering that the 1920s was still the age of Ku Kluxers, who paraded publicly in their sheets, even as anti-Catholic bigots denied Al Smith the chance to be president of the United States.

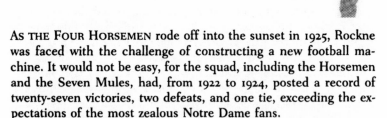

15

After the Four Horsemen

As THE FOUR HORSEMEN rode off into the sunset in 1925, Rockne was faced with the challenge of constructing a new football machine. It would not be easy, for the squad, including the Horsemen and the Seven Mules, had, from 1922 to 1924, posted a record of twenty-seven victories, two defeats, and one tie, exceeding the expectations of the most zealous Notre Dame fans.

In time the Horsemen and some of the Mules would go on to other football assignments. Inspired by the teaching brilliance of Rockne, some chose to become coaching missionaries. Layden, star of the Rose Bowl game, later would become Duquesne and then Notre Dame's coach; Stuhldreher coached at Villanova and Wisconsin, Crowley at Michigan State and Fordham. The only Horseman to desert the football arena was Don Miller, who became a federal attorney, then a judge. All of the Horsemen eventually won election to the National Football Foundation Hall of Fame—Layden in 1951, Stuhldreher in 1958, Crowley in 1966, Miller in 1970. Nobel Kizer, who never played a single game of football before coming to Notre Dame, coached at Purdue. Walsh went to Santa Clara, then to the Cleveland Rams as tutor. Rip Miller became assistant athletic director at Navy, then its coach.

As Rockne pursued the task of rebuilding, most of his South Bend adherents were convinced that it would be only days before he emerged with another gang like the Horsemen and another set of Mules. But, it was never going to be that simple. Rockne warned that it would take time and patience, commodities that were conspicuously lacking in the Notre Dame environment.

There was also another matter that deeply consumed Rockne. Here he was, a Norse Protestant who had coached a bunch of Catholic youngsters to undreamed-of-heights for almost a decade. He had watched his boys rush off to Mass on the morning of every football game. That assemblage also included the non-Catholics on the squad. When these boys prayed on those Saturday mornings, they weren't praying for gridiron miracles, but only for the strength and the will to perform as best as they could.

Many of those who played and prayed under Rockne were aware that their coach was conflicted about his own religious beliefs. But it was a subject that he rarely discussed with friends or associates. From time to time the players would watch Rockne sitting alone in the Notre Dame chapel, though they wished they could have seen him there more often. Many of them hoped that sooner or later Rockne would investigate their own faith. They didn't choose to push him on the subject—they would spare him such pressure— but sometimes they hinted to him about it.

Following the Rose Bowl triumph, Adam Walsh spoke somewhat obliquely about the matter, at a banquet on the Notre Dame campus. "You told us before we played Stanford that any reasonable request is ours—if we beat 'em. That's right, isn't it, Rock?" Walsh asked. "Well," added Walsh, *"well."* Rockne knew what Walsh was trying to say to him.

In response, Rockne told Walsh that he'd been thinking about it for a long time and was pondering his next step. All we want, continued Walsh, is for you to give it a fair test. Rockne assured Walsh and Father Matthew J. Walsh, Notre Dame's president, and others present, including coaches Hunk Anderson and Tom Lieb, that he would do just that.

When the 1925 season got under way, Notre Dame had a new backfield, headed by quarterback Red Edwards. Rockne was under no illusions about Edwards's ability to replace the canny Stuhldreher. As far as the rest of the team was concerned, Rockne had only a few inexperienced men back from the great 1924 squad, but, as usual, he was blessed with a large roster from which to choose his starters.

Rockne works out with his team in 1925. He described football as "sixty percent leg drive and thirty percent fight." Courtesy: AP/Wide World Photos.

However, in its first three games Rockne's team performed better than he had anticipated. When the Irish opened the season by lambasting Baylor, 41–0, then followed with a 69–0 pasting of Lombard, the word around Notre Dame was that Rockne, despite all of his wailing, might have another dynamic team. But in the third game, reality set in as Notre Dame defeated Beloit, 19–3. Beloit wasn't exactly a powerhouse, though they had beaten Northwestern handily the week before. With Notre Dame amassing 110 points in the first two games, Rockne felt that his team and its crowing public might become overconfident. According to a story that circulated at the time, Rockne literally decided to share his secrets with the enemy. He reportedly mailed copies of some of Notre Dame's plays to Thomas E. Mills, Beloit's coach, to give Tommy's team a better chance and perhaps to keep the score respectable. Obviously, he succeeded in his intent, although his tactic would be regarded today with a jaundiced eye.

As Notre Dame prepared to face its traditional enemy Army with a group of aspiring sophomores, hopes were high that the Irish could extend its winning streak to seventeen games. Rockne's own feelings about his team were neatly summed up in a pregame assessment: "We really won't know about our team until this game is over."

This game had now taken on the proportions of one of the major annual events of the Roaring Twenties. At last, too, the game would be staged in Babe Ruth's cavernous cathedral, Yankee Stadium, after Rockne had settled for Ebbets Field and the Polo Grounds the two previous years. The demand for tickets was so insistent that even President Walsh of Notre Dame was overwhelmed with requests from alumni and faculty. Some of those fortunate enough to get tickets were accused of "scalping" them, an accusation that always embarrassed Notre Dame authorities.

On the afternoon of October 17 New York was pelted with rain. The Stadium was drenched, but that did not deter seventy thousand or so hardy fans from showing up. In the press box Gallico, whose personal credo as a sports journalist was that he could write with clarity only if he batted against the curves of pitcher Herb Pennock or tried to tackle a Red Grange or was hit in the nose by Jack Dempsey, shook his head at the tumultuous reaction of the big crowd.

"This phenomenon is one of the most curious and strangest things in this country," Gallico later wrote. "An amazing gathering of self-appointed Notre Dame alumni, which will whoop, rage, and rant and roar through our town in honor of a school to which they never went. The West Point supporters will be numerous and vociferous but of the thousands of spectators three-quarters will be bawling at the top of their lungs for Notre Dame du Lac . . . there are no self-appointed Colgate, St. Mary's, Tulane or Purdue alumni when those teams come to town. . . ."

The 1925 Army–Notre Dame game at Yankee Stadium would be the first of twenty-two such confrontations at the ball park, which would also be the scene of so many Yankee World Series games that New Yorkers would swear that the Bronx facility had squatter rights on the event.

Rockne was well aware that Army was manned to the teeth with talent. The Cadets had players who had apprenticed at other colleges. "Light Horse Harry" Wilson had come from Penn State, Tiny Hewitt had been to Pitt, and Christian "Red" Cagle, who would emerge as one of West Point's greatest broken-field runners, had attended a tiny school in Louisiana before registering as a plebe at Army.

As it turned out, it was one of those days—one of the few—that Rockne conveniently could have forgotten. Though the Irish were able to hold Army in the first period, due mainly to the treacherous condition of the field, the second period was a different matter. The noisy Notre Dame claqueurs in the stands weren't prepared for what happened. Wilson and Hewitt took over the offense for the first touchdown, before halftime, and Harry Baxter, Army's left end, caught a pass for the second touchdown. Not for eight years had a Notre Dame team limped into a locker room down by two touchdowns after two periods.

Rockne had paced up and down the sidelines, gnawing away at his cigar during the first half. Never at a loss for words, there was little for him to say to his men at intermission. He knew that Army was whacking the tar out of his players, much to McEwan's satisfaction. But Rockne knew that nothing in the way of a sardonic pep talk or a bromide could reverse what was taking place on the Stadium gridiron.

The second half was much the same, Rockne employed four quarterbacks in an exercise of futility, but none of them could lead the way to a single score. When the game ended with Army in front, 27–0, it marked the single most one-sided loss under Rockne's aegis. However, Rockne believed that what had taken place was no aberration—his players simply weren't up to the experience and toughness exhibited by the West Pointers. Because of that he was inclined to accept the defeat stoically. In fact, he saved his anger for those Irish fans who had behaved badly in the stands, as they screamed abusive epithets at the West Pointers.

After the loss, Rockne's name appeared on a postgame Sunday column. Although he was a tremendously articulate man, Rockne was not as skilled at writing as he was at "speechifying." The column, probably the work of his ghostwriter Christy Walsh, emphasized that Army's team was the best that Rockne had seen since the end of the World War. It also took pains to describe the Notre Dame squad as "green." Rockne was not in the habit of apologizing for failure, but this seemed as close as he could get to an alibi.

The disappointed students at South Bend realized that their team had been overmatched. When the bedraggled Notre Dame players returned to the South Bend railroad station after their dismal showing, a light snow was falling. But, in the early hours of the morning, a good part of the student body was on hand to lend moral support to their beaten team. Rockne never failed to get sustenance from such student enthusiasm. Whenever he would engage in a tiff with the Notre Dame authorities, he would always remind himself about which side the students were on.

It now remained for Rockne and his "green" team to try to prevent the rest of the season from going down the drain. That had to be especially difficult because of Rockne's tendency to book many of the team's games on foreign fields. However, the Irish rebounded remarkably the next week, at Minnesota. Rockne's old friend Bill Spaulding was no longer the coach of the Gophers; Dr. Clarence Spears was now in charge. But that made little difference as the Irish attack, led by "Red" Hearden, molded a 19–7 victory.

Again on the road the next week, at Georgia Tech, Notre Dame won convincingly, 13–0. It was then on to Penn State, where they would face a team that had barely beaten Marietta and had lost to Georgia Tech and Syracuse. Rockne knew that his men were fatigued because of constant travel, yet he felt that they were able enough to beat the Nittany Lions. But the game evolved into a desperate struggle between two teams going nowhere in the coldness of the Pennsylvania mountains, precisely the kind of battle that Rockne deplored.

Trying to rouse his players at halftime, Rockne broke down and began to sob. He wasn't engaging in any histrionics, either, for he had simply lost control of himself. "What must you guys think of me?" the embarrassed coach asked one of his players. The answer to him was reassuring: He was told that his tears proved that he was as human and fallible as anyone else. The game against Penn State ended in a disconcerting scoreless tie, "which probably bothered Rockne more than any out-and-out defeats," wrote Robert Harron, a Notre Dame publicist.

Back on home soil in mid-November, the Irish woke from their Penn State slumber and thrashed a mediocre Carnegie Tech team, 26–0. With another home game coming up the next week, against the Big Ten's Northwestern team, Rockne was hopeful that his team was on the right track. However, Northwestern was not prepared to roll over for the Irish. By the end of the first half Northwestern had taken a 10–0 lead. If they kept up their good play they were on the road to administering the first Notre Dame defeat at home in twenty years.

As the Notre Dame players walked mournfully into their dressing room at halftime, they expected Rockne to unleash another of his patented wintry blasts. Instead, as they slumped on the benches in front of their lockers, Rockne remained silent. In fact, he wasn't even on hand, having chosen to remain outside of the funereal locker room.

Was Rockne about to pass up a precious opportunity to rouse his troops? With fewer than three minutes to go before his team would return to the field, Rockne suddenly burst into the room. His face was red, the cords in his neck bulged in anger, his words were harsh and dismissive.

"Fighting Irish, you call yourself," he began. "You look more like peaceful Swedes to me. Maybe this game doesn't mean much to you. But it means a lot to *me!* I'd rather win it than any other game this year. Someday you may have the honor of dandling your grandchildren on your knees and telling them that you were on the first Notre Dame team that ever quit. I'm through with you! I'm going to sit in the stands for the second half."

Turning to his assistant Hunk Anderson, Rockne said, abruptly, "You take over, Hunk." With that instruction, Rockne stalked out of the premises. For several seconds not a whisper was heard in the locker room. Then, as if shot out of a cannon, the players bolted from their perches and stormed onto the field, almost running over each other to get out there first.

Myth or magic? All part of the Rockne legend and buildup? Whatever one chooses to believe (this locker-room story was passed along into Notre Dame history by tackle Joe Boland), the result was astounding. For the next eight minutes the Irish stomped all over Northwestern. The Irish were white-hot as they slammed over for two quick touchdowns, all on the ground, led by Notre Dame's newest hero, Rex Enright. (Appreciating the futility of trying to break into the Four Horsemen backfield, Enright had stayed out of school while the Horsemen were riding to glory.) All the while, the sulking Rockne remained distant from his team, as he sat in the stands engulfed in the fumes of his cigar. When the game was over, Notre Dame was victorious, 13–10, and the impeccable record of the Irish on their home grounds had been preserved. Of even larger importance to the mahouts at Notre Dame was that Cartier Field was jammed to the rafters, with the school's receipts coming to sixty thousand dollars.

The windup of the season was scheduled at Lincoln, Nebraska, the site of previous indignities to Notre Dame. There continued to be pressure on Rockne to drop Nebraska from his team's docket. But he insisted that the "big game" nature of the contest, with the resultant healthy proceeds it was bound to produce, was sufficient reason to keep the rivalry in place. Rockne won his point—but with great regret—for the 1925 clash with Nebraska was beset with a crescendo of ridicule directed at the Notre Dame student body and, in particular, at Notre Dame's supposedly lax academic standards. Worse than that, a halftime show was staged by Nebraska students in which the Four Horsemen were portrayed as bricklayers, a common stereotype about Irishmen in those years.

Irish youths crowded Rockne's roster. There were the expected number of Walshes, Flanagans, O'Boyles, and Bolands to go around. "They are as thick on the team as shamrocks in a Dublin bouquet" wrote author Delos Lovelace. But for a rival college and its supporters to portray Notre Damers as ignorant, roughneck, "shanty Irish" was considerably beyond the acceptable parameters of bench-jockeying and needling. It was the most vicious kind of prairie prejudice and demonstrated an insensitivity to the feelings of Notre Dame's players and students. For years middle-class Irish were trying to live down the opprobrium deriving from those in an earlier time who lived in squalid slums under repressive conditions. The rage felt by Notre Dame's authorities was no less diminished by another defeat at the hands of the Cornhuskers—a 17–0 beating.

These continued failures against Nebraska further stoked the fires of Rockne's competitiveness. He burned with the desire to get another crack at Nebraska the following year. Such a game had already been contracted for by him. Nebraska's administrators were also eager for the series to continue, since they had only recently constructed a new, enlarged stadium, which inevitably filled up whenever Notre Dame came to play there.

But Notre Dame's athletic board, incensed at what had transpired at Lincoln, canceled the 1926 game, over Rockne's heated objections. In private, Rockne was as appalled as anyone else at the blatant bigotry displayed in Lincoln. Publicly, however, being as manipulative as he was, he expressed his desire to continue to play against Nebraska. He yearned to even the score on the field and was also aware that many bigots would regard the cancellation of the contest as proof that Notre Dame booked only those teams it could beat. Such insinuations infuriated Rockne, so he worked to reverse the decision to withdraw Nebraska from the schedule. By doing so he incurred the wrath of many at Notre Dame, including President Walsh. Frustrated with his superiors, Rockne reached out to others who had approached him several years before.

It was no secret that for a long while Columbia, eager to match its football team competitively with other elite eastern schools such as Yale, Harvard, Dartmouth, and Princeton, had been casting its net for Rockne. Aside from the talented running back Wally Koppisch, the Lions had met with scant success on the gridiron. Then they had hired the legendary Haughton, only to experience the numbing effect of his sudden death at Baker Field. Rockne had met with representatives of Columbia from time to time. Now it didn't take much to convince him that coaching at Columbia would yield him considerably more money. At Notre Dame he was earning ten thousand dollars a year, while Columbia was prepared to hire him at twenty-five thousand dollars per year for three years, not much less than its famous president, Nicholas Murray Butler, was being paid. In addition, Rockne could then boast that he was the highest-paid football coach in America. It was also certain that Columbia had reminded him that by setting up his household in New York City he would be geographically close to all of those members of the New York press, who had been singing his praises for years.

Although he was under a long-term contract with Notre Dame, Rockne seemed involved in a "get even" scenario with his school. But it was hard for diehard Notre Dame aficionados to accept the notion that their beloved Knute might actually walk out on them.

Columbia's football committee, headed by its director of athletics, Bobby Watt, who brought Lou Gehrig to Columbia a few years before, and by a well-to-do alumnus, James Knapp, were convinced that they had lassoed the services of Rockne. And, for a few crazy days, maybe Rockne did, too. However, the overzealous Knapp jumped the gun on Rockne's "signing" with Columbia by leaking the news to the press. It had been Rockne's understanding that the matter would be kept secret until he could return to Notre Dame to negotiate a release from his contract.

When the news did hit the New York newspapers, Rockne felt a terrible sense of embarrassment. His superiors at South Bend insisted that they had been betrayed by him and opinion at Notre Dame was not particularly kind toward the wayward coach. Much of the criticism was thick with sarcasm. It was also clear that Notre Dame was in no placatory mood to match or top Columbia's offer. They were furious that Rockne might be using the Columbia situation as a wedge to bargain for more money from them.

After several days of accusations and indecision, Rockne, caught with his stubby fingers in the Columbia candy jar, tried to explain to the Lions that having failed to get his release from his Notre

Dame contract, he was not in a position to move to Morningside Heights. At the same time, he felt that Notre Dame might reject him. "I don't know whether I'll have a job left when I get back home," he said wearily.

When the dust finally settled, Notre Dame got back its coach, and Columbia was forced to proceed with Charlie Crowley, whom Rockne was supposed to replace. Nobody emerged from the brouhaha with much dignity. If Rockne was chastened, he also preferred to blame Columbia for all of his difficulties, which wasn't quite the case. There were also those at Notre Dame who were convinced that Rockne might be pried away by still another college. Would that mean, they wondered, that outstanding high school talent would be reluctant to attend Notre Dame for fear that a fickle Rockne would soon depart?

Many in the press who had been automatically admiring of everything that Rockne did now suggested that he'd been in over his head dealing with the big-city slickers. The argument that Rockne was an unsophisticated man, just an unfortunate hick, who had been taken in, at least for a while, by the men at Morningside was rather a laughable proposition; it was probably the last time Rockne would ever suffer such disparagement. True, Rockne, in his petulance, may have misjudged the matter from beginning to end, but a fool he wasn't.

Overlooked in all of this chicanery was the fact that earlier in the season, on the November morning of the Northwestern game, Rockne had at last accepted the Catholic faith and received his First Communion. The ceremony had taken place at the Old Log Chapel, which was a replica of Father Sorin's original Notre Dame building. After much study and introspection, Rockne had received Catholic instructions from a former player under him, Rev. Vincent Mooney, who also performed the service. Those present at the ceremony included Rockne's next-door neighbor Tom Hickey. Father Mooney had thoughtfully arranged for little Knute, Jr., to walk beside his father. During the ceremony Rockne noticed that there was only a single candle burning at the altar. Unable to resist a wisecrack and flashing his lopsided grin, he said, "You know, you guys are awfully tight with the wax."

In later years, whenever Rockne commented on his conversion (his wife, Bonnie, had converted to Catholicism shortly before they were married), he invariably left the impression that his players had been the most compelling force behind his move. He said that he had always been much taken with their strong devotion, as they sometimes arose at five or six o'clock in the morning to attend Mass before football games. They were willing, he pointed out, to sacrifice hours of sleep by walking up to the Communion rail. Such faith, he believed, was a powerful ally to their hard work on the football field. Rockne's act of conversion was not performed frivolously; it was a serious matter to him. There also wasn't much doubt that his conversion had been influenced by the atmosphere of religiosity at Notre Dame, from the priests who took an active role in everyday dormitory life, from the Masses that were celebrated daily, from the ubiquitous crucifixes that were prominently displayed in all of the classrooms, and from his own desire to achieve peace of mind. Thereafter he would always be there with his players in the chapel, rather than remaining a quizzical bystander.

After he left Notre Dame, Enright, the star of the 1925 Northwestern game, insisted that there was a link between Rockne's conversion on the day of that game and the vigorous performance of Notre Dame in the third quarter. Not a Catholic himself, Enright was convinced that the players had responded to their coach's acceptance of the Catholic faith. "It was not an exaggeration to suggest," he said, "that Notre Dame won that one for Rock." He added that Rockne's influence on his own life and on others who had crossed his path at Notre Dame was enormous.

16

The Coach Plays Hooky

A DRIVEN, WORK-ORIENTED MAN like Rockne had a need to take
some time out, as many of his friends kept reminding him. After
the tempestuous 1925 year, after the Columbia debacle, and after
other job proposals (which he rejected summarily) to come out to
Southern California, Rockne was encouraged to take a European
trip. Though football was hardly the main recreation of the French
or the British, Rockne was treated endearingly in both places, especially by the French. After all, wasn't Notre Dame a French
name, and wasn't it started by a Frenchman? The British, although
more blasé and not always accepting of celebrated Americans, were
unusually warm toward him.

He used his guidebook French to rattle off French dishes and
to ask questions in the street. While on board ship going to Europe
he became acquainted with Helen Wills, who dominated the world
of women's tennis the way Bobby Jones ruled golf. He made friends
wherever he went and loved to regale other touring Americans with
his tall stories. For a few months his restless mind was removed
from the intricacies of football and the problems he'd had with
Notre Dame's wise men. It appeared that he would be able to begin
the 1926 season with renewed vigor. "The Swede is himself again,"
one of the members of the 1926 squad remarked to Francis Wallace

after there had been comments that Rockne appeared to be a fatigued and troubled man.

It was fitting that among the players who reported to Rockne in 1926 one was named Parisien, although it was unlikely that he'd been recruited while the coach was roaming around the Louvre. But there were others, such as Butch Niemiec and Christy Flanagan, both backs of considerable skill, who promised to keep the Irish on a winning path.

There remained hope at Notre Dame that the Big Ten would relent and open the doors of its self-important conference to the Irish. Rockne himself did a good deal of lobbying with various members of the Big Ten. However, such efforts may have been counterproductive, for his reputation with schools such as the University of Chicago and Michigan was not positive. Some in the Big Ten might have been willing to forgive Rockne's so-called recruiting excesses, as well as Notre Dame's questionable (to them) academic standards. But what they weren't willing to forgive was Rockne's tenacity and ability to win, plus his adroit handling of the press.

Ultimately, Notre Dame's bid to join the Big Ten was turned down despite the fact that the Irish, at the end, had four supporters. Surprisingly, during this period, there were those at Notre Dame who charged that it was Rockne who actually stood in the way of Big Ten admission. They felt that coaches such as Yost of Michigan and Chicago's Stagg regarded Rockne as somewhat lower than a dachshund's belly and would oppose Notre Dame under any circumstances. Rockne's retort to such people was that the opposition to Notre Dame was based primarily on anti-Catholicism. He was right up to a point, but his own role served to firm up the enmity of some conference members.

Despite the unpleasant hurdles constructed by the Big Ten, Rockne's reputation with the general public was solid. He was increasingly in demand to make speeches all over the country; he was always available to give advice to other coaches, who sought his counsel; he was exceedingly kind to youngsters who hung around the South Bend campus hoping to catch a look at Notre Dame's stars in practice sessions. Ironically, Rockne may have paid more attention to such urchins than he did to his own children, for he believed that Bonnie could tend to the needs of his kids.

Rockne the speechmaker was an especially quick study when it came to adapting for his own purposes the words and neologisms of others. Naturally, he always felt free to use his friend Francis

Wallace's expressions, such as "intestinal fortitude" and "suicide schedule." After a while he was convinced that such phrases had originated with himself. What Abe Lincoln, H. L. Mencken, Daniel Webster, Will Rogers, or Freud might have thought about such studied "borrowing" is yet another matter. However, even without dipping into the word arsenal of others, he had an original flair for public speaking that was probably exceeded only in his time by New York's mayor Jimmy Walker. A voracious and eclectic reader when he had the time, Rockne was an erudite fellow who managed to hide his penchant for culture behind his pugilist's face.

In the first eight games of the 1926 campaign Notre Dame, employing mainly second-year men, was overwhelming. The team yielded just one touchdown, against Minnesota, in the second game. They barely squeaked by Northwestern, 6–0, in the fourth game. But against all the others, including Beloit (77–0), Penn State (28–0), and Indiana (26–0), the Irish put on a show that was dazzling. Their success underscored the basic Rockne doctrine: straight football, emphasizing speed. In this system, which was not widely copied, a blocker was obliged only to brush his man hard once, with the expectation being that that would permit the runner to go for his opening. To Rockne every play was a potential six-pointer, and he usually disdained the field goal, even when he had experts in the art on his squad. "It takes three field goals to beat one touchdown," he frequently explained.

The game with Minnesota was closer than the final score indicated, for at halftime the Gophers led, 7–6. But at the start of the second half Christy Flanagan raced for a sixty-eight-yard touchdown. After that, the Irish were never headed.

In the victory over Indiana, Rockne suffered a weird injury on the sidelines when an Indiana back, hell-bent for yardage, barged into him. In the crush, Rockne was badly shaken up. When he was a younger man Rockne might have been able to overcome the impact of the collision more readily. But in this instance, he was more vulnerable. In later years, when he suffered from a serious phlebitic inflammation in his legs, it was believed that this unfortunate episode might have triggered it.

Following the Indiana game, Notre Dame prepared to face Army for the thirteenth time. The Irish were protecting their unbeaten mark as they engaged the Cadets for the second straight year in Yankee Stadium. The hoopla surrounding this clash had now reached such proportions that whole platoons of personnel had to tend to the care and feeding of the press. Rockne himself was so besieged for tickets and complimentary passes that he had some difficulty concentrating on the task at hand: beating Army, in retribution for the disastrous defeat suffered the previous year. In his book *Dementia Pigskin*, Francis Wallace tried to describe the symbiotic relationship between the two rivals. "Army and Notre Dame is a masculine friendship, like two guys who meet on a golf course on a quiet Tuesday afternoon," he said. "Army, the older member, invites the new chap to play. They have a good game, like each other and it grows and grows." Even at this stage, there were some critics who thought it had grown too much.

This time Army arrived at the mammoth ball park in the Bronx led by a new coach, "Biff" Jones, a former All-American tackle who had attended West Point and then had served in France during the Great War. Jones was blessed by the presence in Army's backfield of two spectacular performers, "Light Horse Harry" Wilson, who was so instrumental in destroying Rockne's team in 1925, and Christian Keener Cagle. Curiously, for a good part of the year, Cagle had seemed lackadaisical, which was unusual for such a spirited runner and passer. When Jones persisted in searching for the cause, it was discovered that "Red" Cagle was nursing a tapeworm, which presumably had deprived him of much of his energy. The doctors at West Point at once started medical treatment, and by the time the November 13 date with Notre Dame rolled around, he was ready to spark the Cadets—which was bad news for Rockne.

The Cadets had won eight games in a row, over two seasons, as they came into this game. They also had the entire monarchial, in-a-brace Corps of Cadets, more than a thousand strong, marching and shouting in their support. The game was Yankee Stadium's second transcendent sports event to take place within a few weeks, for on Sunday, October 10, on a bleak afternoon, the veteran pitcher Grover Cleveland Alexander came to the rescue of the St. Louis Cardinals in the deciding game of the World Series against the Yankees. Alex struck out young Yankee slugger Tony Lazzeri in the seventh inning with the bases loaded, sewing up the Series for the Cardinals.

Like all Army–Notre Dame games, the 1926 clash was grimly fought. But unlike the '25 game, when Army scored almost at will, the first half ended in a 0–0 deadlock. The ground game exhibited by both teams yielded almost the same yardage. Wilson was stopped cold every time he carried the ball.

In the third quarter Army kicked off to Notre Dame, and full-back Harry O'Boyle scampered to his own thirty-three-yard line. One play later, O'Boyle moved the ball to the thirty-seven-yard-line. At that point Rockne called for a play that was known among his men as no. 51—an off-tackle "bread and butter" maneuver past the outstretched arms of Army's big Texan Bud Sprague. With Flanagan lugging the ball, each Notre Dame blocker performed his role to perfection. Down the sidelines Flanagan went, for the only touchdown of the day. Strangely, the same "perfect play" was attempted seven times in that '26 game before it finally worked—or, at least, before Flanagan's blockers made it work.

In the last quarter, as a chill settled over the field, the Cadets fought gamely to tie the score. Cagle threw seven passes, missing on six of them. As the game came to an end, halfback Ray Dahman of the Irish intercepted the last of Cagle's desperate aerials. Rockne's intense preparation against a last-minute air offensive had paid off.

Flanagan played well again the next week, against Drake University of Iowa, in the Irish Homecoming Game. The final score was 21–0, which caused most of the sports seers to anticipate that the Irish would be named the top eleven of the season. There were only two games remaining, one against Carnegie Tech, the last versus USC.

The game with Carnegie Tech was regarded by almost everybody as a routine contest. In those days it was common to call such games "breathers" and, obviously, Rockne also considered it in that light. But he made one of the worst tactical blunders in his career—and it turned out to cost his team an unbeaten season. With some urging from the omnipresent promoter Christy Walsh, Rockne decided that he should go to the Army-Navy bloodletting in Chicago instead of traveling to Pittsburgh, where the Irish were playing Tech. Presumably Rockne went to see the interservice game to scout a Navy team that was on Notre Dame's schedule the following year. But that was only one side of the story, for Walsh wanted Rockne to pose for some publicity photographs alongside Stanford's Warner and Tad Jones, late of Yale, two other celebrity coaches of that era. Both were scheduled to be on hand in Chicago. As a matter of fact, they were seated next to Rockne in the press box. Overconfidence had never been Rockne's besetting sin, but that day he absented himself from his squad in Pittsburgh. Having misjudged Carnegie Tech's potential for mischief, Rockne felt, no doubt in all sincerity, that it was safe to leave his charges in the hands of one of his assistants. Hunk Anderson was anointed with that role and lived to regret it.

Rockne hadn't reckoned with the skills of Tech's part-time coach, Wally Steffen, who had a full-time post as a judge in Chicago and had learned his football at the knee of Coach Stagg. Before the start of the game, Steffen received information that Rockne had chosen to be 411 miles away in Chicago to watch the service rivals. Thus, when he addressed his players, Steffen said that Rockne apparently thought so little of Tech's chances that he arrogantly deserted his unbeaten team. Reacting in outrage, the Tech kids went out and played the Irish off their feet, in a display of "constructive fury."

In the preceding week Rockne had given Anderson a set of instructions to follow against Tech. Rockne had noticed that Tech employed a deep punt formation, so he told Anderson to use a close box defense, much tighter than the 7-2-2 arrangement that was

In 1926 Rockne posed with two coaching idols of his time, Pop Warner of Stanford (center) and Tad Jones of Yale. Courtesy: Don Honig.

generally favored by the Irish. Noticing this, Steffen had his team quick-kick on second down early in the game to take advantage of Notre Dame's bunched defense. The Irish never seemed to recover from that tactic, or from the cold, miserable day, with snow and rain lashing into their faces. Throughout the game the Irish played lethargically.

Was it Hunk's fault? Or was it Knute's fault, for not being there when his team apparently needed him? As Rockne sat in Chicago, at halftime, one among 110,000 people, a sportswriter with a telegrapher beside him tapped the coach on the shoulder.

"I have some bad news for you," he said.

At worst, Rockne figured Tech had scored a touchdown. But he never bargained for what he heard next.

"The final score is Carnegie Tech 19, Notre Dame 0," the writer added, with a touch of *schadenfreude*.

Rockne could hardly speak; he hadn't believed such a result was possible.

Line coach Hunk Anderson, second from left, with Rockne on the sidelines in a 1930 photo. Courtesy: UPI-Corbis-Bettmann.

185

In the days that followed the disaster at Pittsburgh, Rockne never once criticized Hunk Anderson, nor did he belittle Carnegie Tech's achievement.

"I would have fired Hunk if he had changed that defense," remarked Rockne. "It took a lot of courage for Hunk to stand up there and take a beating for the sake of following orders."

Two days later Rockne sent a telegram to Clarence Overend, the athletic director at Tech. This is how it read: "From what the boys told me when they got back home, Tech deserved to win. I was more than sorry not to be able to get there but my little bit of help could hardly have been able to change things. . . . Knute Rockne."

Newspapers played up the Tech win as one of the monumental upsets of the year—but none of them cared to mention that Rockne's absence, to perform some publicity chores, was the main reason he wasn't present at Forbes Field. They offered the official excuse that he was in Chicago to scout Navy. Some of these reports went so far as to describe him as furiously scribbling notes in the press box. Rockne's human weakness in this situation, which may have deprived Notre Dame of an unbeaten season, served to point up the complexity of the man. Nobody cherished victory as much as he did, yet he had actually obliged Carnegie Tech by not showing up.

Many of the men who played under Rockne worshiped him—and wouldn't have wanted to play for anyone else. "He was an inspiring force," John Kieran of the *New York Times* once wrote about him. But on that November day in Pittsburgh he wasn't on the bench to inspire anyone.

Embarrassed by their setback, the Notre Dame squad chose to take an earlier train than planned back to South Bend. They didn't want to face a student body that was always there to greet them. But in the few days before the next game, with the University of Southern California, the players were serenaded in the student halls, proving that Rockne was not surrounded by "fair-weather friends."

Were Notre Dame—and Rockne—now sufficiently resilient to redeem the season? The final game with USC, a team with a record of 8–1, including victories over California, Washington State, and Montana, and only a one-point loss to Stanford, was scheduled for Los Angeles Coliseum. Despite Notre Dame's defeat at the hands of Carnegie Tech, the tickets for the USC game—eighty thousand of them—went as if some half-witted press agent were flinging them about.

Before the Irish left for the West Coast, Rockne held a special Monday practice at which he addressed his players. Again he repeated that Anderson was not to blame for what had happened; it was his way of apologizing for his absence. He reminded the team that the season could still be a successful one, with a victory over USC. "We can redeem ourselves," he informed them, with a measure of guilt.

The trip to the West Coast did not rate as a triumphant pilgrimage, yet Notre Dame rooters all along the way came out to greet Rockne and his squad. Whenever the train stopped to permit the players to loosen up, people emerged from the woodwork to welcome the Notre Damers. Despite the defeat by Tech, the mystique still held—and Rockne knew it.

It was scaldingly hot that November day in California, but at the start of the final period Notre Dame still led, 7–6. Then, with only a half-dozen minutes to play, USC seized the lead. A fast-wilting Notre Dame team was on the verge of losing two straight games for the first time under Rockne's leadership. Had Flanagan, Niemiec, and Company run out of gas? Or was it time for Rockne to pull another one of his miracles out of his hat?

Rockne peered down the line of his grim-faced players, and his eyes fixed on the 145-pound Art Parisien, a fourth-string quarterback from Haverhill, Massachusetts. Parisien, who had a heart murmur and wouldn't even earn his varsity letter that year for lack of playing minutes, could throw a football with either hand. In the closing minutes, Rockne thought, this particular talent might befuddle USC. So he motioned to the young man to go into the game. It was worth a try.

As the clock ticked down to the final minute, Parisien's passes landed the Irish within striking distance of USC's goal line. With thirty seconds remaining, Parisien faded back, dodged several would-be tacklers, and threw a perfect strike into the outstretched hands of Niemiec on the five-yard-line. Butch stumbled for a second, then rumbled over for the winning touchdown as the crowd roared in disbelief.

This time it was no steaming locker-room oratory that had turned the tide. Instead, the game was won by the type of careful preparation to which Rockne was addicted. This slight substitute quarterback had been brought along by his coach almost in anticipation of such an emergency. Most major teams probably would have ignored a youngster like Parisien. Many would not even have included him on their squads. Yet here was this unlikely hero rising to the occasion in the California heat. Rockne had faith in the boy and was willing to use him. "He had the spark to do it," Rockne said later to the sportswriters, who were in awe of his genius—and his luck.

There was an interesting footnote to this dramatic game. It was the presence in the USC line—if only for a few minutes—of a lanky young giant named Marion Morrison, who hailed from Winterset, Iowa. Morrison had made his letter on USC's freshman team, but when he moved up to Coach Howard Jones's varsity, his lack of speed deprived him of a first-string post. Jones had switched Morrison from guard to tackle, for the guard position on USC was one that required a player to act as interference in the coach's running game.

Several USCers, who had played alongside Morrison, claimed that he was on the path to becoming an All-American when he suffered an injury. There was little truth to this claim, for when Morrison left USC in 1927, he was considerably less than a star.

Where Morrison did become a star was on the silver screen. Going to Hollywood, where he became known to the world as John "Duke" Wayne, he evolved into the prototypical cinema cowboy, an exemplar of raw machismo. In time he became a superpatriot and an icon of the right wing, encouraging the film industry's press agents to spread the word that he had been a mainstay of USC's fine football teams. Rockne could have told them it wasn't anything like that.

17

Ten Years at the Helm

By THE TIME 1927 rolled around, a year that sports historians invariably have blessed as the Mount Everest of the Roaring Twenties, Rockne had been head coach at Notre Dame for a decade. In the eyes of many observers he had become the preeminent coach of his time, even as his teams had won ungrudging acceptance across the nation.

It's no exaggeration to suggest that although Babe Ruth, Jack Dempsey, Bobby Jones, Bill Tilden, Helen Wills, Tommy Hitchcock, Gene Tunney, Earl Sande, Lou Gehrig, and countless others of that sports-dizzy decade had their cheerleaders in the press corps, Rockne still managed to gain the lion's share of attention. He continued to win more unabashed idolatry than most of them, and the man in the street seemed to have a special place in his affection for him.

This reverence stemmed more from Rockne's attractive persona than it did from his unceasing chain of victories. He was the supersalesman of sports, a student of the classics, and constantly the source of quotable quotes, witticisms, and wry, self-depreciating remarks that were often subtle and profound. Typical of Rockne's humor was his reaction to the frequent jesting over the fact that his Fighting Irish team was composed of such "Irishmen" as Carideo, Bondi, Savoldi, Brill, Schwartz, Metzger, Polisky, etc. When a New York writer suggested, in light of this irony, that there should be a slight change in the Latin quotation *Non omnis moriar* (I shall not altogether die), Rockne was quick with his riposte: *Non omnes Moriarty.*

There were many advantages that accrued to Rockne as a result of his widespread celebrity, not the least of which was money. Never noticeably allergic to dollar bills, he was able to cash in, to an extraordinary degree, on his fame and popularity, showing the way to other aggressive entrepreneurial coaches and athletes. If one seeks the roots of today's millionaire sports figures, Rockne must receive credit—or blame—as an early catalyst. He was never shy about involving himself in various outside means to increase his wealth, although he was not eager to have members of the press draw attention to this proclivity. When columnist Pegler wrote, "I see Mr. Rockne as a modest man who does not think much of himself, who is amazed to find himself a great national celebrity and who wants to make all the money he can, while he can, lest the public suddenly get next to him," Rockne was furious. Although the Notre Dame fathers suffered some embarrassment about the far-reaching extent of Rockne's business activities, there was not a word in his contract that prevented him from engaging in such pursuits.

Rockne's basic salary of ten thousand dollars per year was handsome remuneration for a college football coach in that era. But compared to Babe Ruth's sixty-thousand-to-eighty-thousand-dollar range and the million-dollar gates attracted to prizefights featuring pugilists such as Dempsey, Tunney, Luis Angel Firpo, and Georges Carpentier, it was relatively lean pickings. Thus Rockne was constantly tempted to invite other means to augment his income. His articles and syndicated columns, turned out with the help of Christy Walsh, brought him as much as five thousand dollars per year, and his speeches to diverse business and educational groups earned him as much as four hundred dollars per speech. In some years he made hundreds of such speeches, in all parts of the country. He was one of the first coaches to endorse products and football equipment, and he did promotional work for the Studebaker Auto Company, which had South Bend as its headquarters. (After Rockne's death a two-door Rockne coupe, which was essentially a small Studebaker, was manufactured and distributed. It was a flashy little car, with whitewall tires, and was available in a wide range of body styles. The car was withdrawn from the Studebaker line in 1934, after 30,293 of them had been sold.)

Rockne opened coaching schools, which sometimes yielded him as much as twenty thousand dollars per year, and he put his name on an instructional book that earned him close to seven thousand dollars. Toward the end of his life he reluctantly turned down a bid to go on the vaudeville circuit, where such luminaries as John J. McGraw, Babe Ruth, Bill Tilden, and pitcher Rube Marquard, who had much less to say than Rockne, had made surprising sums of money. (Rockne's decision was based on an already overcrowded schedule, as well as frowns from the Notre Dame administrators.)

Rockne had plenty of competition for headlines in 1927. Some of it, of course, came from other sports titans in this wildly extravagant period. During the whole year of 1927, for instance, Ruth belted towering home runs at a furious, record-setting pace. By the end of the season he had reached the sacrosanct sixty figure as the Yankees spread-eagled the American League field. After the Yankees beat the Pittsburgh Pirates four in a row in the World Series, such dominance caused them to be adjudged as "the greatest baseball team of them all." It also provoked the shrill and aimless cries

A Rockne two-door Studebaker went on sale after his death.

of "Break up the Yankees!" Nobody ever had to direct such appeals about the Notre Dame football team, for, after all, All-America players graduated sooner or later—nobody had to break them up.

The second Dempsey-Tunney heavyweight fight took place at Soldier Field in Chicago on September 22, 1927. Comedians cracked jokes suggesting that five-dollar seats for the brawl would be as far off as Milwaukee. Chicago's "Scarface Al" Capone, the mythic archgangster of them all, led a contingent of celebrities who were seated near the action, among them Doug Fairbanks, Charlie Chaplin, Al Jolson, Harold Lloyd, John Barrymore, Bernard M. Baruch, Florenz Ziegfeld, David Belasco, and Otto Kahn. Rockne was absent from the scene, as he was busy preparing his team for the season's opener against Coe College, of Cedar Rapids, Iowa, on October 1. He would have been present, except for this prior commitment. He knew most of the show business people and politicos who congregated at such events, and enjoyed their company. He was also a fight buff, who had great admiration for the boxing skills of Tunney.

Tunney won this 1927 fight, which assumed legendary proportions due to the infamous "long count" in the seventh round. Dempsey, who had been regarded as a World War I draft dodger until that night, suddenly emerged as an appealing underdog figure.

Herbert Asbury called 1927 the year of "The Big Shriek," but he wasn't referring to Rockne's locker-room effusions. "Scarcely had one stupendous occurrence been emblazoned in journalistic tradition as the greatest story of this age than another appeared in its place, to goad frenzied editors and reporters to new heights of hysteria and hyperbole," he wrote.

Soaring over all events in 1927 was Charles Lindbergh's dramatic solo flight across the Atlantic Ocean to Paris in May, accompanied only by a couple of sandwiches. The country went crazy over this slim, enigmatic young air-mail pilot, who struck a chord, wrote reporter Elmer Davis, with a "public which had seemed to find its highest ideal in Babe Ruth, Rudolph Valentino, Gertrude Ederle or perhaps in Peaches Browning and Ruth Snyder." Lindbergh became the most acclaimed figure in the world overnight, surpassing all of the heroes of the sports pages. He was "Lucky Lindy" to admiring Americans, just as Rockne was "Rock" to all those who followed the less sublime field of college football.

Expectations for Rockne's 1927 squad were high, with a number of experienced players on hand, including Niemiec and Flanagan.

With the season approaching, Rockne put aside his skirmishes with Notre Dame's administrators, who remained sensitive to the accusations about over-emphasis of football. Rockne had played a part in it but in the pervading atmosphere, where there was a good deal of hypocrisy and corruption to go around, he was not out of step with the time. "Any time they all want to come out in the open on all this business," Rockne said, "I'll take my chances."

Before the season began, Notre Dame still did not hold membership in any official conference. But some schools, such as Missouri, Kansas, and Kansas State, held out the possibility that a Missouri Valley Conference might be organized, including Notre Dame as a member. Rockne expressed his gratitude for such a proposal, though he wasn't enthusiastic about it. But among Notre Dame's satraps there was a consensus that such participation would work to downgrade the Irish and reduce their claims for a national ranking. They felt that membership in a Missouri Valley Conference, with a schedule including fewer teams of muscle and renown, would forfeit Notre Dame's reputation as a "national team." In a Missouri Valley Conference many of the teams on Notre Dame's docket would have been similar to Coe College, hardly a challenge to the Irish.

After defeating Coe, 28–7, in a home opener that failed to entice many local supporters (there were fewer than ten thousand on hand), Notre Dame went on the road the following week to play Detroit in their new stadium. Guiding the Detroit team was none other than Gus Dorais, who had become head coach there two years before and who would remain in place until 1944. Dorais's style of attack, borrowed basically from the Notre Dame box, was augmented by a passing attack led by Lloyd Brazil. There was plenty of pregame bantering, back and forth, between the old teammates and warriors. Rockne went so far as to suggest that Detroit could conceivably upset his team, pointing to Detroit's near-miss the week before against Army. However, Detroit fell rather easily, 20–0, in spite of the pleading of a sellout crowd of thirty thousand.

The battle with Navy came next. It was staged at Baltimore, a neutral site, and attracted more than forty-five thousand. Baltimore had whole neighborhoods of Catholics, so the Irish were more welcome there than in other communities they occasionally invaded to play football. This game, long pursued by Rockne, began a long-running series with the Midshipmen, becoming almost as prestigious on Notre Dame's yearly schedule as Army. In spite of all the hectoring over his absenteeism from the Carnegie Tech game, Rockne must have learned something in his ill-timed scouting trip the year before, for the Irish beat Navy, 19–6. They were led by Niemiec against a Navy team coached for the first time by "Navy Bill" Ingram.

This appearance of the Naval Academy on Notre Dame's schedule presented a somewhat ticklish problem for Rockne. For several years Navy authorities had been raising the issue of Army's policy of permitting graduates of other schools to play football for them. The relationship between the two service schools became so inflamed that Navy dropped Army from its schedule in the late twenties. Desirous of keeping the Cadets on board, as well as maintaining a good yearly association with Navy, Rockne was forced to play a cool diplomatic hand. He knew that Army did, indeed, benefit from the bearded veterans who dotted their roster. Obviously, too, such players had helped Army against Notre Dame in recent games, starting in 1924. But Rockne had been accused of doing the same thing, so he refused to take a position in this argument. Later, Navy picked up Army again on its schedule, but not before a further exchange of angry words passed between the two academies. All the while, Rockne continued to schedule both of them. He was a man on a tightrope, if ever there was one.

As the season progressed, Rockne appeared to have the makings of another unbeaten year, although he was aware that Notre Dame didn't have quite the mixture of talent it had had in other years. Yes, Notre Dame had plenty of ethnic mixture, as Rockne always testified cheerily. But was it good enough? When writers continued to refer to his men as the "Fighting Irish," Rockne was amused and accepting. "As long as they play with true Irish spirit," he said, "it doesn't matter what they are, or where they come from."

Indiana fell at its home in Bloomington, 19–6, and Georgia Tech journeyed to Cartier Field, only to lose, 26–7. With Minnesota coming up next, Notre Dame was confident it would extend its unbeaten streak at home, where they hadn't lost in twenty-two years. However, that nasty bugaboo—an unremitting snowstorm—descended on Cartier Field, and so did an uncommonly large sophomore (6 feet, 2 inches, 235 pounds) named Bronko Nagurski. Destined to become a Minnesota all-time legend, Nagurski had never played any high school football before registering at Minnesota. But in a few months he developed into a player who could dominate at fullback or on the line.

In the '27 game against Notre Dame, Nagurski, born in Rainy River, Ontario, played all sixty minutes on the line, messing up Rockne's offense about as well as any single man ever had. One of Rockne's special talents was scouting the opposition. But in this instance, his perfectionism failed him—he had overlooked this "beginner."

For three periods it appeared as if Notre Dame would be able to nurse a seven-point lead to victory. The Irish's single touchdown had resulted after Minnesota had fumbled a punt on its own twenty-yard-line. However, with only two minutes to go in the contest, and the players as wet as trout, Nagurski leaped on a fumble he had provoked. From there the Gophers employed several plays, including a crucial pass that went over the head of defender Niemiec (only five-nine) into the hands of an end who was seven inches taller. When the Gophers kicked the extra point the game was tied at 7–7. That's the way it ended. When it was all over, twenty-eight thousand aggrieved Notre Dame fans, who had filled every inch of space at Cartier Field, sat silently as the snowflakes washed their faces. There went Notre Dame's infallibility at home. Not long after that, Rockne, and many other coaches, were picking Nagurski on their All-American teams, while Grantland Rice, in time, would insist that eleven Nagurskis could beat eleven Red Granges or eleven Jim Thorpes.

As Notre Dame licked its wounds, Rockne tried to prepare his men to rebound against Army. But even as the coach worked on his men in practice, he was again forced to cope with the accusations of overemphasis that came from many quarters. Such cries were a constant burr in his pants. Invariably he had a ready response, for he was never shy about presenting what he believed to be his legitimate argument in behalf of his game and the way he pursued it and coached it. He attacked the reformers in no uncertain terms, charging that they were simply scrambling to get on the front pages of newspapers. He asserted that these negativists didn't fully comprehend the positive aspects of college football.

"Isn't it far better to have a group of boys working off their excess energy, after hours of classroom work, on the football field, under capable instruction in organized athletics, than it is to have the same young men dashing around in automobiles, cluttering the street corners or poolrooms or the drugstore?" he asked. "What we try to do is to develop these boys so that their physical triumphs go hand in hand with their mental achievements in the classroom."

(What Rockne failed to address was the fact that many players, despite their supposed exhaustion, *still* managed to run around at night or "dash around in automobiles.")

In his day there were few more insistent advocates of college football than Rockne. But sometimes he went too far, when he tried to portray his critics as evil fools, as they accused him, and others like him, of underemphasizing the educational importance of college.

Rockne chose to be the man in the arena, as he threw his wordy rebuttals at the reformers. But occasionally he got into trouble due to his propensity for tongue-in-cheek humor, which could be easily misinterpreted by others. One day a reporter asked him to comment about the "decline" of football in the East, the section of the country where the game had originated and still was played with unusual zeal. On this issue Rockne had some fun by playing populist. Maybe these eastern kids, he offered, live in the lap of luxury and choose to shy away from the rigors of physical combat. Certainly Rockne must have known he was engaging in stereotypes, always a foolish practice.

Naturally, the newspapers snapped up the story, for almost anything that Rockne uttered was fodder for the columns. So the chastened Rockne had to back away. After all, how could a coach whose roster featured at least a dozen first-rate kids from the East make such a case? He said he was appalled that anyone could have translated his jocular remarks in such a way. Generally a man open to the press, he was paying a penalty for his glib tongue. His refuge then was to suggest that he was misquoted.

Needling statements about the effeteness of Easterners was especially ill timed, for the game against Army was at hand; nobody had to be reminded that West Point was perched up on the Hudson River, only an hour or so from New York City, the Babylon of America.

Each year, with Army and Notre Dame jousting at Yankee Stadium, tickets were more difficult to come by. In fact, it is no exaggeration to state that two hundred thousand tickets could easily have been sold for the November 12 game. As it was, the usual eighty thousand or so were there, a majority of them members of the diehard "subway alumni." The Cadet Corps again paraded in all of its stiff-backed grandeur, while Rockne's men took the field dressed in green instead of their usual blue and gold. They had worn the colors of the Irish countryside before, but never against

Army. New York's dandy little mayor, Jimmy Walker, who wrote love songs in his spare time and was a friend of Rockne, did his best to subdue his Irish partisanship by sitting on the West Point side for one half, then switching over to the Notre Dame side for the other half.

Rockne counted on the resiliency of his team in this game, for in the past they had rebounded strongly after a setback or a tie. In this instance, however, it was not to be, for Army was fielding one of the best teams in the country. Five of its regulars, including the ineffable Cagle, had accumulated fifteen years of playing time at West Point among them.

Nothing on that balmy afternoon at the Stadium could stop Cagle, who experienced one of the most productive days of his career. He literally tore Rockne's defenses apart with his running as well as his passing, helping Army to win handily, 18–0. On one play Cagle ran forty-eight yards for a touchdown; on another he went fifteen yards for a touchdown.

In the lingering moments of the game, Notre Dame still refused to give up, abiding by the dictum of a latter-day baseball hero, Yogi Berra, that "it's never over till it's over." When the game ended the Irish were on Army's five-yard-line and still trying hard to score their first touchdown of the day.

The proof of just how good Biff Jones's Cadets were through the last three meetings with Notre Dame was that they had tallied forty-five points against a lonely seven for the Irish. Ironically, the seven points had been enough for Notre Dame to win one of those games. Despite the disparity in those years between Army and Notre Dame, Rockne continued to love the challenge. Even as some critics screamed to high heavens about Army's permissive policy, allowing men from other schools to play for them, Rockne had no intention to drop West Point from Notre Dame's docket.

As was his custom, Rockne visited the West Point dressing room after the game. This time his purpose wasn't solely to congratulate the Cadets. He also wanted to take exception to a rough tackle made by a Cadet against one of Notre Dame's backs, as he returned a punt. Rockne said that he wasn't offering his complaint as an alibi. On the contrary, he was inclined to give credit where it was due.

"They played heads-up football," he said of Army, "and they deserved to win. They made their own breaks and were alert. That isn't luck. That's good football."

Fortunately for the Irish the next week they had a relatively easy opponent in Drake. At that moment, Notre Dame wasn't prepared to take on another team with Army's talent. Playing under Ossie Solem, Drake was having a poor year, having won only a single game up to that point. But when the Irish arrived in Des Moines, they found that the weather was colder than the tundra and the playing field resembled a skating rink. Rockne took one look and briefly toyed with the notion of keeping his best backs, Flanagan and Niemiec, on the bench, so they wouldn't risk injury and would be available for the final game, against USC. He quickly changed his mind about this tactic when he reflected on the recent experience he'd had in underrating Carnegie Tech.

After the first few minutes of the game it became clear that Notre Dame would win easily. They did, by 32–0, before a sparse, hardy Iowa crowd of eight thousand. But Rockne's fear was realized: The one negative note in the game was that Niemiec was badly hurt and would not play again until 1928.

As Rockne readied his team to wind up the 1927 season against USC, in a game scheduled for Chicago's cavernous Soldier Field, the oddsmakers had a difficult time trying to figure this one out. The Trojans were undefeated, with only a 13–13 tie against Stanford marring their season. But the rivalry between Howard Jones and Rockne had become intense, despite only one previous meeting between the two teams. Jones was a stickler for tough, aggressive football and was a taskmaster in training his men. In fact, Jones trained himself as hard as any of his players and was known never to have taken a drink of any kind. Rockne told his men that they'd better be ready for anything USC could throw at them.

When the teams took the field, 120,000 people were in the stands, although it is likely that many in this astounding crowd had not paid to get in. The Irish had become accustomed to performing before big crowds, but this was the biggest of them all. At the time it was purported to be the largest assemblage ever gathered for a football game in the United States. It also marked the first time that a top Pacific Coast team had scheduled a contest at Soldier Field—and pregame ticket sales were better than any other game ever played at that stadium, including the Army-Navy game.

By the fourth period Notre Dame held on to a 7–6 lead. The game ended that way, but not until after a bitter controversy that arose in the final seconds. USC, and Jones, claimed that USC should have been awarded a safety on a play in Notre Dame's end zone, thus giving USC an 8–7 victory. The officials ruled otherwise, declaring the disputed play a touchback.

Thus the year was concluded on a tenuous but high note for Rockne. But the naysayers continued to spread tales that he was engaged in too many outside activities that distracted from his main role as football coach.

18

Twelfth Man

FOOTBALL COACHES, like baseball managers and presidents, have traditionally been subjected to withering criticism, whether deserved or not. A few missteps, a few misjudgments, a few imprudent remarks, a few losses, a few changes in the weather of opinion, a few enemies—those are all it has ever taken. Some have been abused and pilloried more unmercifully than others, but most of those who have worked in these professions have accepted this state of affairs as an unpleasant fact of life.

But it must have come as a painful surprise to many people that by 1928, after a Horatio Alger-like career, from Voss to Chicago to South Bend, with a life story full of achievement and vision, Rockne was being openly and severely castigated. At Notre Dame he may have been "St. Knute," but Rockne had his detractors— and as time went by, that band of dissidents became more vocal. Only Rockne's unparalleled success, on and off the field, had managed to silence them.

But now, even within the confines of South Bend, they were complaining that he hadn't produced an all-winning season since 1924; that he was spread dangerously thin off the gridiron; that he wasn't able to recruit good players the way he had in the past.

The last criticism was laughable, for it was due to Rockne's fame that many aspiring young men took their football pads elsewhere, feeling that they'd get only a slight chance to play because of Rockne's overstocked roster.

While scouting a Notre Dame team for West Point, Earl Blaik, in the company of announcer Graham MacNamee, overheard a group of Notre Dame panjandrums whining about Rockne and his "faults." These critics were in loud agreement that Rockne had somehow "lost his touch" and that the game had gotten ahead of him. They claimed that he had stayed with the box formation too long and had lost his enthusiasm and "zing" (whatever that was) for the game. At age thirty-nine, Rockne was said to be too old! They agreed that Rockne had been acceptable in his day but now had lost his way. They blustered that new blood was needed at Notre Dame and refused to acknowledge Rockne's ability to adapt to new situations and to introduce new techniques and strategies.

It was true that Rockne had a full dinner plate of outside commitments. At the same time, he was a prime mover at South Bend for a new stadium to replace Cartier Field. However, on any number of occasions he made it clear that he didn't want his name to be affixed to the facility, which was expected to be finished by 1930. (So involved in the project was Rockne that he even supervised the parking arrangements, as the stadium was being constructed.)

At one point Rockne became so angered at President Walsh's negative attitude about a new stadium for fifty thousand people ("We must not present a first-rate production in a third-rate setting," Rockne wrote) that on November 27, 1927, he tendered his resignation as coach in a letter to Walsh. Walsh ignored the offer.

Such a maze of activities required enormous vitality, and concentration on Rockne's part—but President Walsh, coming to the end of his six-year term, had grown increasingly hostile to Rockne's runaway extracurricular program. In addition, Walsh felt that an enlarged dining hall should be a first priority at South Bend, rather than a football stadium.

Because Rockne constantly pointed to the moral and spiritual values of college football, he was painted into a corner as something of a hypocrite, although he had never said that he didn't fully appreciate the many advantages of uninhibited capitalism. "Football supports all the minor sports in most colleges," he argued, "and because football doesn't take in sufficient receipts at many colleges, these institutions have been forced to abandon their athletic activities." The powers-that-be at Notre Dame were willing to concede that Rockne had put their football team on the map, with profits coming to more than $250,000 annually. But they also thought that much of Rockne's outside programs had little if anything to do with enhancing the reputation of Notre Dame as an important educational institution. Also, almost every time Rockne's name appeared on a commercial product, the name of Notre Dame was prominently featured. Was this a proper use of the school's name? Was Rockne using the school's reputation to augment his personal income?

Reacting to the charges that he was spending too much time away from the campus, both in-season and out of season, Rockne was pressured to turn down a number of offers to deliver out-of-town speeches. Instead, he still managed to reap the dividends from a new ten-thousand-dollar contract he signed with Studebaker Motors, a firm that employed a large number of locals.

In Studebaker's behalf Rockne became a nonstop apostle of hard-sell marketing, the first football coach to be lured for such a purpose. His sales talks were generally delivered to the company's dealers and salesmen and were spiced with football anecdotes and analogies that tended to emphasize the psychological aspects of running a successful business organization. Because these talks, which were similar to his locker-room exhortations, took place all over the country, Rockne was away from South Bend more than he would have been had he pursued the other offers from his lecture bureau.

However, according to author Murray Sperber, Father Charles L. O'Donnell, the new Notre Dame president, a poet and World War I chaplain, who had replaced Father Walsh, "did not complain, in part, because Albert Erskine, the president of Studebaker, was head of the lay trustees and a great patron of the university, as well as of the famous coach."

In this acrimonious atmosphere Rockne began assembling his team for the 1928 season. If he had any premonitions of failure, due to the noisy accusations, as well as his own unaccountable carelessness, Rockne never let on to the press. Even if he nursed anxieties about the coming season, he couldn't have dreamed how bad things would get on the field. Those who had charged that the parade had passed Rockne by were hardly prepared for such a year of woe. They may have secretly wished for it; but when it happened, they were stunned.

Even the emergence of Frank Carideo (pronounced Cari*dayo*), a stocky, undersized (five-seven) quarterback who came to Notre

Dame from Dean Academy in Mount Vernon, New York, failed to stem the tide of disaster for the Irish. After watching Carideo in a few practice sessions, Rockne was convinced that he had another Gipp or Stuhldreher on his hands. In the next couple of years he turned out to be right in his assessment. Carideo had great poise and confidence, could kick a football as artfully as anyone Rockne had ever seen, and was born to be a leader on the gridiron.

Carideo was one recruit Rockne couldn't take credit for—and he didn't. A Mount Vernon lawyer named Roy Mills, who never made the varsity at Princeton, discovered Carideo and taught him the secrets of punting and dropkicking. Mills believed that long, high, soaring punts were counterproductive, for they would be run back more easily by the safetyman, whereas low, scudding kicks would hit the ground and were unpredictable in their bounces. Under Mills, and then Rockne, Carideo would develop into one of the most skilled corner kickers of his day. When Carideo came to Notre Dame, Rockne acknowledged that he knew little about angle punting and thus refused to tamper with Carideo's style. "Do it your way," he told the young man.

But Carideo wasn't enough in his first year to make Notre Dame into a winning team. Rockne knew that Carideo had to be supported properly, and that's where Notre Dame came up short in 1928. For one thing, Niemiec, still the top threat in the backfield, never fully recovered from his injuries of 1927. There were other key injuries besides Niemiec's, causing Rockne to rely on a crop of newcomers. But now, at this late stage in his career, Rockne was made to appreciate that inexperienced sophomores could not be rushed into the breach. Like anything else, football is a learning process—and these neophytes hadn't learned enough at this stage from Rockne and his coaching staff to be winners.

The opener in '28 was an away game in New Orleans against Loyola, a weak team coached by Clark Shaughnessy, another old friend of Rockne. Rockne had booked Loyola as a favor to Shaughnessy, who had earned the nickname of "Man in Motion" because he kept moving from one school to another. Loyola held on to a six-point lead at the half, but then Jack Elder brought the Irish back with a forty-eight-yard touchdown dash. Late in the game Niemiec passed to Johnny O'Brien at the Loyola eight-yard-line. Then Niemiec scored the winning touchdown from the two-yard-line, giving the Irish a squeaker, 12–6. The writing was on the wall for Notre Dame, for Loyola shouldn't have given Rockne's men such a close battle.

Rockne wasn't in need of any further distractions at this point, but now he found himself confronted with another dilemma that had nothing to do with his football team. A presidential election was being fought that autumn between Republican Herbert Hoover, a Quaker from Iowa, and Democrat Al Smith. Inevitably, Rockne, as the celebrated representative of the most publicized Catholic school in the country, was urged by many prominent Democrats to throw his support to Smith. As governor of New York Smith had been an enterprising, hardworking executive, and he strongly believed that America was a land of opportunity for all, including Irish immigrants. He was the kind of politician who should have appealed to Rockne's sense of fairness. Other icons of the sports world, led by Babe Ruth, a Catholic, had been willing to openly endorse Smith. Ruth even went so far as to pose with a derby cocked on his head and a big, brown cigar clamped in his jaw, both trademarks of the raspy-voiced Democratic candidate. Rockne's familiar face would have made an attractive photo opportunity for Smith's backers. However, after much troubled conversation, Rockne, and the Notre Dame authorities, chose to remain on the sidelines.

Although politics was not Rockne's main interest, he was aware of the subtext to this presidential race: bigotry and anti-Catholic bias. He had a keen recollection of how his teams had been abused in certain areas of the country, and he remembered his difficulties with Big Ten coaches who had made no secret of their hostility to Catholicism. When the Ku Klux Klan reared its ugly head in the South or in his home state of Indiana, he had not hesitated to speak out.

But in the heated matter of Smith versus Hoover he was reluctant to make a commitment. Such a political endorsement, he was reminded by his superiors at Notre Dame, would, by implication, involve his school. Therefore he was advised to back away from Smith, and he dutifully did. The Democratic National Committee proposed that he head a campaign subcommittee for Smith. More important, they were eager for him to go out on the hustings and make his inimitable pep talks for the New Yorker. But Rockne felt it was wise for him to stay out of politics. There was also a pragmatic edge to this turndown, for knowledgeable observers were convinced that two central issues—Smith's Catholicism and Prohibition (which Hoover favored)—were bound to plunge the Democrat into defeat.

Perhaps there was little commendable about Rockne's passive stand on the election. But in a country populated by many who spread the word that Smith's election (he was denounced as a "thick Mick" by the bigots) would have him sharing the White House with the pope, it represented a conveniently safe posture.

With the formerly Solid South crumbling and going to Hoover, Smith went down to a resounding defeat, by 444 to 87 in the electoral college. Forty states voted for Hoover, who was about as colorless as the mute actor Buster Keaton on the speaker's platform. Hoover's popular vote margin was six million, a bit less than the margins rung up by Republican Warren G. Harding in 1920 and Republican Calvin Coolidge in 1924. Doubtless, Rockne felt distressed about his careful neutrality in this campaign. But he also felt worse about his team's record, for by the time of the November election Notre Dame had dropped two games to Wisconsin and Georgia Tech.

The Wisconsin loss, at Madison, by 22–6, before thirty thousand people, was especially irritating to Rockne because it might have been attributed to the expert coaching of Tom Lieb, who learned his football under Rockne and was also the director of Rockne's summer camp in Wisconsin. Lieb was an assistant coach under Wisconsin's Glenn Thistlewaite, who relied, in this instance, heavily on his advice. As it turned out, Notre Dame's shocking seven fumbles did more to unsettle the Irish than Lieb's insights. Only Jack Chevigny managed to score a touchdown for Notre Dame, who surprisingly clung to a 6–2 lead at the half. But then Wisconsin's strong passing and ground attack blew the Irish out of the game in the second half, giving a Big Ten team the first victory over the Irish since 1921.

Notre Dame revived itself, but barely, the following week against Navy. Playing before 120,000 spectators, Notre Dame scored its single touchdown in the fourth quarter on a slant-in pass from Niemiec. It was hardly an artistic 7–0 triumph for Notre Dame—but the huge stadium was sold out, proving once again the tight grip that Rockne's teams had on the emotions of the public.

For this game and others, Rockne handled the distribution of complimentary tickets for the occupants of the press box, an imprudent policy if ever there was one. He never was able to remove himself from the minutiae of his job, whether it was handing out free passes, designing new uniforms for his warriors, or arranging for employment interviews for needy players.

At a well-attended alumni dinner after the Navy game, Rockne was applauded to the echo, a reassuring reaction that he should have enjoyed. But instead of expressing his appreciation for such support, Rockne snapped that "after the Wisconsin defeat eight trucks could have driven abreast down the street outside our dressing room without hitting any alumni." It was not like Rockne to lash out at his natural constituency, but these were not the best of times for him.

After the close call with the Midshipmen, Rockne shepherded his team again to the Deep South to tangle with a powerful Georgia Tech squad. In two months Tech would visit the Rose Bowl, where they would conquer California, in a game that was forever remembered because of a classic mistake committed by California's Roy Riegels. Riegels ran sixty yards the *wrong* way with a fumble, thus paving the way for Tech's victory.

With the national election only three weeks away, the atmosphere in Georgia was tense and angry, with much of the anti-Catholic venom of the locals rising to the surface. The battle against Notre Dame had become the Georgians' own substitute for the contest between Hoover and Smith. The Ku Kluxers in the area joined with many of the "decent folk" to bait the Notre Damers. It was an agonizing situation for Rockne but, oddly, this time his usual loquacity deserted him. He confined his pregame remarks to a facetious dismissal of his team as "my Minute Men—they'll be in the game for a minute and the other team will score." That wasn't providing much moral support for his men, even if Rockne only meant it as a joke. He would have been better off encouraging the Irish to go out and win it for Al Smith—but he wasn't in the mood for such politicking.

Tech had an easy time of it that day with Notre Dame, aided by Father Lumpkin's two pass interceptions and a bad injury suffered by Irish guard John Law, who would later become one of Rockne's great linemen. On the first scrimmage play Tech passed for a touchdown over the head of Jumpin' Joe Savoldi, who was in the lineup for the first time. It would take another year for Savoldi to emerge as a fine back, but against Tech his inexperience was costly. The 13–0 victory of the Yellowjackets over Notre Dame had Atlantans jumping for glee, as if General Sherman had been repulsed at the gates of the city. Rockne also came in for his share of put-downs in the press, which didn't improve his brooding state of mind.

Returning home to Cartier Field against Drake, the Irish licked their wounds and walloped the Iowans, 32–6. Rockne's team was proving to be in-again, out-again, a situation not inclined to improve the coach's disposition. But he remained hopeful that a mediocre Penn State squad the next week would be cannon fodder for his improving players, such as Moon Mullins and Carideo.

There were no miracles in the mud against Penn State in Philadelphia, but Rockne felt that the final score of 9–0, with the Irish on top, could have gone higher. Carideo sneaked in for a score, and Rockne was relying more and more on this young man to lead the troops. Several days after the Penn State triumph, Smith took his drubbing from Hoover. It was not, despite the win over State, a euphoric time for Rockne. But still he looked ahead to the Army game at the end of the week, to redeem Notre Dame's season and to gain revenge against the Cadets for the plastering the Irish had taken in 1927. Even Grantland Rice, a man with deep-rooted southern sympathies, suspected that Rockne was engaged in a personal battle to wipe out the indignities of the year, including the pummeling at Atlanta. If Notre Dame, wrote Rice, could bag unbeaten Army, all would be forgiven back at South Bend.

Despite Notre Dame's inconsistency in '28, the annual Army–Notre Dame clash at Yankee Stadium remained the pièce de résistance of football's Roaring Twenties.

More than any other factor in the hysteria surrounding this game was Rockne's seductive personality. It was his reputation, and Notre Dame's yearly performance, that raised this game to such a level of hysteria. New York's journalists, willing purveyors of the myths and folklore of the sport, did nothing to subdue the rampant frenzy. In such extravagant times, when college football had become the ne plus ultra of Saturday afternoon entertainment, Rockne had the words to stimulate and the vision to excite millions.

The rush for tickets became so chaotic one year of the Army–Notre Dame game that Rice, the éminence grise of the press box, actually failed to receive his credentials in the mail. "He went down to a ticket scalper on Broadway," Red Smith said about his friend, "and watched the game from the stands, with his typewriter on his knees." When Rice was asked why he didn't try to throw his weight around, he said, "To tell you the truth, I don't weigh very much."

There was no mistake about it—in 1928 Notre Dame was not a great team. Its record, including the two defeats by Wisconsin and Georgia Tech, showed that clearly. Now Army, with a splendid team built around Cagle, was prepared to handle the Irish. A betting man would have put his money on Army, and those who wanted Notre Dame could have gotten odds of at least four to one. The best bet of the year was that Cagle would be designated that season's top player.

In spite of such a pregame appraisal, Rockne appeared surprisingly confident in the days before the game. At a luncheon with the eastern sportswriters at a Westchester country club, where the Irish players camped down prior to the game, the coach was optimistic. Rockne hinted he had something special up his sleeve for Biff Jones's team. He wasn't letting on about it but Ed Healy, one of his assistants, who had been at the luncheon, later said that Rockne didn't act like a man who was about to be thrown to the lions.

The Friday night before the game, Rockne called Rice at his apartment on Fifth Avenue, according to Rice's recollection of the matter in his memoir *The Tumult and the Shouting*. In a cheery voice Rockne asked Rice if he'd care to spend some time that evening shooting the bull. "Want to sit around with me and Hunk for a while?" asked Rockne. Rice always loved to swap stories with Rockne, so he said he was game for Rockne's proposal. He then invited Rockne to come to his apartment, where "we can warm up our sides at an open fire and have a spot of Tennessee 'milk' and watch the rest of the world go to hell." Not too long after that, Rockne arrived at Rice's apartment.

"The game tomorrow is going to be a tough one for us," acknowledged Rockne. Then he proceeded to tell Rice about George Gipp's last hours on earth. "He died, practically in my arms, eight years ago this month," said Rockne. "But I may have to use him tomorrow."

At first Rice was puzzled by Rockne's remark. But Rockne then said, "Grant, tomorrow I may ask the boys to pull one out for Gipp." Rice understood then that Rockne had made up his mind to use the Gipp story to exhort his squad against the Cadets. He had been hearing from Rockne's lips the prelude to the most dramatic game in Notre Dame's history.

If anything is clear about the Rice story it is that this motivational moment was premeditated by Rockne. Obviously Rockne had been thinking about unleashing his yarn long before the start of the game. The question that remains is how respectful of the truth Rockne had been in his recitation of the facts between the dying Gipp and himself. It might be fair to conclude that Gipp may have expressed such feelings to Rockne at some point and then the coach had doctored the remark to add drama, something that was very much in character.

When Rockne and Rice said good night to each other, the latter wished his friend good luck against Army. "We'll need it," said Rockne with a laugh.

All of the foregoing makes a sweet and, perhaps, compelling story. Yet research into this homely anecdote, as remembered by Rice, has knocked the tale into the proverbial cocked hat. Murray Sperber matter-of-factly points out that Rice was *not* in New York the Friday night before the game at Yankee Stadium. He happened to be on assignment in Atlanta, covering the Georgia Tech vs. Vanderbilt game for the *New York Herald Tribune*. While Rice was supposed to be listening to Rockne's words, he was actually en route to his reportorial job in the South. There was no way he could have been exchanging tall tales in his New York apartment with his favorite football coach. Sperber's detective work has also revealed that Hunk Anderson, supposedly in the company of Rockne that evening, was never there. He was the coach of the University of St. Louis team that year, and his squad would play Loyola of Chicago the next day in Missouri and lose, 7–0.

More than likely it was Rice's failing recollection when, in his early seventies, he dictated his "sometimes fading memories" (Rice's own acknowledgment) to an earnest fellow named Dave Camerer. Camerer, a fine former Dartmouth tackle, who had become a sports writer, worshiped Rice and faithfully reported every anecdote that his mentor ever recalled, or thought he recalled.

"I guess it's possible that Granny had heard the Gipp story from Rockne at another time," Camerer has said. "So he might have confused the exact date of the meeting with Rockne. After all, Granny moved around a lot in those days, and he went to a lot of parties and interviews." Sperber's own explanation is more caustic. "A few thousand miles of railroad track," he writes, "never kept Rice from inventing an imaginary meeting, particularly one that gave him an exclusive preview of the most famous locker-room speech in football history."

There had been some rain in New York on the day preceding

the game. But Saturday, November 10, turned out to be a crisp fall afternoon, and the Yankees' big ball park was crammed with all of the greats and near-greats of politics, the military services, the movies, and the theater, as well as Notre Dame's vast legion of fans. Nearby apartment houses whose roofs overlooked the Stadium could have rented space. Every fire escape and window ledge in the neighborhood sagged under the weight of fans, who strained to see the action. The elevated platform of the subway that ran past the Stadium was so crowded that the police feared it might collapse into the street.

After the Cadets marched, as usual, the two team captains, Notre Dame's Freddy Miller, a rich man's son, and Bud Sprague of Army, met at midfield, shook hands briskly, and the game was on. For the first two quarters the vaunted Army attack was stymied. But Notre Dame could gain little ground. Fortunately for Notre Dame, Niemiec's long punts kept Army bottled up in its own territory. All the while, Rockne watched the proceedings quietly on the bench as a mist settled over the gridiron. Was he musing about the imploring words he was about to utter in the chilly dressing room underneath the Stadium?

As the teams retired for the halftime intermission, Notre Dame's first-half docket showed five first downs to just three for Army, and the score was deadlocked at 0—0. The Notre Dame players, including Law, Ed Collins, Fred Collins, Miller, Moynihan, Carideo, Chevigny, Niemiec, Twomey, and Frank Leahy (a first-year 185-pound tackle from Winner, South Dakota, who would become one of Notre Dame's most successful post-Rockne coaches), sat silently in the dressing room. They would have only a dozen minutes or so to mull over what they had just been through and what they might be able to do in the last half of this struggle.

For a few moments Rockne busied himself with the Irish wounded. Then he took his place in the middle of the group of players, his eyes seeming to fall on each one of his men. "He knew the physical, mental and moral qualities of every boy in the room," wrote Francis Wallace. Rockne was convinced that Notre Dame had a wonderful chance to win this game, with just enough persuasion.

So the coach started to talk. He spoke more slowly than he had in the past. "Before he died, Gipp said to me," began Rockne, "I've got to go, Rock. It's all right. I'm not afraid. Sometimes, when things are going wrong, when the breaks are beating the boys, tell them to go out and win one for the Gipper. I don't know where I'll be then, Rock. But I'll know about it and I'll be happy.' "

With those words Rockne walked quickly toward the door, leaving his battered group of athletes. The scene that then took place—the yelling, screaming, and swearing of a healthy, sweating gang of men as they stormed to the exit of the dressing room to get back on the field for the second half—has been chronicled by any number of those who were there.

"We couldn't wait to get on the field," said one lineman. Ed Healy said that there wasn't a dry eye in the room, including Rockne's, as "the players almost tore off the hinges of the door." Another eyewitness reported that a big tackle "knocked himself out by running into a concrete overhead, as he rushed blindly from the room." Mayor Jimmy Walker was a guest in the locker room along with several policemen. They all had tears in their eyes, according to another observer.

There probably hasn't been a Hollywood football movie since that afternoon that hasn't included such a scene of halftime emotion. These episodes have been melodramatic, others have been outright satire. When viewed today by a more cynical, sophisticated society, such goings-on border on the ludicrous and often evoke laughter rather than credibility. But those who were there in 1928 insist it happened that way.

There were no immediate miracles produced by Rockne's oration. In the opening moments of the second half triple-threat Cagle ran and passed until the Cadets reached the one-yard-line. From that point Johnny Murrell inched over for the first touchdown of the game. When Sprague missed the extra point, Army held a 6–0 lead.

Led by a charged-up Chevigny, the Irish mauled and pushed their way back into the ball game. After Chevigny scored the tying touchdown from the two-yard-line, he held the pigskin up in the air for all to see and shouted, "There's one for the Gipper!" Had Chevigny been hypnotized by the old chemistry teacher? Whatever Rockne had said in the locker room, it certainly had worked with Jack Chevigny. Several of the players nearest to Chevigny, as he barged across for the six-pointer, testified that he actually shrieked the name of the Gipper. So historians will have to make their own judgments.

On the extra-point try, Army blocked the kick, putting the score at 6–6, with the fourth quarter coming up. When Carideo came in at quarterback for Notre Dame, replacing Jimmy Brady, the Notre Dame contingent in the stands set up a din. Carideo proceeded to move his team inexorably toward the Army goal line, with Chevigny and Niemiec playing the leading roles in the drive.

Trained to do small things correctly by Rockne, the Irish committed a bad mistake on the next play. The ball from center sailed high over the head of Chevigny, who hustled back twenty yards to recover it. Several Army players pounced on the poor fellow in the scramble. When Chevigny got back on his feet he didn't appear to know what year it was or the name of the ball park he was playing in. So Rockne removed him from the game. As everyone watched Chevigny walk slowly off the field, a gangly, fragile sophomore named Johnny O'Brien, a whippet on his feet but not much heavier than your local scarecrow, was sent in at end by Rockne. At that moment referee Walter Eckersall signaled that there were just two minutes left in the game.

Without being told, Carideo knew exactly what Rockne wanted to do with O'Brien. On third down, with twenty-six yards to go from the Army thirty-two-yard-line, Carideo called for a pass from Niemiec to O'Brien. Taking off for the right corner of the field as Niemiec faded to his left, O'Brien ran past the defending Cagle. At this stage of the game O'Brien, fresh and determined, was the fastest man on the field. Cagle knew what his man was up to, but having played the entire game at full speed, his body was exhausted. He was left behind as Niemiec's soft pass looped overhead. O'Brien never stopped running until he had camped under it. For a split second, he juggled the ball, then swallowed it up a few yards from the goal line. As he pranced into the end zone, unmolested, the crowd went berserk. Forever after at South Bend, O'Brien would be known as "One Play" O'Brien—even though Army's assistant coach Blaik argued that if Army had defended that day with a zone, Johnny O'Brien never would have been adored as "One Play" O'Brien.

Back on the bench after his big play, O'Brien was pounded heartily by Rockne and anyone else who could get close to him. But Notre Dame, now ahead 12–6 (the extra point was missed again), still had to survive the last minute of play.

On the kickoff, Cagle, summoning his remaining strength, picked up a cordon of Army blockers and ran fifty-five yards to Notre Dame's thirty-five-yard-line. The redhead wasn't through yet.

One of his passes failed; then he bulled his way to the ten-yard-line with the seconds ticking away. But 59 minutes of physical pounding had taken its toll on Cagle, and Biff Jones elected to remove him from the game. The crowd roared its appreciation for the man, while a collective sigh of relief rose from the Notre Dame adherents.

Dick Hutchinson, in for Cagle, passed to the three-yard-line. With only a few seconds left, Hutchinson hurtled into the line, moving just inches from a score. The roar in the Stadium approached the noise level that Babe Ruth provoked with his blasts. The Cadets lined up quickly in the semidarkness as the center tried to pass the ball back for one more play. But at that instant the chief official blew his whistle: time had run out. The game was over.

After a game that may have been the most grueling in Notre Dame history, Rockne remained philosophical. "My boys were great—at least for one afternoon," he remarked. This was not Rockne's best team, but it was one that he respected for its refusal to give up. As for his own role, Rockne preferred not to talk about a triumph that might have been attributed to a *twelfth man*—Gipp. Had Rockne been the chief actor in a fable?

Two days after the game, on Monday, November 12, the *New York Daily News* featured a story that for the first time credited Notre Dame's victory to Rockne's spellbinding words in the locker room. But Francis Wallace's report in the *News,* under the headline GIPP'S GHOST BEATS ARMY, raised still another issue. Did Rockne deliver his remarks to his team *before* the game or at *halftime*? Not having been present in the locker room, Wallace relied on an eyewitness to tell him about Rockne's Gipper story. That person told him that the beseeching words were issued *before* the game. What calls this account into question is that Rockne had asked the former heavyweight champion Jack Dempsey to say a few words to his boys before the game. Under the circumstances, it was unlikely that Rockne would have followed the Manassa Mauler's cheerleading comments with his own speech about Gipp. Rockne never believed in anticlimaxes.

When Rockne read Wallace's description of his pep talk, instead of being pleased, he expressed his annoyance to Wallace. "Why did you violate a confidence?" he remonstrated to Wallace, who was regarded as a loyal friend and confidant of the coach. Wallace was upset with Rockne's disapproval, but he reasoned that such honest sentiment emanating from the Gipper tale was not foreign to the Notre Dame tradition. According to Wallace, Rockne then withdrew his objections. The final irony of this tempest between Rockne and Wallace was that the Gipp story ultimately evolved into Notre Dame's most enduring legend, enhancing the reputation of all parties concerned—Notre Dame, Gipp, Rockne, and even Ronald Reagan, who would play Gipp on the screen, exploiting the slogan "Win One for the Gipper" while campaigning for the presidency.

If Notre Dame's season had ended with the Gipper game it would have been the happiest of situations. But the schedule included two final games, against Carnegie Tech and USC. This time Rockne's oratorical magic was insufficient to rescue the Irish. Tech came into Cartier Field with a record of six straight victories. Coached by R. N. Waddell and led by a 230-pound fullback, John Karcis, they were determined to plague the Irish, as Tech teams had done in the recent past.

Rockne was aware that the emotional pitch his men had reached against Army would be hard to sustain. "If there are two games that you have to win you can point for those, especially if one is the final game of the schedule," he said. "But you've got to try to take the others in stride." Leery of a letdown against Carnegie Tech, Rockne's fear proved to be based on reality. This was not a sound Notre Dame team to begin with. Against an inspired Tech team they played listlessly. By the time Tech went ahead, 27–0, in the last quarter, many of the diehard Irish fans in rain-soaked Cartier Field started to leave the premises. They missed Notre Dame's only touchdown, a play by Moon Mullins, after he recovered a fumble. Rockne didn't have to be reminded that it was the first Irish defeat at Cartier Field in twenty-three years. It also marked the first time that a Rockne team had dropped three games in one season.

As Notre Dame then prepared to end its year against a powerful University of Southern California team, at Los Angeles Coliseum, the old rumors about Rockne again began to percolate. Was Rockne still unhappy at Notre Dame? Was he ready to leave Notre Dame for another school—perhaps Ohio State or even USC? When Ohio State officials were asked if the Buckeyes were pursuing Rockne, they were cautious in their response. They remembered how Columbia had lost Rockne and rested their case with a prudent "No comment." For his part, Rockne remained unusually quiet.

Stung by the three defeats in 1928—with another tough game in the offing—Rockne fully realized that he had many critics "out there"—some in the press, and others who were simply chronic Notre Dame-haters or Rockne-haters. Now that his team had lost three games, despite his assiduous pursuit of playing talent, he was chided both for losing and for overemphasis. It was also no secret that Rockne was determined to get his new stadium to allow for larger crowds and to reduce the nomadic status of his team. (With increased capacity at home, Rockne wouldn't have to search for a bigger stadium elsewhere, in which to play his games.)

Rockne had come to personify Notre Dame, the institution, which didn't sit well with all of the administrators of the school. They would have much preferred that Notre Dame be regarded as a respected educational resource rather than as a manufacturer of All-American football players.

In such an environment Rockne faced the final game of the year, with USC. For another, personal reason, it was not an easy time for the coach. His little son, Jack, was in a South Bend hospital on the critical list, after having inhaled a peanut that had lodged in his lung. This time Rockne did not reach out for any histrionics in the locker room. He was subdued and didn't engage in false dramatics in front of his squad. In addition, USC's Howard Jones was commanding a first-rate team that opening day of December. Nothing that Rockne said or did could have stemmed the tide of a convincing USC win, 27–14.

The Irish played gamely but were never really in the contest, before seventy-two thousand fans. However, Rockne's compensation was that the game provided a showcase for several future Notre Dame stars, including Carideo, Jack Elder, Leahy, and Mullins.

With the defeat by the Trojans, Notre Dame concluded its season with a 5–4 mark. For the only time in his coaching career, Rockne's team scored fewer than 145 points and was outscored by its foes. Rockne's overall record of excellence—including the 1928 campaign—would have been wildly acceptable everywhere else in the world of college football. But at South Bend the 1928 numbers were considered a disaster, even though the school ran up a profit of over half a million dollars after all expenses were deducted.

Whether they won or lost, the Irish, still playing most of their games on the road, remained one of the most magnetic attractions in sports. Everywhere they went, fans came out to see them. They filled foreign stadiums. They were a charismatic team handled by a charismatic coach long before that expression was in popular usage. One question worried Notre Dame: Would the Irish continue to draw large, enthusiastic crowds if they became a losing team, or only a .500 team?

19

On the Rebound

As 1929 CAME ALONG, millions of Americans remained on a get-rich-quick joyride. The dollars rolled in, and profits skyrocketed. President Hoover had promised "two chickens in every pot and a car in every garage," and many people believed in his political affidavit. America appeared to be the Rock of Gibraltar in the world economy.

By engaging in sly adjustments to the Eighteenth Amendment, it was possible to "make whoopee." For most citizens the violence of the era was something that occurred only in the lynching zones of the Deep South or on the front pages of the tabloids or in the gangster movies.

It was the last year of the noisy, brash, frenzied Roaring Twenties, and in the worlds of show business, the cinema, journalism, literature, politics, racketeering and high-and-low finance, everyone seemed to be having one helluva good time.

Then, suddenly, all the moorings broke loose; the stock market came crashing down on everyone's head in October 1929, and with it, soon after, the economic stability of the country. "Brother, Can You Spare a Dime?" became the national anthem, and hungry apple-sellers dotted the landscape of the big cities. Millions were thrown out of work, banks went under, and fear permeated the once-optimistic land.

In the baseball world the lordly New York Yankees also came crashing down, their dynasty temporarily sidetracked by Connie Mack's team of Athletics from Philadelphia. And early in the football season Rockne's robust health, always taken for granted, took a wicked downward turn just when he was on his way to restoring the team's glory in a new stadium, now under construction, at South Bend. The stadium, without his name adorning it, would be Rockne's enduring monument at the school. He was not a humble man, but he had a certain modesty about being memorialized. (At that point only a swimming pool at Notre Dame was garnished with his name!)

Rockne was confident that the grueling 1929 schedule of nine games, including both service schools, USC, and the two rambunctious Techs—Carnegie and Georgia—would turn out to be the high mark of his career. All of these games were to be played on enemy territory or at neutral sites as the finishing touches were being applied to Notre Dame Stadium. Rockne had also been eager to book Nebraska again. But he was overruled by those who insisted that the Cornhuskers should be excluded because of the rabid anti-Catholicism previously encountered at Lincoln.

During spring practice at Notre Dame Rockne worked with a team that would be sparked by Carideo, already tested during the 1928 season. Now Carideo was ready to take over as the signal-caller and heir apparent to the quarterbacking tradition of Stuhldreher. Elder could be counted on to provide speed at halfback, while Marty Brill, a transfer student from Penn, was determined to prove that Penn's coach, Lou Young, had made an egregious error by not using him in the backfield. Mullins was still available at fullback, while Joe Savoldi waited in the wings. For the first time Rockne was inclined to employ heavier backs—his operatives were nearly twenty pounds heavier than the Four Horsemen set.

The line may have been as good as any ever produced at Notre Dame, headed by Jack "Boom Boom" Cannon, a throwback who insisted on playing guard for sixty minutes without relief and without a helmet—one of the last big-time players to do so. Cannon was undoubtedly Rockne's toughest lineman since Adam Walsh; Grantland Rice believed that Cannon was the best guard ever to play for Rockne. Captain John Law was the other guard, while Frank Leahy and Ted Twomey were at the tackles.

It had always been Rockne's policy to surround himself with skillful, competent assistant coaches who would be thoroughly grounded in his system and psychology. Such a man in 1929 was Tom Lieb, who had played under Rockne several years before, and then had apprenticed at Wisconsin as a line coach, Rockne was wise enough to persuade him to return to South Bend. The move turned out to be a happy choice in an unhappy situation, for in the early days of the season Rockne's health broke down. Thus Lieb, in effect, became the coach, the man on the field with the troops. However, Rockne still managed to work in close concert with Lieb, on the phone and by message.

Lieb has received relatively scant attention in the annals of Notre Dame football, but if ever a person deserved more credit, he is that man. He was able to employ Rockne's plays and diagrams, as well as any last-minute advice, without any noticeable resentment or alteration of their relationship. A good-natured extrovert, Lieb seemingly didn't mind playing second fiddle to the great man, much as Lou Gehrig did with Babe Ruth in the Yankee lineup, or the worshipful Harry Hopkins did for President Roosevelt in the White House of World War II years.

Rockne's ailment, which was diagnosed as a phlebitis attack, with a life-endangering blood clot in his right leg, originated after a summer and fall of strenuous entrepreneurial activity. The driven Rockne was a tired man. But whether that had anything to do with his physical condition has never been clear. One report hinted that Rockne received a punishing blow in the leg while he was engaged in a spring practice session with his players. (Many coaches, including Rockne, often volunteered to mix it up with their players in practice.) However, this scenario may not hold up in the full light of day, for Rockne was away much of the time during the spring period, mostly on his outside work for Studebaker. At such times Lieb was already filling in for Rockne, with Rockne's full support.

More likely, the blood clot resulted from that sideline incident in the 1926 game against Indiana at Bloomington. With so many muscular arms and legs thrashing about it was possible that Rockne received a stiff kick and a painful bruise. It was one of those inadvertent episodes that take place in football games, but the impact of the pileup was more important than the result of the game.

It was beside the point that Notre Dame, starting its shock troops and then going for assistance from its regulars, such as Schwartz and Savoldi, won its opener against Indiana, 14–0. The larger, more dramatic news was that the coach was placed on the injured list, with doctors advising him to go to bed and remain there. Such a prospect was anathema to Rockne—that is, until he picked up a slew of medical textbooks, including *Gray's Anatomy,* and concluded that he did indeed have phlebitis. Agreeing with the doctors that he might be at risk if he became overly excited (the medical theory underlined the possibility that undue stress could cause a massive heart attack or an aneurysm in the brain), Rockne chose to act prudently. For the first time in his hyperkinetic life, Rockne was a full-time patient. He was instructed not to think about his team, or of Notre Dame's mission, or of victory or defeat, which was like slicing the wings off a sparrow. He understood the gravity of the situation, yet found it difficult to divorce himself completely from his normal environment.

Rockne promised that he would not appear at the Navy game the next week, in Baltimore. But he devised a system of communication with Lieb and his players that probably did not pass muster with his concerned doctors. During the week prior to the game Rockne invited key players to his house, including Carideo, who had become "a coach on the field." Supported by Mrs. Rockne's cooking, the coach carefully went over strategy to be employed against the sailors. On the night before the game Rockne sent a long letter to Lieb, outlining what he thought would be the most advantageous plays to be used. But the pièce de résistance was yet to come. On the morning of the game Rockne was in touch with each one of the regulars on the team by telephone—pep talk over the air, if you will. He delivered pregame instructions and admonitions. There were no references to Gipp or sick little boys; this time it was his own disability that was being used, subtly and poignantly.

In person Rockne had always represented a strong goad for his men. Now, by telephone, he aimed to provide the same inspiration. When Navy scored first, it appeared that Lieb's presence wasn't enough, that Rockne was needed. But that situation proved to be ephemeral, for Carideo rallied Notre Dame quickly. He hit Elder with a touchdown pass thrown while he was on his knees, then picked off an interception as many of the sixty-five thousand fans screamed their delight. Brill pounded away for key yardage, and finally Mullins carried the ball across from the one-yard-line, giving Notre Dame the victory. Another legend had been born: "pep talk by telephone." And it worked, even if there was some polite snickering in the press box about the power of Rockne's golden voice.

In 1928 Wisconsin had overwhelmed Notre Dame, adding to the

misery of that campaign. Would Notre Dame now be able to reverse that result despite Rockne's absence? Prior to the rerun with Wisconsin, the Big Ten authorities, maliciously vigilant in their attitude toward Irish football, criticized the fact that the game was to be held in Chicago's Soldier Field. This was nonsense, for other Big Ten teams consistently performed before large audiences—but in games that didn't happen to feature Notre Dame. Wisconsin refused to heed the small minds in the upper echelons of the Big Ten and went through with the engagement. Perhaps the Badgers had privately considered that with Rockne absent from the bench they stood an excellent chance of repeating their 1928 victory. But it didn't work out that way.

Though Chicago wasn't that far from South Bend, Rockne still chose not to make the trip, in this instance obeying the ukase of his doctors. However, Lieb, already steeped in knowledge of Wisconsin's athletes and Coach Thistlethwaite's formations, was briefed further by Rockne on every aspect of the encounter. In the days preceding the game Rockne began to chisel away at the caveats from his doctors: He arranged to be taken to several practice sessions in a specially equipped hearse from a local funeral home.

Helped considerably by Savoldi's heroics and a long dash for a touchdown by Elder, Notre Dame won easily, 19–0. Thus far the team had survived brilliantly with Rockne remaining at a distance.

Now it was a question of how long Rockne would continue to obey the dictates of his doctors and their warnings about the seriousness of his ailment. With the fourth game of 1929 scheduled against Carnegie Tech on October 26, Rockne had become increasingly restless with his self-imposed exile. He was also aware of the vast improvement that his team had made over 1928.

Not a man to carry grudges for long, Rockne still nursed strong feelings about the two defeats suffered at the hands of Carnegie Tech in 1926 and 1928. He also had a lingering sense of guilt at not having been present at the 1926 game. Thus Rockne made up his mind that nothing would keep him away from Pittsburgh for this latest tussle with Tech. During the week preceding the game he coached from a platform erected on the practice field, using a loudspeaker and a megaphone. His voice was not as crisp and metallic as usual, but his spirit was ebullient. The sole concession he made to his doctors was not to go on the practice field and scrimmage with his boys!

Rockne hadn't announced to anyone whether he would be on

the bench for the game with Tech. With his flair for theatrical gestures, he kept his decision to himself. But when the team left for Pittsburgh, Rockne was on the train, although it was Lieb's understanding that Rockne would remain ensconced at the Pittsburgh Athletic Club during the game.

When Notre Dame conducted a practice session at the Tech gymnasium, Rockne was there, a wan figure slumped in a special wheelchair. (At this time, according to author Delos Lovelace, "a willing attendant had been recruited from the undergraduates . . . wherever Rockne went the chair and bearer followed. Rockne never bothered to look down, but his chair was never missing, when the coach decided to give his legs a rest.")

The night before the game, when Rockne might have been regaling his friends in the press or scheming in a last-minute skull session with Lieb, he stayed in his hotel room. This set off a fever of rampant speculation. Rumors spread that Rockne was dying and that he might be rushed off to the hospital.

However, the script took another turn the next afternoon. As a jammed house of sixty-six thousand waited impatiently for the game to begin at Pitt Stadium, an automobile drove to the entrance of the Notre Dame locker room. Having heard all of the rumors about their coach, the Irish players were fearful but expectant. With only minutes to go before they would take the field in this grudge match, the door to their sanctum opened. Lieb appeared in the entrance. In his arms, cradled like a baby, was Rockne, who, at best, could walk only a few steps at a time. He wore a heavy overcoat that seemed much too large for him and black, high-top overshoes. The players stared at him respectfully; not a word was uttered. As the seconds ticked away, Rockne remained silent.

In the rear of the locker room Francis Wallace stood next to Dr. Maurice Keady, who had been attending to Rockne's case. Dr. Keady turned to Wallace and shook his head. "If he lets go and that clot dislodges and hits his heart or brain," he whispered, "he's got only an even chance of ever leaving this room alive."

No sooner had Dr. Keady confided this morose assessment to Wallace than Rockne started to speak. His voice was surprisingly strong, and he didn't falter. "A lot of water has gone under the bridge since I first came to Notre Dame," he began. "But I don't know when I've ever wanted to win a game as badly as this one. . . . I don't care what happens after today. Why do you think I'm taking a chance like this? To see you lose?" He paused for a moment, then his voice rose to a shout and he literally spat out the next words. "They'll be primed, they'll be tough. They think they have your number. Are you going to let it happen again? You can win if you want to." There was a brief pause as Rockne drew a deep breath. Then, in rapid-fire fashion, he unleashed a barrage of barked challenges.

"Go on out there and hit 'em, crack 'em, crack 'em, smack 'em! Fight to live. Fight to *win, win, win, win!*" In the years to come, generations of moviegoers would hear this staccato style mimicked by veteran actors such as Pat O'Brien and J. Farrell MacDonald, performing as Rockne in their maudlin worst.

But in that 1929 locker room Rockne's words sent the players rushing for the door as beads of sweat poured from their impassioned coach's face. Realizing that Rockne was choked with emotion, Dr. Keady felt for his racing pulse. Wallace, a writer sometimes addicted to hyperbole, didn't exaggerate in the least when he later reported that *"Rockne wanted to win more than he wanted to live."*

Had there ever been a football coach with such a need to win? Or such a compulsive drive to emerge on top in an athletic event? Had there ever been a man so unwilling to accept defeat?

The game with Carnegie Tech was every inch the bitter battle that Rockne had anticipated. On the sidelines, sitting uncomfortably in his wheelchair, often grimacing with pain, Rockne watched the proceedings. He tried to direct the play as closely as if he were a well and vigorous man. But he knew that the game was really in Frank Carideo's hands and in Carideo's brain.

"I don't believe in running a game from the bench," Rockne would say. "That's the quarterback's job. The quarterback should know what to do and when to do it. He's out there. If he doesn't know what to do, he doesn't belong there." In time Carideo, everybody's All-America choice in both 1929 and 1930, would become almost as much of a Notre Dame myth as Gipp.

One story told about Carideo was that Rockne, who loved to administer impromptu quizzes to his disciples, cornered Frank's substitute quarterback one day in practice and put the following hypothetical situation to him: "It's our ball on our opponent's two-yard-line, fourth down, with goal to go. What would you do, young man?" The backup quarterback didn't hesitate for a second for his reply. "I'd move over on the bench a little so I could see the touchdown better," he said.

Crippled with phlebitis, Rockne directed his team from a wheelchair in a 1929 game against Carnegie Tech. Courtesy: AP/World Wide Photos.

The first half of the Tech contest was scoreless. Coach Wally Steffen of Tech may not have matched Rockne for inspiration, but he did have a crushing defense. He also had figured that if Carideo could be stopped, Tech might be able to defeat Notre Dame again. However, in the third quarter Carideo returned a punt to midfield, Elder sped to the seventeen-yard-line, and Brill bulled through to the eight-yard-line. From there Carideo turned the fortunes of the team over to Savoldi, a young man who had once been in Notre Dame's doghouse. The press had written that Savoldi, also known as the "Wandering Italian," had an IQ so low that he couldn't grasp his coach's offensive theories. But the powerful fullback, carefully nurtured by Rockne into stardom, was handed the ball three straight times by Carideo. Each time he advanced the ball closer to the goal line. On a fourth and final effort, Savoldi took the ball again and pushed it into the end zone. It was the only touchdown of the afternoon—but it was enough to give Rockne his precious victory.

Physically exhausted, Rockne returned to Notre Dame on an

emotional high. But he was so weak that Bonnie Rockne immediately put him to bed. A deluge of congratulatory mail greeted him, including one from Westbrook Pegler, who had more than once bruised Rockne's feelings. This time the acerbic journalist wished Rockne well and reminded him that he should pay more attention to his health than to winning football games.

As weakened as he was, Rockne still wanted to be present for his team's fifth game of the season, against Georgia Tech, which had been recognized as the national champions in 1928. But his ailment, as well as his reckless expenditure of energy, had caught up with him. Some nonmedical people, such as Grantland Rice, were convinced that Rockne's preseason clinics for high school football coaches had contributed to his debility. "He was the whole show," Rice wrote about one of Rockne's extracurricular activities.

When Rockne made another plea to his doctors to permit him to travel to Georgia for the game, they refused to grant his request. To add to Rockne's discomfiture, before the contest with Georgia Tech, another publicized brouhaha emerged concerning his tactics. It had always been known that Rockne, as well as other formidable coaches of his era such as Warner of Stanford, Gloomy Gil Dobie of Cornell, Bob Zuppke of Illinois, Stagg of Chicago, Jock Sutherland of Pitt, Wallace Wade of Alabama, and others, could be "trimmers" when it came to obeying the strict letter of football law. They didn't want anybody else to gain an edge on them, so they often marginalized their adherence to the gridiron codes; evasive recruiting techniques were the order of the day, and most of them ran their shops in violation of normal academic and scholastic standards. Paul Gallico had constantly deplored the ethics practiced by college football powers in the 1920s and 1930s.

Rockne had informally agreed to a no-scouting concordat with Georgia Tech in 1929. This meant that neither school would employ scouts to watch the other team perform. However, two scouts from South Bend showed up to witness an early-season game featuring Georgia Tech. When Rockne was informed of this flagrant violation of the agreement, he cleared up the matter—at least to his own satisfaction. He promised that he'd *forget* everything that the scouts had passed along to him about Tech's team! Whether Tech's powers-that-be bought into this mystifying logic or not, the Irish managed to win anyway, 26–6.

Getting off to a fast start when they recovered a Notre Dame fumble, the Georgians led briefly. But Cannon blocked a punt with his bare head, Carideo ran seventy-five yards for a touchdown on a punt return, and Marchy Schwartz, coming into his own, went eight yards for another touchdown. Rockne didn't need the scouting reports after all.

After each victory Rockne's health seemed to improve. But his doctors still didn't think it was advisable for him to journey to ball parks and become involved with the emotional tumult surrounding each game. On November 9, when Notre Dame faced Drake at Soldier Field before fifty thousand, Rockne was nowhere in sight. Rockne already had made a Faustian deal with his doctors: He'd stay away from Soldier Field for the Drake game if they would give him a green light to attend the game against USC the following week. With a victory over Drake, 19–6, Notre Dame approached the USC clash with an unbeaten mark in six games.

Although California had edged USC the previous week, USC came into the Notre Dame game with victories in all of its other games. This included a horrendous thrashing of UCLA, 76–0, an astonishing score that coach Howard Jones might have enjoyed more than Rockne, as Rock disliked the notion of "rolling up a score" on weak foes. In Rockne's mind this upcoming game with USC was the second biggest game on Notre Dame's schedule. Only the annual brawl with Army exceeded USC in importance. An added incentive for the coach was that the Trojans had defeated the Irish in 1928.

Aside from the general madness that invariably accompanied each version of the yearly Army–Notre Dame clash, nothing could have equaled the six days in November that preceded Notre Dame's meeting with Southern California in 1929. Of course, it reflected the manners and morals of this hyperventilating decade, with its wild excesses, its overindulgence, its zaniness, and its cockeyed sense of values. Ignoring his infirmity, hundreds of Notre Dame alumni and would-be alumni besieged Rockne for anything resembling a ticket to the USC game. He always had a hard time saying no; this time it was worse than ever before. He would have done himself a favor had he hired an agent. Since the game was to be played in Soldier Field, almost every football fan in Chicago claimed to be an Irishman or descended from an Irishman. New York may have had its devoted "subway alumni," but Chicagoans were closer to South Bend in miles. Every day the Chicago press hyped the event with stories and features, plus the usual pregame predictions from coaches Rockne and Jones.

Before the Notre Dame squad embarked for Chicago, they were hailed by thousands of Notre Dame students at a pep rally and a giant bonfire. The enthusiasm wasn't dampened in the least by a steady downpour the whole night. The idea of Notre Dame versus USC had caught on in the Midwest, even if the rivalry was only in its fourth year.

When the day arrived—a brilliant, crisp November afternoon— an enormous crowd of 120,000 people rocked every portal of Soldier Field. No matter how ill Rockne may have been, he wouldn't have missed being there for all the money that had been lost in the stock market crash the last week of October.

As Rockne gazed at the proceedings from his wheelchair, USC got off to a quick lead on a long pass. Bucky O'Connor, the Notre Dame defender, permitted the USC pass catcher to get behind him, a dereliction that Rockne had repeatedly warned about in practice drills. When it turned out that O'Connor had a swollen black eye that blurred his vision and contributed to the touchdown, Rockne had to restrain himself. Why hadn't the young man informed Lieb that he couldn't see properly? Did he want to play so badly that he kept the information from the coach?

However, even in his weakened condition, Rockne had prepared some surprises for Coach Jones. Throughout the year Rockne had limited the use of the forward pass by his team, despite his own early devotion to that weapon as a Notre Dame player. Aware that USC had been scouting all of Notre Dame's games, Rockne purposely kept a leash on the Irish passing attack. Now, in this big game, he changed tactics and encouraged his team to utilize aerials. Nobody expected that Elder, whose reputation was gained for his track feet, would suddenly unwind and throw a beautiful fifty-four-yard pass for a touchdown to Tom Conley. That made the score 6– 6 at the half.

As the Irish retreated to their locker room, the players wondered if their coach would deliver another emotional effusion. Paul Castner, a former player under Rockne, didn't expect that Rockne would repeat his oratory from the Carnegie Tech game, so *he* stood up to remind the players about how much Rockne meant to Notre Dame tradition and how much he was risking—perhaps his life—to attend this game. It was a moment that Rockne simply couldn't resist. He pulled himself up in his wheelchair. Recharging his batteries, he summoned up almost the exact exhortatory phrases he had employed at Pittsburgh. If they had worked then, why not now?

Within minutes after the second half started, Savoldi, who had reportedly broken into tears at Rockne's words, scored a touchdown, moving Notre Dame ahead (after the extra point), 13–6. Russell Saunders, like Elder a racehorse, then took the kickoff and ran it back for a USC touchdown. Inexplicably, the Trojans again failed to kick the extra point. Both teams had been carefully schooled in fundamentals, but when Notre Dame finally emerged victorious, 13–12, it marked the third time in four games against the Irish that USC wound up losing by a single point. Something had gone awry in Howard Jones's preparations.

That night, as Rockne tried to rest after the excitement of the day, the dangerous clot in his leg broke loose. This was what the doctors had feared and warned against. Amazingly, the clot passed through Rockne's heart, missed his brain, and settled in the other leg. The near-fatal experience was enough to keep Rockne away from the last two games of the season, against Northwestern and Army.

If the newspapers had been quickly informed about Rockne's precarious condition following the USC game they might have gone easier on him. As it was, some of the stories in the Chicago press, principally the *Chicago Daily News,* were mockingly unpleasant about Rockne's locker-room speeches. It was almost as if Rockne were being equated with Scarface Al Capone, one of Chicago's most unsavory characters. This wasn't the first time Rockne had been subjected to such ridicule. But now that he suffered from such poor health, his admirers were deeply angered. They insisted again that such uncalled-for baiting was a subtle form of anti-Catholic bias. There was no reason, they said, to cast Rockne in the role of a sentimental fool even if there were those in the press who laughed at the coach's tearful appeals.

Northwestern's Wildcats were usually competitive with Notre Dame. But, in 1929, Notre Dame was a much superior team, even with Rockne staying home to heed the warnings of his doctors. However, Rockne's influence was still pervasive, even when he was among the missing. It remained in subtle ways. His search for perfection on the gridiron included the way his boys looked on the field, the way they carried themselves, and the way they dressed. He never claimed to be a fashion arbiter. As a matter of fact, his own wearing apparel, with wrinkled pants and old sweaters, invariably resembled a bum's discards. But when it came to his own players, he wanted them to "look like football players." "He put the old canvas pants away and substituted gold satin. "The luster and fit of this material made a striking combination with the blue and green of the jersey," wrote Harry Stuhldreher. "The whole uniform had a tapering effect. The pants fitted well at the thigh and the knee. The jersey was very snug so it couldn't wrinkle. When they sat on the bench, they wore huge golden coats of a leather material and were wrapped in blue blankets, trimmed in gold."

Before the Irish left for Chicago to face Northwestern, Rockne told his men to win "the one-hundredth victory" for him. He was a bit premature about the exact number of victories under his aegis, but again he was free to use poetic license. Notre Dame didn't have much trouble with Northwestern, tallying three touchdowns in the second quarter, by Savoldi, Schwartz, and Carideo. Savoldi added another touchdown in the waning stages of the game, making the final score 26–6. (The hundredth win would be registered the next fall, against Indiana.)

With another all-winning season at stake the next week against Army at Yankee Stadium, it wasn't certain until the last minute whether Rockne would defy his doctors and show up in "the House That Ruth Built." Speculation about his presence or absence continued for the whole week preceding the game. However, when long-range weather reports predicted that Saturday, November 30, would be icy cold, with blustery winds, Rockne bowed to the forecast and reluctantly decided not to accompany his team to New York. By this time Rockne had great confidence in Lieb; after all, how could one argue with eight triumphs in eight games? In the hour or so before the game got under way in New York, Rockne put in his phone call pep talk from South Bend to his boys, as they waited to engage the Cadets. Again he emphasized how much the game meant to him and to all Notre Damers. The message never changed.

Many in the sold-out house of more than eighty thousand had paid as much as $50 each for their scalped tickets. Boxes went for as high as $350, which in those days might well have fed a family of three for a couple of months. (At about this time, the novelist Erskine Caldwell had arrived in New York with only a dime in his pocket; "Hoover Hotels," where the homeless sought refuge, were opening around the country, and restaurants advertised "all that you can eat for sixty cents.") But at Yankee Stadium that afternoon the grimness of the Depression was nowhere in evidence. A special train brought in Notre Dame's eighty-piece marching band, and hundreds of South Benders came along with them. The Army brass, warmly dressed in everything from greatcoats to woolly blankets, and topped off by furry hats and earmuffs, journeyed for miles to cheer on Biff Jones's team, which hadn't had much luck in 1929. Even at an extortionate rate for tickets, another 150,000 probably could have been sold.

In the moments before the game got under way the temperature dipped to a few degrees above zero, accompanied by a thirty-five-mile-per hour wind that quickly froze the Stadium turf. "A congealed crowd sought relief in bottles," recalled Army's assistant coach Blaik. "After the game there were sufficient empties borne away by garbage trucks to decorate several city dumps. . . ." Prohibition was still the so-called deterrent law of the land, but many ignored it—especially when Notre Dame–Army games were played in an igloolike atmosphere.

This was truly a Rockne-produced event, except on this occasion the producer was at home listening to the play-by-play on radio, along with millions of others. For a few hours other millions of fearful Americans might get surcease from reports of a faraway football game.

This game, the sixteenth between the fierce rivals, settled at once into a struggle that those in the cavernous ball park would never forget. Because it was Jones's last game at West Point's helm and also the great Cagle's final performance for the Cadets, the West Pointers were determined to upend the Irish and, in the process, ruin their unbeaten season. For a while, in the first quarter, it appeared that the Cadets were going to wear out the Irish defenders. Their line stubbornly refused to yield much yardage, while, on the offense, Cagle scampered from one end of the field to the other, but without picking up a score.

In the second quarter Army got a break when tackle Jack Price blocked Carideo's punt, with the Cadets gobbling up the ball on Notre Dame's thirteen-yard-line. With third down and eight yards to go on the eleven-yard-line, Cagle swung wide to the right, whirled suddenly, and tossed a crossfield pass to Carl Carlmark in the northwest corner of the end zone. At the last second, a strong gale of wind held up the floating pigskin, enabling Elder to move in front of Carlmark and pick off the ball. In commenting later, Jones said that as soon as he saw the wraithlike figure of Elder intercepting the ball, he knew that the play would quickly boomerang into a touchdown for Notre Dame. As Elder, an Olympic-caliber runner who held the world's sprint record for sixty yards, sped by the Army bench and down the sidelines, Jones was sorely tempted to throw a bucket of water over his head. But nothing could have stopped Elder that afternoon. He picked up speed and blockers as he ran. At the finish of his long gallop for a touchdown he was scarcely out of breath.

For years Elder's legendary dash had been listed between ninety and ninety-eight yards. But along came Notre Dame football historian Steve Boda, years later, to set the record straight. He obtained original film of the blazing return by Elder and had it reproduced onto videotape. By running the film in slow motion, Boda revealed that Elder had actually run the ball back *one hundred* yards. The original estimate was due, said Boda, to the fact that the press box at Yankee Stadium was at a bad angle, causing most sportswriters who were present to judge the figure to be anywhere from ninety to ninety-eight yards.

At halftime almost every player on both teams had to be treated for frostbite or chills. They were football players—but they looked like they had been challenging Mount Everest. In the final half Cagle, in his valedictory performance against the Irish, made several bids to break away, but each time the slippery footing contrived to thwart his efforts. Notre Dame, by contrast, played a defensive game, sitting on its lead and protecting its slim 7–0 margin. For years Rockne had come in for criticism because he was inclined to resort to such strategy, which minimized taking risks. He always explained that he played to win—as if anyone needed to be reminded of that—and he was not in the business to trounce foes or roll up a score.

In the last seconds of the game Cagle tried a long, desperation heave that was knocked down. The game ended with Notre Dame stubbornly in possession of the ball. "The frozen crowd," wrote author Jim Beach, "realized that they had witnessed one of the greatest standoff games in football history."

In weather that would have driven Eskimos to despair, Army used only *eleven* players throughout the entire game, a feat seldom matched for durability. On the other hand, Notre Dame shifted a few players around on the line and in the backfield, in keeping with Rockne's shock troop tactics.

So 1929 and the Era of Wonderful Nonsense came to a close, with Rockne, battered but unbowed, sitting on top of the football world with another unbeaten team.

20

The Last Season

IN 1930 FRANCIS WALLACE, who aspired to write novels and screen-plays about college football, showed the manuscript of his first book, *Huddle,* to a producer at Fox. As one might suspect, the coach in Wallace's book bore a strong resemblance to Rockne. Wallace informed the producer that it might be possible to get Rockne himself to play his own part on the screen. Even when they engaged in arguments (a process that Rockne keenly enjoyed), Wallace always managed to remain close to Rockne. The producer took the manuscript to Sol Wurtzel, then the chief of Fox. Wurtzel cast a cursory glance at the text and shrugged.

"Football, football?" Wurtzel said. "Who cares about football?"

"But we could get Rockne in the movie," the producer said.

"Rocky, who's Rocky?" Wurtzel responded.

(Ten years later producer Sam Goldwyn professed equal igno-rance about Lou Gehrig, who had just died. However, Goldwyn did get around to producing *The Pride of the Yankees,* based on Gehrig's life, while Wurtzel never did produce a movie based on Wallace's book.)

If Wurtzel didn't know who "Rocky" was in 1930, most Ameri-cans, including those with only a remote interest in football, were aware of Rockne and his achievements. His name and his fame had become inextricably entwined with Notre Dame and Notre Dame with him. But to a public that was not yet watching television, the intensely empathetic side of Rockne was barely perceived. People knew that he was a successful coach, they knew he could talk a blue streak, they may have known about the Four Horsemen and the Gipper.

But they didn't know that he responded to people with generosity and understanding, making friends wherever he went. Constantly besieged by friends and strangers alike for tickets, he tried to accommodate everyone, but naturally that was impossible. Even his archfoes at West Point, including the ruling military class at the Academy, became Rockne's drinking companions and intimates, as did much of the press. He liked them, liked being around them, and they liked him and enjoyed his company.

Rockne's kindness toward ordinary people who admired him did not receive much attention in the newspapers, mainly because Rockne didn't volunteer to publicize such matters. There was, for example, Ray Fornier, a fifteen-year-old boy who worked in the business office of the *New York Times.* Fornier was involved with a local 135-pound football team and wrote a letter to Rockne, a man he didn't know, seeking advice about how to build himself up physically, considering that he worked in an office all day. Back came a reply from Rockne:

"I admire your pluck very much," wrote the coach, "but from what you write, you must be holding your own and better. . . . I hope you can inspire your players to greater and lasting efforts . . . brains will always win over brawn, and there is a lot of satisfaction in this for all of us."

Fornier cherished Rockne's response for the rest of his life.

Robert Harron, in a biography of Rockne, imagined that the Fornier incident could have been "multiplied hundreds of thousands of times in Rockne's career."

Inmates in a penitentiary in Pennsylvania once wrote to Rockne asking if he'd be able to furnish them with football uniforms that may have outlived their usefulness at Notre Dame. Within a few days the convicts, who presumably followed the fortunes of Notre Dame, received a batch of uniforms—all *new*—from Rockne.

After Notre Dame played Army in one of their games in the late twenties a blind man, who had attended the game, bumped into Rockne on the way out of the ball park. The crowd had dispersed from Yankee Stadium, making it easier for the sightless fellow to navigate. Rockne expressed surprise to this man that he would come to "listen" to a football game. But the blind man responded that he could "see" what was happening, with the assistance of a few informative words from his companion at the game. Rockne congratulated the blind man for his interest and enterprise, then revealed that he was Knute Rockne. Rockne then invited him back to the dressing room.

"He introduced me to a lot of the players," said the sightless man, "then he sat down next to me and talked for a while. Everyone was packing and in a hurry to get away, but Rockne kept talking. It was apparently characteristic of the man to do things like this. The talk was the beginning of a new lease on life for me."

Since becoming ill with phlebitis Rockne, too, needed the support of others. For the most part he received morale-building aid from Bonnie, Tom Lieb, and the Notre Dame players. But during the winter of 1930, when Rockne went to Miami Beach, Florida, to soak up the sun and laze on the beach, he was dissatisfied with his seeming lack of progress. He appeared restless and disgruntled to those who came to spend time with him. His usual charm and wit were not in evidence. He simply was not used to a life without activity, a cause, and a purpose. Here he was, coming off a season of enormous achievement, his name was a household word, but he couldn't be sure what was going to happen to him next. It was the uncertainty that had gotten his spirit down more than anything else.

Then, almost overnight, Rockne's general condition started to improve. As the season approached, with the new stadium nearing completion, and with a ten-game "suicide schedule" in the offing, Rockne thought about making radical changes in his work patterns. He was willing to give up control of certain parts of the football operation, those things tangential to the game itself, such as equipment, doctoring, tickets, training table, publicity, etc. In the past he had involved himself with all of these elements. By now divorcing himself from these chores he knew that he could conserve his energy and remain focused on the task at hand—coaching his men on the field. Reluctantly, too, he agreed to cut back on his recruiting efforts, which had always played such a signal role in Notre Dame's football successes.

Aware that their coach was deserving of more help on the field, Rev. J. Hugh O'Donnell, Notre Dame's president, approved of hiring several new assistants for Rockne. Hunk Anderson, always close to Rockne, was brought back as an aide, and Jack Chevigny and

The first practice of what would be Rockne's final season. Courtesy: AP/World Wide Photos.

Ike Voedisch were also put on as assistant coaches, thus lessening the burden on Rockne.

The coach did not totally reject other peripheral matters, such as writing articles and making speeches. In 1930 his "autobiography" was completed with the help of a freelance writer named John B. Kennedy. Exactly how much of the text was directly attributable to Rockne's efforts was not clear, but the best guess is that it was limited. Rockne was a confident public speaker, but when it came to writing, that was another matter. The autobiography, published by Bobbs-Merrill in 1931, was probably almost entirely the work of Kennedy.

In a better mood than he had been for a long while, Rockne was now able to joke about his phlebitis. He referred to the large rubber bandage that enclosed his bad leg as "my spare tire." Rockne seemed to have gained a new life from the diminution of some of his duties. Those who knew him best were convinced that his bout with phlebitis had been won. They were supported by the findings of the Mayo Clinic, which, after a thorough examination of the coach, announced that he was in good shape and could resume his job on a full-time basis. For a man who a year before had been reported to be near death, this was quite a transformation—and it certainly contributed to Rockne's mellowness.

Equally important as his regained health was the completion of the new stadium with a bunch of exploding stars to put in it. It had usually been Rockne's policy to underplay the prospect of each of his teams. There was no way he would ever boast about how unbeatable his squad was. If anything, he would underplay their potential. Sitting with Curly Lambeau, the coach of the Green Bay Packers, at the Oliver Hotel, Rockne was asked to describe the kind of team he had. A grin creased Rockne's face. "It may be the best team I've ever had here," he answered, "but I'd never tell anyone that."

Many observers, even the most jaundiced, realized that Rockne had assembled a team that was capable of repeating the unbeaten season of 1929. Headed by quarterback Carideo, who was now being acclaimed as the best team leader in the nation, Notre Dame also had a line featuring Bert Metzger, a 149-pound guard, plus Tom Conley and Al Culver. The other members of the backfield, probably surpassing the Four Horsemen, were Marty Brill and Marchy Schwartz at the halves and the enigmatic Savoldi. All of these men were capable of breaking a game open at any time. By the time the 1930 season came to an end most of these players won nomination to any number of All-America teams.

As Rockne regained his health, he remained vitally interested in the new stadium, which had been financed by selling all of the ten-year leases on the prime seats and the stadium boxes. This was a remarkable feat, for the country was entering a period of wide-spread economic misery. Watching Notre Dame and rooting for it was obviously a splendid Depression-time catharsis. To this day there are those at South Bend agitating to have Notre Dame Stadium renamed for Rockne, and calling it "the House That Rockne Built."

The formal dedication of the stadium was scheduled for October 11, with Navy as the opponent. But prior to that game with the Midshipmen, Notre Dame met Southern Methodist University on October 4 in what was called "an informal opener." Although Rockne had been relieved, for the most part, of acting in behalf of friends and associates who wanted tickets, he didn't mind dealing with his own players when they requested complimentary tickets. Before the game with Navy, Savoldi approached Rockne and asked: "How about two for Saturday?" Rockne responded: "Relatives?" "No, tickets," riposted Savoldi, who didn't always get the point.

SMU's Mustangs, led by Coach Ray Morrison, an ex-Vanderbilt quarterback, had topped the Southwest Conference several times prior to the 1930s. They featured an adventurous offensive, espe-

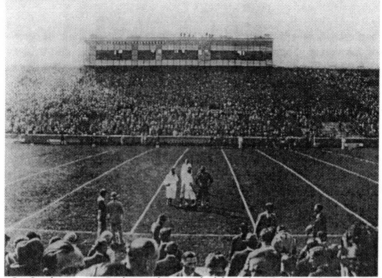

On October 4, 1930, Rockne, in hat, watched from the sidelines as his Fighting Irish played their first game at an expanded Notre Dame Stadium. Courtesy: Department of Sports Information, University of Notre Dame.

cially with the forward pass. Four plays into the game they scored on a forty-eight-yard pass play as the crowd of fewer than fifteen thousand began to think that they were witnessing the end of the Irish winning streak of nine games.

But as the afternoon waned, Savoldi sped to a touchdown on a long kickoff return and Schwartz went off tackle for six points. At halftime the score was tied at 14–14. However, with fewer than five minutes to play, the old Rockne magic once again asserted itself. During an Irish time-out trainer "Scrapiron" Young, himself something of a legend at Notre Dame, asked Rockne if he wanted to send in any last-minute instructions that might turn the tide of the game. The coach's "inspiring" retort was considerably less than that.

"Tell 'em any play will work if the blocking is good," Rockne told Scrapiron. When Scrapiron dutifully relayed Rockne's message to Carideo, the quarterback shrugged and called for a pass play. Schwartz thereupon let loose a long aerial to Ed Kosky, who made a stunning catch close to SMU's goal line. From there, Schwartz punched over left end for the winning touchdown. No doubt the Irish had followed Rockne's bland prescriptions with good blocking.

But without three late interceptions by Tommy Yarr, Notre Dame would have gone down to defeat.

The weather cooperated neatly on the weekend of October 10–11 for the dedication of the new stadium. The event had a glittering touch, worthy of Florenz Ziegfeld, although it was the locals who had put it together. The night before the game with Navy the Notre Dame campus, under a full Indiana moon, became one vast celebratory arena. Anyone who didn't show up among the twenty thousand or so students, dignitaries, and fans must have been sick or treasonous. Carrying flaming red torches and "waking up the echoes" with the rousing lyrics of the Notre Dame Victory March, the three-thousand-strong all-male student body fell into lockstep for three blocks behind the Irish marching band. Once in the stadium everyone applauded wildly as air bombs went off, the Notre Dame monogram was spelled out by the students, and the American colors were unfurled. Rockne spoke, but only briefly, for he chose to let others do the official anointing. Navy's relationship with Notre Dame, which now covered four games, was hailed by an admiral. President O'Donnell borrowed from a campus poet's eulogy for George Gipp.

According to Father O'Donnell, Gipp was the true architect of the new stadium, a reference that must have made Rockne wince, for he had done more than anyone to bring this to fruition. Gipp's deathbed words, said Father O'Donnell, had earned him the right to be acknowledged as Notre Dame's "spiritual guardian." Father O'Donnell knew as much as anyone at South Bend the true, somewhat profane details of Gipp's short life, but he preferred to present the Gipper's transformation as "an uplifting spiritual tale."

The next day, with the help of special excursion trains from Chicago, more than forty thousand people collected at the stadium for the dedication game. The afternoon was crisp and clear, thus providing a pleasant stage for a game that seemed an anticlimax to the ceremonies that had preceded it. Prior to the game Frank E. Hering, who had been the Irish coach from 1896 to 1899 and who was now president of the Alumni Association, threw a verbal bouquet at Rockne. Hering declared that "those thousands of athletes who have been inspired by him, have added to the fame of Notre Dame, making this ceremony more than a dedication—it is a testimonial." Hering added that "tradition is a compound of reverence and pride and unselfish service. Notre Dame traditions live. Notre Dame teams have thrilled millions and inspired the youth of the nation to play the game of football—and the game of life—in the spirit of the rules."

One of the players who was outstanding that day in an easy 26–2 victory over Navy was Savoldi, who ran for three touchdowns. But Savoldi, following in the untamed footsteps of Gipp and West Point's Cagle, had violated two prime Notre Dame rules: The school forbade students to be married, and, because it was a Catholic institution, divorce was verboten. Shortly after the Navy game, Savoldi filed suit for divorce. Outside of a few intimates of Savoldi, nobody at school, including Rockne, was even aware that he had a wife. But with the issue now out in the open, the problem had to be resolved in the midst of an unbeaten season.

There was a sharp division of opinion about what to do with Savoldi. The priests at Notre Dame, placing religion and principle ahead of football triumphs, insisted that the young man should be expelled. On the other hand, many subway alumni, a part of the press, and a number of the more rabid Notre Dame graduates thought there might be a way out if Savoldi could be encouraged to drop his petition for divorce. Having been vulnerable in the past to charges of overcommercialization and to squeezing good football players past the admissions office, even when they had inferior academic records, Rockne this time played his cards masterfully. He remained open with the press in providing the details of Savoldi's difficulties, even as he pointed out that there were football players at other schools who were married. But he also underlined that he appreciated how serious many at Notre Dame regarded Savoldi's flouting of the rules. He emphasized that he was not prepared to conduct a public fight to keep Savoldi, a player he had molded into a destructive force on the gridiron. Instead, he sat down with Savoldi, and like the father figure he was with many of his men, explained that to avoid being expelled he should leave school. Savoldi followed Rockne's advice. Several weeks after the controversy exploded on the South Bend scene, he departed. Rockne helped Savoldi start his new post–Notre Dame life with a personal check for fifteen hundred dollars. In no time at all, Savoldi was ripping off yardage as a professional footballer. Later he became a professional wrestler, in an era when Jim Londos and Strangler Lewis lent a patina of respectability to that occupation.

Through all of the stress over Savoldi, in addition to the grinding week-to-week challenge on the field, Rockne remarkably appeared to have regained the full vigor of his earlier years. He was still young in age and at the height of his career, and other men might have been more inhibited by his ailment. But he had chosen to confront it in his own fatalistic way, never giving in to it. If anything, as each game approached, he seemed more involved, more inventive than ever before.

With another grudge match coming up against Carnegie Tech on October 18, Rockne employed all of his psychological magic on Brill, one of two Jewish boys playing in Notre Dame's "all-Erin" backfield. Reporters and old grads didn't hesitate to make jokes about the non-Irish origin of the four men who comprised this talented group. When Carideo and Savoldi were in there with Brill and Schwartz they were hardly celebrating the glories of Dublin.

In previous games Tech's "human cement barrel," Johnny Karcis, had delivered some tough lessons to Brill. Rockne constantly prodded Brill about that, suggesting that it was time for Marty to give it back to Karcis. With only minutes gone by in the 1930 game, Brill seized an opportunity to smash Karcis head-on, in a collision that reverberated back in the South Bend dormitories. After that moment Tech's purpose diminished—but Rockne's reverses, spinners, and laterals also had something to do with it. With a lead of 21–6, Rockne "kindly" sent in his reserves, although one could not always be certain how much less talented the second- and third-stringers were than the varsity.

With Pitt next on the agenda, Rockne was determined that there wouldn't be a letdown for his club. The game was perceived in many quarters as a national championship contest. Coached by Jock Sutherland—like Rockne, one of the master strategists in the game—Pitt had gone through 1929 undefeated, until they were beaten by USC in the Rose Bowl. They had begun the 1930 season with four straight victories, scoring 134 points while yielding none.

Notre Dame hadn't faced Pitt since Rockne's student years. But what chiefly concerned Rockne was that the game would be played in Pitt's new multimillion-dollar stadium. There would be seventy thousand people there, most of them rooting for the Panthers, which wouldn't make it easier for the Irish. To make matters worse, a funny thing happened to Rockne on his way to the game. Figuring that his face was sufficiently familiar around the country's football arenas so he didn't have to present identification or a ticket to gain entrance, Rockne found himself barred by a suspicious policeman. A brief argument ensued between the vigilant gendarme and the coach until a Notre Dame official arrived on the scene. This fervent

Notre Dame supporter didn't relish the idea of the Irish riding into combat against Pitt without Rockne on the bench, so he offered him an extra ticket that he had in his pocket. If Rockne believed that this contretemps was a bad omen for that afternoon's proceedings, he was proven wrong. Rockne switched his offensive strategy to a concentrated ground attack after Sutherland had cautioned his men to be alert to Notre Dame's passing offense.

On the first play from scrimmage Schwartz broke through for a sixty-yard touchdown gallop with the help of several key blockers. There was no better way to deliver a knockout punch, even before the boys could work up a few beads of perspiration. Pitt was never in the contest after that. Savoldi, still on the Notre Dame roster, bulled his way to two touchdowns, and Moon Mullins scored another before the half was over. Going into the locker room, the Irish held a 35–0 lead, meaning there was no need for Rockne to deliver any uplifting remarks to his charges. The second half was simply a consolation match, with Notre Dame choosing to coast on its lead. Sutherland's team put together nineteen points but that served only to make the final score of 35–19 look better in the newspaper stories. The Panthers had literally been defanged, and Sutherland knew it. He shook his head in disbelief after the game, assuring the press that if Rockne had ordained it "Notre Dame could have run up a hundred points with ease." That was probably only a slight exaggeration. But Sutherland had benefited from the fact that Rockne, stubbornly dedicated to winning, also was not one for rubbing it in.

The next week Rockne was happy to have his team back home at Notre Dame for an engagement with Indiana. When a small crowd of eleven thousand showed up, such a seeming lack of support puzzled Rockne. As well, it appeared to influence the lackluster play of his team in the first half. The Hoosiers battled Notre Dame to a 0–0 stalemate in the first two quarters, causing Rockne to suspect that his men may have run out of gas. To bring about the appropriate brio, Rockne addressed his embarrassed team in the locker room. He wondered out loud what had come over them. Within a few minutes, after the second half began, Rockne got his answer. Savoldi and Schwartz raced for touchdowns and Brill added two as the sparse crowd came alive. The final score of 27–0 didn't tell the whole story, for the Irish ran for 432 yards, about six times Indiana's output.

The disappointing turnout against Indiana was forgotten the

next week, when the Irish journeyed to Philadelphia for their first game ever with Penn. An overflow crowd of seventy-five thousand jammed Franklin Field for what had been rated as a relatively even game. Many had journeyed from New York to cheer on the Irish. That included the flamboyant Mayor Walker of New York, who never failed to show up at sports events that promised to take him away from the drudgery of City Hall.

Minutes after the game got under way Rockne ordered "Scrapiron" Young, to clear the area around the Notre Dame bench of people who might threaten the physical safety of his players. Young spotted one scrawny fellow, in a derby and dressed to the nines, with a green blanket wrapped around him. When Scrapiron commanded this gentleman to move, he was ignored. It didn't take much to set off Scrapiron's Irish temper, so he picked up the "intruder" by the seat of his pants and unceremoniously pitched him in the air several yards from the bench.

Rockne had been paying strict attention to the action on the field when suddenly he noticed this dapper man bouncing off the turf. "Come over here, Scrapiron!" yelled Rockne. Then, pointing at the upended man, Rockne said, "I want you to meet the mayor of New York. He's my good friend. Please treat him properly." Scrapiron almost fell over in embarrassment. But Jimmy Walker was never at a loss for words. "You were only doing your job," he said soothingly to Rockne's aide-de-camp.

Coming into this game Penn had run up four victories against one defeat. They had beaten a powerful Kansas team the week before. But the newspapers concentrated on the vendetta angle involving Marty Brill. It seems that Brill had gone to Penn to play football but had failed to win a regular berth on the team. Humiliated and angered by Coach Lou Young's dismissal of his talents, Brill transferred to Notre Dame, even though Rockne had never actually recruited him. Much ado was made of the report that Brill's well-to-do father had offered his son a thousand dollars for each touchdown he could score against his former school. That tale turned out to be apocryphal, but that didn't prevent the Notre Dame students from labeling the game against Penn as "Marty's Day."

Brill had already put together a brilliant year for the Irish, even getting mention on several All-American teams. But his performance on the afternoon of November 8 was right out of a hokey movie scenario. As Notre Dame romped to a shocking 60–20 victory, an exceedingly high score in those days of tight defensive football, Brill was unstoppable. Carrying the ball ten times, he ran for three of Notre Dame's nine touchdowns, with runs of sixty-seven, thirty-eight, and twenty-five yards. That put the Irish ahead by 43–0 after only thirty minutes of play. When Brill was removed from the game, a roar of approval went up from the Notre Dame supporters. They had found a new hero in a Jewish kid who could have been elected mayor of South Bend on the spot.

"In addition to his eighteen points, Brill also paved the way for another touchdown by intercepting a pass," wrote Allison Danzig in the *New York Times*. "His defensive work and blocking also were of a high order and, all in all, it was a great day for the hometown boy who came back to make good . . . it wasn't a football team that struck the Red and Blue, it was a cyclone and who is going to stop it?"

Already having immortalized the Four Horsemen, Grantland Rice had to grope for new zoological analogies. "Carideo, Brill, Savoldi, and Schwartz were a combination of four antelopes, four charging buffaloes, four digdigs and four eels," he wrote. A bleak year by any other standards, 1930 had turned into the most spectacular of years for Rockne.

Few expected Drake the next week to give the Irish much of a battle. Rockne, himself, apparently agreed with this assessment. He chose to scout unbeaten Northwestern in its game against Wisconsin, instead of being on hand for Drake—this despite the fact that Hunk Anderson was quick to remind him of what had happened in 1926, when Rockne had played hooky from the ill-fated Carnegie Tech game. However, this time Rockne's absence didn't make any difference. Drake simply didn't belong on the same gridiron with this Notre Dame team and went down to defeat easily, 28–7. The Irish were helped considerably by the sophomore Dan Hanley, who had been named to replace the departed Savoldi. Once again Notre Dame's stadium was relatively empty, with only ten thousand on hand. Reality had hit the Midwest, for now it was apparent that the depressed economy was having a dampening impact on attendance, even while Rockne's men were reaching heights of football perfection.

If this was Notre Dame's fiercest array of gladiators in their history, they now faced a rigorous test—three games with Northwestern, Army, and USC, all away from home. Northwestern, undefeated and leader of the Big Ten, was coached by Dick Hanley, who was rated almost as talented as Rockne at halftime preachments. Although interest at South Bend may have flagged, it had reached a high level in Evanston, Illinois, and in the Chicago area, where Northwestern was based. Tickets were in such demand for the game—three-dollar seats going for as much as a hundred dollars—that Northwestern's athletic department considered transferring the game from its own Dyche Stadium to Soldier Field, where they estimated such a change of venue would more than double the crowd.

Although Notre Dame's officialdom agreed that such a switch might be a sound idea (with part of the receipts set aside for charity), the Big Ten made a request that the game *not* be moved. The ruling was another manifestation of the anti-Notre Dame prejudice of the Big Ten. Rockne felt that the best way to confront such stupidity was to defeat the Big Ten teams on the field.

Another issue that Rockne faced from time to time was the suggestion, widely disseminated by Big Ten officials, that he tried to "influence" the selection of officials who worked Notre Dame games. There had been occasions when Rockne experienced difficulties with referees. What coach hadn't? But Rockne never baited officials or tried to intimidate them. There was no reason to believe that he held the upper hand with such a man as Walker Okeson of Lehigh University, who, for some years, had presided over the appointment of officials for football games in the East. Okeson said that if Rockne was satisfied with the overall competence of an official, he never objected to that person's assignment to a Notre Dame contest. But Okeson also pointed out that "Rockne was a far cry from being careless about the selection of officials in Notre Dame's games . . . we had voluminous correspondence before being able to come to agreement. But Rockne never held it against an official who might have called one against Notre Dame, provided that that man was qualified to do his job."

Ed Thorp, a prominent football referee who worked many of the Irish games, said that Rockne was "one of the greatest sportsmen he'd ever met . . . he rarely exchanged words with me between halves." Thorp recalled how he had called back a play in the Rose Bowl game of 1925, when Elmer Layden's toe had flicked across the sideline marker, after Layden had snared a long pass. In such a tight game the play could have been crucial, but Rockne never whispered a word of dissent against Thorp's ruling. When Rockne respected an official, such as Thorp, he tried to control his tongue and his emotions.

Rockne's approach to the Northwestern game was unusual. As a master of timing, he was not inclined to burden his players with pregame palaver as well as halftime speeches. It was generally one *or* the other, depending on his mood and the circumstances. The best way to lose his audience, he thought, was to talk too much. As prolix as Rockne could be, he was smart enough to know when to exercise restraint in the locker room. But against Northwestern that November day, he didn't observe his own unwritten rule.

Sensing that his players were fatigued, Rockne gathered them together in Dyche Stadium's locker room before the game. Quietly he urged them to do their best. Their "best" turned out to be a o–o halftime tie against the Wildcats. However, Notre Dame's defense held; twice they stopped Northwestern on the five-yard-line. With Rockne sensing that his unbeaten season was drifting away, he made up his mind at the half to deliver a second pep talk of the afternoon. It wasn't easy for him to do this, for he had lost the febrile energy he once possessed. As well, he suspected that his players might not want to hear from him again. As he began to speak, the locker room was as quiet as a mortuary. Sotto voce at first, Rockne then started to bite off each phrase for dramatic effect.

"Maybe you're having an off day," he said. "But if you do better, you'll win." Then he told his men how much this game meant to them, to him, and to Notre Dame. At the finish he was almost roaring. "I want you to go out there and fight, fight, FIGHT!"

The entire performance took less than a minute, but it galvanized the team. Those who heard Rockne that day swore it was the best halftime speech he had ever delivered.

In the second half Northwestern, suddenly grown anemic, couldn't advance past the forty-yard-line. Meanwhile, the Irish were still having a hard time moving the ball. As the clock ran down, it looked like the Irish would be forced to settle for a tie. As the loss of Savoldi had obviously hurt Notre Dame's running game, Rockne suggested to Carideo that he switch to a passing attack. After the long afternoon, the strategy started to work. When the Irish reached Northwestern's eighteen-yard-line, Schwartz set off for the goal line. Only Northwestern's safetyman barred Schwartz's progress. But Johnny O'Brien proved that he was more than a "one play" athlete by leveling a devastating block. As Schwartz scampered to the first touchdown of the game, Rockne, on the sidelines, raised his arms over his head in celebration.

With the dam broken, Notre Dame quickly advanced to a second touchdown. Notre Dame's unbeaten streak had held. But it was a wrenching loss for Coach Hanley, who, off the field, was a close personal friend of Rockne. In Northwestern's locker room Hanley cried bitter tears as his team's own unbeaten season had been tarnished.

Now Rockne could look ahead to Army, in the ninth game of a schedule that for most teams would have been pure torture. The game had originally been scheduled, as usual, for Yankee Stadium. But it was moved to Soldier Field, even though Rockne would have preferred to battle it out in The Bronx. Because the last game of Notre Dame's season was scheduled to be played against USC on the West Coast, a game in Yankee Stadium the week before would have necessitated a trip to the East, then out to California. By placing the contest in Chicago, Notre Dame's team would be saved considerable wear and tear.

The usual hoopla surrounding Army–Notre Dame pervaded the press in the days before the game, with some soothsayers predicting that the largest crowd in football history would assemble in Soldier Field. It wasn't difficult to beat the drums for a game in which Notre Dame would arrive undefeated, to play a West Point team that had yielded only two touchdowns in nine games, with only a 7–7 tie with Yale marring an otherwise perfect docket.

Despite all the preparations that always preceded the Army game, the coach also consented to head a group of Notre Dame "All-Stars" in a charity game at Soldier Field. The opponents would be an assemblage of Northwestern "All-Stars." The game was scheduled to be played on Thanksgiving Day, just two days before the Army clash! Conceding that the cause was a good one, many openly questioned Rockne's sanity. How could he participate in such a time-consuming distraction only hours before West Point would battle his team? The answer was that Rockne was a man who just couldn't say no.

Fewer than two thousand people showed up for the charity game, as a driving snow beat down on the participants. Many who had given their time for the game also had neglected to do any real training. Some of them had been belting down beer the night before and were in no physical condition to gambol on a field that was in miserable shape. Nobody bothered to keep score, and the final result remained unknown. The biggest loser turned out to be Rockne himself. He ended up signing a check for three thousand dollars to cover some of the costs of the charade.

Army against Notre Dame remained special. But on that November 29 afternoon in 1930 the most memorable feature of the event was the weather. A steady downpour of rain became sleet. Although the field had been protected prior to the game by hay and a large tarpaulin, once the protections were removed a coating of ice that would have had more appeal to the skater Sonja Henie threatened to turn the running game into a slippery farce.

Rockne's health again was questionable and had not been completely restored at this point; thus his mood before the game matched the grimness of the day. In a hoarse voice, he spoke to his players as they readied themselves to take the field. But he failed to muster the necessary zeal. Following Rockne's less-than-compelling words, his team went out to face the stern elements and Major Ralph Sasse's team. Not even the fact that Red Cagle had already played his final game for Army against them could rouse the spirits of the Notre Damers. As the game got under way, Rockne sat in his wheelchair, bundled in long underwear and a heavy overcoat, his hat pulled down low over his forehead.

For almost a week the press had been trumpeting that this would be the greatest crowd ever to watch a college football game. But the actual attendance of 105,000 was considerably below expectations. What the sportswriters had failed to properly assess was the mood of a country that had now been plunged into a state of melancholy over "Mr. Hoover's Depression." However, there was no way they could have predicted that other attendance assassin—the foul weather.

As the chilled, sullen crowd looked on for three quarters, huddled in the mist-shrouded stadium, the two teams wrestled in the mud for an advantage. But it was impossible to accelerate any attack under such conditions, and Rockne might even have settled for a tie as the fourth period got under way.

However, as so often was the case during his tenure, Notre Dame rose to the occasion as the game wound down to its bitter end. This time it was Marchy Schwartz who came to the rescue. With only minutes left in the game, Schwartz took the ball and churned through the muck on Old 51, one of Rockne's basic plays. Once he passed the line of scrimmage, he was in the clear. With this fifty-four-yard-touchdown gallop, Notre Dame appeared to have its victory. Carideo kicked the extra point, which, at the time, seemed superfluous.

But that was not the case. Not long after Schwartz's run Dick King, a substitute Army end, blocked a Carideo punt and alertly followed the ball all the way across Notre Dame's goal line. The score suddenly became 7–6, with Army awaiting the opportunity to tie the game.

On Army's bench, Assistant Coach Blaik argued vehemently that Army should try to pass for the game-tying extra point. Because Rockne was employing a nine-man line to rush the pants off the kicker, Blaik figured it would be relatively easy, despite the weather, to float a pass over the defenders for the extra point. (There was no two-point conversion then.) But Ralph Sasse refused to take Blaik's advice. He wanted to go for the point in an orthodox way, as he emphasized to Blaik how slippery the ball was for passing. So in came the undersized Chuck Broshous, Army's dropkicking specialist, who, in an earlier game against Yale, had tied the game with an extra point in equally dismal weather. Decked out in warm, dry clothes, with dry shoes on his feet, Broshous used his sweater to wipe off the pigskin. Then he stepped back to the twelve-yard-line, where he waited for the pass from center. But the swarming forward line of the Irish never allowed Broshous to swing his foot against the ball. Thus, several plays later, the triumph belonged to Notre Dame by a single point.

Rockne was overjoyed at the victory, despite the narrow margin. But in his euphoria he also appreciated how distraught Broshous must be. So he paid a visit to the gloom-filled West Point locker room after the game. First Sasse came over to him to extend congratulations. Then the Notre Dame coach approached Broshous, sitting hunched over on a bench, with tears streaming down his cheeks. Putting his arm around Broshous's shoulder, Rockne spoke to him softly. "Don't let this get you down," he said. "There'll be other games for you to win."

The moment was typical of Rockne. Most assuredly he loved the taste of victory, but he never forgot how difficult defeat was for others. Rockne's ability to empathize with his foes, even after a game as brutal as this one, was his finest character trait.

Rockne's relationship with West Point, its players, and its ruling class, had always been congenial and exemplary. His understanding of Broshous's feelings underlined the continuing nature of that relationship. Seventeen years earlier Rockne, as a player, had helped to initiate the rivalry with Army. As a coach he had expanded and nourished this fusion between two great schools to the point where it had become a fixture in the minds of millions of college football fans.

It remained for Rockne to face the last hurdle in the path of another unbeaten season. With eighteen consecutive victories over two years, Notre Dame would now play the University of Southern California, which had won recognition as a "wonder team" of the era. Under Jones, a Phillips Exeter Academy and Yale product, USC had a remarkably efficient team in 1930. Two of their backs, Ernie Pinckert and Gus Shaver, were of All-America quality. Though the Trojans had lost one game to Washington State, 7–6, they had trounced other teams by mind-boggling scores. UCLA went down by 52–0, Utah State by 65–0, Stanford by 42–12, California by 74–0, and Hawaii by 52–7. By racking up such horrendous margins—even though some of these badly licked foes were working at de-emphasizing their football programs—USC came into the game with Notre Dame as the favorite. This was a strange state of affairs, for many, including Grantland Rice, regarded this Notre Dame team, with its splendid leader, Carideo, as the best collection of football talent ever assembled. "They have done all that was asked of them," wrote Rice, "considering that they were not mounted on motorcycles and armed with machine guns . . . they had all the in-gredients, but its four main features were speed and skill, brains and courage."

That USC was favored suited Rockne just fine. Playing an un-derdog role was perfect for him, especially because his team would be playing in USC's Los Angeles backyard, with more than seventy-five thousand fans screaming at them. However, it was not certain that the coach, still plagued by phlebitis, would accompany the team to California. He acknowledged that he wasn't feeling up to par, and the team doctors had been urging him to report for an-other checkup at the Mayo Clinic. But Rockne always acted on his feelings and emotions. Those, of course, dictated that he would go with his boys to the West Coast. How could he not be around for a game that was being hyped everywhere as "another battle of the century" and in which his team was seeking to put the finishing touches on perhaps its greatest season? With the glamorous Hol-lywood community scrambling to buy up the best seats for the game (by this time many of the film community's stars had come to regard Rockne, that consummate actor, as one of their own), how could Rockne deny himself the chance to be a signal part of all of this melodrama and ballyhoo? While USC's players were constantly pursued by Hollywood's flappers and would-be Clara Bows, Rockne made certain that his own players were all business.

On the way to California the Notre Dame squad stopped off at Tucson, Arizona, for a strategic pause in the journey and also to conduct "secret" practice sessions. A main problem facing Notre Dame now was finding an adequate replacement for Savoldi. "Moon" Mullins had been filling in well, but in the Army game his knee had been so badly bruised that he couldn't possibly play against USC. The only back left on Rockne's roster was sophomore Dan Hanley, who had no game experience as a fullback.

Before the first practice session at the University of Arizona Stadium Rockne, playful as ever, summoned a few friendly reporters. He informed them that he had concocted an "innocent" little scheme about which he'd been thinking for a few days.

"People always expect me to pull a rabbit out of my hat," he said. "So I'm going to give them one. I'm switching Bucky O'Connor from halfback to fullback, but keep that under *your* hats. . . ." So five thousand people showed up to watch the practice, an extraordinary number of folks, enticed by all of the pregame flummery, and they saw "Hanley" at fullback. In reality it was Paul "Bucky" O'Connor, wearing Hanley's usual number. Rockne kept playing along with this deception as he continued to tell other members of the press (who hadn't been let in on the fact that Hanley was really O'Connor) that "Hanley" was going to be a fine replacement for Savoldi and Mullins. Meanwhile, O'Connor kept up his side of the bargain as he brandished Hanley's number to certify the gag. When writers clustered around "Hanley" and asked him how he felt playing under such pressure in such a monumental game, Bucky O'Connor performed his role with finesse.

In a final practice session in Arizona, Rockne revealed that it was still possible for him to return to Notre Dame before the game with USC. His gut feeling, he said, was that his players weren't charged up sufficiently for the USC game. If that was the case, he grumbled, there was no reason for him to hang around. Again Rockne was up to his old tricks, employing his keen understanding of the psychology of the football battlefield.

The reaction of the players to Rockne's gambit was strong disagreement with his remarks. They wanted to win every bit as much as he did, and they demonstrated this by loudly chanting the Notre Dame Victory March in the locker room. Rockne had to be impressed by such esprit de corps, though he had probably never doubted it for a minute.

However, he wasn't through getting into the psyches of his men. Before the game he conspired with his former associate Tom Lieb in another round of skulduggery that was designed to stimulate rage among his troops. Now coaching at Loyola (in California), Lieb issued a statement to the newspapers averring that USC was too strong for Notre Dame and that Rockne had no talented substitute for Savoldi and Mullins. Lieb did everything but declare that his revered mentor was shy on brains and desire. When the quotes appeared in the Los Angeles papers, Rockne clipped them and posted them on the locker-room bulletin board. This was not the first or the last time that a crafty manager or coach had used such a device to get his players aroused. The suggestion that Lieb had turned on his former team, and its coach, was swallowed whole by the Notre Dame boys. They angrily accused Lieb of selling out.

In time, Lieb made it plain that he had actually joined with Rockne in this chicanery. Writing to Francis Wallace, Lieb declared: "A thing that has never been cleared up and left me a black sheep with some Notre Dame alumni and friends is that I picked USC to win . . . we played the act well and it was one of Rock's greatest team preparations. The boys were really poisoned against Lieb."

Considering what occurred on the afternoon of December 6, Rockne didn't have to bestir himself with his conspiracies. Whether or not his team had been inspired by his goading, the Notre Damers turned out to be entirely too much for the favored USC. And O'Connor emerged at the center of the masterful victory—almost as if Rockne had planned it. On an early play in the game O'Connor ran eighty yards for a touchdown, in what has been described as a "poem of gridiron power and poise." For the remainder of the day O'Connor, running like a man possessed, ate up almost as much yardage as all of USC's backs combined. Whether Hanley could have done the same thing is beside the point; O'Connor *did* it, while masquerading as Hanley. USC was never in the ball game, going down to defeat, 27–0.

There were postgame comments in the press about Rockne's flimflamming. Some reporters were critical of Rockne's tactics. Were such tricks necessary? these writers asked. Did Rockne really have to pull such a stunt with O'Connor, when his team was obviously so crammed with talent? Did any one of the Notre Dame players believe Rockne when he threatened to go home?

However, in Notre Dame circles the victory, the tenth of the season, and the rousing valedictory to still another unbeaten season under Rockne, was greeted with acclaim. Even beyond the elms and oaks of South Bend, the supportive roars went up from the general public. This Catholic institution, now regarded as college football's dynasty, seemed to have broken down many barriers of bias and ignorance.

When the team arrived back in Chicago, thousands paraded and lined the streets in the team's honor as ticker tape flew as thick as a snowstorm. There was a parade a few days later in New York, in the chill of early December, as a prelude to still another expression of warmth in South Bend. It seemed like everyone in the Indiana town was there, as all business came to a standstill. Pre-Christmas cheer was in the air, but this celebration was not for Santa Claus. It was for Rockne and his remarkable squad, now acknowledged by the experts as the country's greatest team. Grantland Rice, the ultimate fan of Rockne, had been writing this for a long time. Frank Carideo, himself, thought this was the best team he'd ever played on. Who could disagree with him?

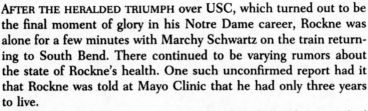

21

A Final Flight

AFTER THE HERALDED TRIUMPH over USC, which turned out to be the final moment of glory in his Notre Dame career, Rockne was alone for a few minutes with Marchy Schwartz on the train returning to South Bend. There continued to be varying rumors about the state of Rockne's health. One such unconfirmed report had it that Rockne was told at Mayo Clinic that he had only three years to live.

"How much longer are you going to coach?" Schwartz asked Rockne.

Rockne gazed out of the train window. Then he looked at Schwartz. "When autumn comes and the leaves fall off the trees," he responded, "I'll be on the football field."

What followed in the last days of 1930 was confirmation of Rockne's continued commitment to football. After all of the stress of the campaign, Rockne was approached by his pal Mayor Walker, who sought to raise money for those who had suffered from the Great Depression. Things had gotten so bad, remarked comedian Groucho Marx, "that I saw pigeons feeding the people in Central Park." If Rockne could help the people of New York, Walker, who "wore the city like a lapel in his boutonniere," as author Gene Fowler wrote, would be delighted. Especially taken with Rockne and Notre Dame, as so many other New Yorkers were, Walker proposed a charity game between some of Rock's former stars and the professional New York Giants. The contest would be held at the Polo Grounds on December 14.

At first Rockne, fatigued from the ordeal of the season, turned Walker down. But when Walker assured him that such a contest could raise needed money for unfortunates living in "Hoovervilles" on the banks of New York's rivers, Rockne relented. Walker's other argument was also persuasive: Once and for all, he said, such a game would determine how good the upstart pros really were, even though the Giants of that year weren't a particularly good team.

Walker made Rockne agree that the entire Four Horsemen backfield would show up for the game. These fellows, as well as other former Irish stars, with their bulging waistlines and shortness of breath, didn't find the prospect of such a game very appealing. But when Rockne sent out the clarion call, they came.

New York's dapper playboy mayor, Jimmy Walker, got Rockne's help for a 1930 charity contest at the Polo Grounds. Courtesy: Associated Press.

Prior to the game, Walker presided over a much-publicized reception for the Notre Dame volunteers. The glow left from this event caused Rockne openly to suggest that this game might actually resolve the college boys versus pros controversy, always good for a rainy-day story in the newspapers. Or was the grand old salesman just helping to sell tickets?

As he had done before, Rockne held a secret practice for his men at the Polo Grounds, with no press permitted on the premises. Even the desks of the secretaries who worked for the Giants' baseball club were turned around so they couldn't view the proceedings through the windows. "We've got something up our sleeves," promised Rockne, singing his same old refrain.

Rockne delivered a pregame pep talk in which he emphasized that the Giants were slow, overrated, and overweight. Obviously he hadn't paused to inspect the girth of his own players. "Go out there and score a few times on passes," he advised, "then go on defense." It all sounded good and it was typical Rockne. But it was also totally unrealistic, as Rockne must have known. Under the direction of the dour Oklahoman Coach Steve Owen, and Benny Friedman, a former All-America quarterback from Michigan, the Giants quickly romped to a 15–0 halftime lead, sparked by Friedman's pinpoint passing and aided by Stuhldreher's inability to get off a pass from behind his own goal line.

Sensing that the second half would be equally disastrous, Rockne literally threw his team at the mercy of the Giants. He dispatched an emissary into the Giants' locker room, with a plea to Coach Owen. "For heaven's sake, I came here to help charity and at a lot of trouble," was Rockne's message. "You're making us look bad. Slow up, will you? I don't want to go home to be laughed at."

Owen's response was as charitable as the event itself. He withdrew Friedman and most of his other regulars from the game, keeping the final score to 22–0, which seemed to be a tribute to Owen's compassion and Rockne's reputation. The game did turn out to be a financial success—a check for $115,000 was put in Mayor Walker's hands. But it was hardly a way for Rockne to end his greatest season, one in which Notre Dame became the first school ever to win consecutive national titles in college football.

As the winter came on, Rockne had to decide, once and for all, what his future would be like. He was still troubled about his phlebitis, as were his doctors. The lure of big money, without having to coach or win football games, was very seductive. However, how long could Rockne go on being a marketing executive for Studebaker if he wasn't the world's greatest, *active* football coach? Once he disappeared from the limelight of the gridiron game, would his syndicated columns, his football clinics, his investments and movie offers remain steadfast?

However, it would be difficult for any man who was at the peak of his profession to turn his back on a milieu that had won him such fame, glory, pleasure, and money. Now Rockne was up there, in a nation that cherished its sports icons, with the Babe, the intrepid transatlantic flier Lindbergh and dethroned heavyweight champ Dempsey. In his own profession Rockne had risen above all others. To reject this game and no longer to work with young men was simply too much to ask of him, even if continuing with it was bound to take a heavy toll on his body and mind. After all, in 1931 Rockne would only be forty-three years old.

"They tell me that I have to learn to rest," said Rockne, who was still instructed to wear a long rubber bandage around one leg, "but it's one of the toughest things I've ever handled."

In mid-March of 1931 Rockne's yearly arrangement with Studebaker was continued, thus assuring him of extra money. His role mainly was to travel around the country addressing sales meetings of the company. He generally used airplanes in his travels, for, like another popular figure of the era, Will Rogers, he had become part of "the movable feast for the famous," as writer Richard Schickel had once described the group. Rockne was one of those corporate trailblazers in the air, long before the average person had investigated the insides of an airplane. In his desire to save time and energy, Rockne had been willing to accept the risk of air travel, which was not insignificant at the time.

Those who knew Rockne well realized that he thrived with constant competition. But his desire for money wasn't far behind competition in his priorities. His yearly coaching salary at Notre Dame was still only ten thousand dollars, although he had been promised more money in the near future. However, regardless of how much Rockne needed and wanted income, he still drew the line at the vaudeville stage, even when he again was offered a lucrative deal for a ten-week tour at a reported seven thousand dollars per week. Rockne would only go so far in the exploitation of his own considerable talent.

Constantly badgered by his friends in the press to sum up his years at Notre Dame and to give personal evaluations of his teams and players, Rockne voiced his opinions, scarcely suspecting that such words would amount to a valedictory. His teams of 1929 and 1930, he said, probably were his best. Carideo, the quarterback of those teams, was his favorite, despite his "cockiness." Quarterbacks earned the right to be cocky, he pointed out, "especially when they sincerely believe in themselves. Carideo did believe in himself. When the game started, I let Carideo run it."

But Rockne insisted he still had a soft spot in his heart for the "old Four Horsemen." He had great admiration for them and the team that they led for their "poise, mentally and physically . . . somehow they seemed to be able to go to town whenever the occasion demanded. In their senior year they had every game won even before they played it." He regarded the Horsemen as wonderful athletes who understood the psychology of keeping the other fellow off balance.

Did Rockne have any misgivings about anything in his career? Yes, he said, singling out an instance when he castigated a player whose injury he had once questioned. At a victory dinner for his national championship squad he made a public apology to this Notre Damer. But there was one thing that Rockne would never apologize for to his critics—that was for "overemphasizing" football or for any of his battles with Notre Dame's athletic board and faculty. These were involvements that represented his basic philosophy; he was not about to undercut his own lifetime of effort. In addition, he always believed that by opening up Notre Dame's schedule to schools all over the country, including the Far West, he was raising money for Notre Dame's future. Also, it was his firm belief that the more his young men traveled the length and breadth of America, the more people would come to appreciate Notre Dame as an institution. (The negative aspect of Rockne's emphasis on football was that in many circles South Bend came to be regarded as little more than a place to play football.)

Although Rockne rarely chose to talk about it, his most invaluable contribution to college football was his role in the development of a whole colony of coaches. He was responsible for the coaching careers of more men than any other coach of his time, or any time. His disciples coached from coast to coast, at Holy Cross and Columbia in the East, to Santa Clara in the Far West. One of his ex-players even coached at Sing Sing prison in upstate New York. Elmer Layden went to Duquesne and later to Notre Dame; Marchy Schwartz to Stanford. Clipper Smith had any number of ports of call, from Gonzaga to Lafayette. Frank Thomas became famous at Alabama; Jim Crowley was at Michigan State and Fordham; Harry Mehre was at Georgia and Mississippi, Eddie Anderson at Holy Cross and Iowa. Curly Lambeau coached in the pros for years. Noble Kizer was at Purdue, Rip Miller at Navy. Lieb went to Loyola in Los Angeles and Florida. Carideo coached at Missouri. On and on the list went. In all, forty-one undergraduates became head coaches at other schools, as well as Notre Dame.

He was a teacher par excellence and reaped great enjoyment out of seeing his disciples move into the front ranks of the coaching field. The most dramatic example was that of the intense Frank Leahy, who played tackle on Rockne's last three teams. Leahy's final year at Notre Dame was marked by a leg that had been badly damaged in a preseason scrimmage. Leahy's playing time was cut down severely, but he never lost his spirit. Rockne was so impressed by Leahy's attitude that he invited the young man to join him when he went to the Mayo Clinic. In the few days that Rockne was there the two roomed together. It was during that time that Leahy revealed to Rockne that he wanted to become a coach.

The first chance that Rockne got, he helped Leahy to realize that ambition. Rockne had always been well connected at Georgetown, where his good friend Lou Little had coached before moving to Columbia. Little's successor, Tommy Mills, hired Leahy as an assistant, thus beginning a most productive career for Leahy. He was head coach at Boston College in 1939 and 1940. By 1941 Leahy was called to Notre Dame as head coach. He stayed until 1943, when he joined the Navy during World War II. Returning to Notre Dame in 1946, Leahy coached until ill health forced his retirement in 1953. While at Notre Dame, in his two tours of duty, Leahy put together six unbeaten seasons and five national championships, coming close to outdoing his own mentor.

Marchy Schwartz, who put in a stint at Stanford in the 1940s after working as an assistant coach at Notre Dame and Chicago, said he owed everything to Rockne. "We were everywhere," Schwartz once remarked, referring to the ubiquity of Notre Damers teaching football across the land. But he added, with great conviction, that there was never another Rockne.

In 1931 Rockne's superiors were firmly against his accepting outside work. They feared for his health and also thought it might be a distraction from his coaching duties. Rockne's spectacular overall record of 105 victories, 12 defeats, and 5 ties, for a percentage of

.881, should have been enough to deflect such reasoning. None-theless, some of the administrators at Notre Dame wanted to curtail his moonlighting. When they heard that he had an offer from Universal Pictures in Hollywood to appear in a football movie for a reported fifty thousand dollars, they suggested that he turn it down. But Rockne appeared to welcome the proposal, even after informing Father O'Donnell that he wasn't really interested. More accurate proof of his intentions was an airplane trip to Hollywood that he scheduled on his agenda for the last day of March.

Before going to the West Coast, Rockne flew down to Coral Gables, Florida, where his family was spending the winter in a small rented house. Bonnie shared her husband's enthusiasm for the racehorses at Hialeah racetrack, and she felt it was a splendid way for him to relax. For a while he didn't have to think of his players, or hatch new strategies for the coming season of 1931. However, the notion that Rockne's fertile mind could ever be removed from his duties at South Bend was preposterous. With an eye always on tomorrow, he simply didn't enjoy "doing nothing."

Following a week in the sun at Coral Gables, Rockne returned to Notre Dame to make further preparations for his journey to California. By this time he had also informed Father O'Donnell that any motion picture in which he participated would be "instructive and educational" and thus a benefit to all Notre Damers. From South Bend he went to Chicago, where he spent a few hours with his mother. Then he took a night train to Kansas City, where he could visit with his sons, Bill and Knute, Jr., who were attending Pembroke Country Day School there. An old friend, Dr. D. M. Nigro, who knew Rockne from his early days at Notre Dame, was also on hand in Kansas City to spend some time with him. One of the last things Rockne had to say to Dr. Nigro was that he was sure the weather would be fine for flying.

Rockne's doctors were not enamored of his flying around the country, for they believed it could be a further strain on his physical condition. But they couldn't talk him out of it, for Rockne felt that air travel was the most practical way for him to travel. "With a good pilot and a good plane, it's as safe as any other method," he insisted. (In the year before Rockne's flight there had been six major accidents in planes, a fact that Rockne must have known.) He argued further that planes were certainly more comfortable than trains or cars. Rockne never appeared in the least anxious about the possible dangers of flying. However, when friends wished him "soft landings," he would remind them politely that they really meant to say, "happy landings."

At the Kansas City airport on March 31, 1931, Rockne met his five fellow passengers, as well as the two pilots, Robert Fry and Herman "Jess" Mathias. At thirty-two years old, Fry was a veteran of more than four thousand hours in the air. Rockne was the most famous of these travelers, who represented varied occupations: sporting goods salesman, interior designer, advertising man, insurance salesman, and produce man.

As the group waited to take off in the plane, an eighty-thousand-dollar Fokker Super Trimotor commissioned in October 1929, a light snow began to fall. Rockne had expected that his boys would come to the airport to wave good-bye, but they arrived shortly after the plane left the ground at 9:15 A.M. Eight short of capacity, the aircraft had no difficulty ascending, for it carried only two hundred pounds of luggage, including a mail load of fewer than sixty-five pounds. Generally, the Fokkor, one of Transcontinental and Western Air's fleet, cruised at 120 miles per hour. As the craft approached Chase County, in eastern Kansas, it became immersed in a thick fog, causing Fry to bring the plane down low. Mathias was still in contact with Wichita by radio. Nothing untoward seemed to be happening until he sent an ominous message that he "didn't have time to talk."

Several ranchers working with their cattle near the tiny town of Bazaar looked up to see the plane emerging from a big cloud. The snow had stopped, but the clouds still hung low over the drenched tall grass country, later made famous by Dorothy and Toto in the movie *The Wizard of Oz*. Ninety degrees off course, the plane suddenly lost part of its left wing and seemed to be circling aimlessly.

"It sounded like a couple of cars racing down the road," said one observer, who was shelving bags of corn in the area. The stuttering and backfiring had been caused by Fry closing down the throttles to lessen the chances of an explosion on impact. As it neared the ground, the plane turned over in one last violent spasm. Crippled and out of control, the aircraft plunged into the prairie snow.

Rushing to the scene in his father's 1930 Chevy, Easter Heathman, then fourteen years old, vividly recalled what he saw for the *South Bend Tribune:* "The tail was sticking straight out of the ground. There were five bodies that had been thrown west of the plane. Three bodies were still in the wreckage. The ambulances showed up and were carrying them off in stretchers. I remember seeing a rubber wrap that had fallen out and put it back on a stretcher. That was Rockne's. The wrap was for his phlebitis."

A call had gone out to nearby Cottonwood Falls, to the west of Emporia, for emergency medical assistance. Within a short time, the morbidly curious, as well as souvenir hunters, started to gather at the scene of the crash. Within a three-hundred-foot radius, the bodies, most crushed beyond recognition ("like jelly," wrote one observer), were strung out, along with the plane's detritus of mailbags, letters, baggage, and articles of clothing.

The local sheriff assigned a group of prisoners to the ghoulish task of picking up the debris, but a number of Kansans from the surrounding area had beaten them to the punch. "It was like a great carcass scavenged by hyenas," wrote author William Least-Heat Moon.

Not long after the tragedy a Kansas columnist wryly suggested that "if Rockne's pockets contained all the articles which local souvenir hunters claim to have removed from them, it must have been that extra weight that brought down the plane." When Rockne's remains were assembled, one report stated that his rosary was clamped tightly in his hand. This dramatic detail, adding to the growing Rockne legend, was never confirmed by those who were engaged in placing the bodies in caskets.

For many the shattering news of Rockne's demise became an unforgettable moment, triggering expressions of sorrow that would normally have been reserved for one's own family. Later, millions of people could tell you where they were, and what they were doing, when they heard that this extraordinary man had been killed. Americans would react similarly to the deaths of such figures as Will Rogers, Marilyn Monroe, Franklin D. Roosevelt, John F. Kennedy, Robert Kennedy, Martin Luther King, Jr., and Princess Diana. But Rockne's death in an accident marked the first time that an entire country appeared to be united in its grief.

Obviously, Rockne had touched millions with his achievements, his competitiveness, his quick wit, his nimble mind, his optimism, and his outstanding leadership qualities. Somehow, his personality had connected with people who had never even seen a Notre Dame football game. Included in this group were numbers of Irish, Catholics, Protestants, Jews, and lower- and middle-class working people who sensed that Rockne's values and aspirations were their own. To some, his violent death at such an early age sadly signaled

The great coach died in the twisted wreckage of a Fokker Super Trimotor on March 31, 1931, in Bazaar, Kansas. Courtesy: UPI-Corbis-Bettmann.

the end of an era, in which he was one of those larger-than-life personalities who had seized the country's imagination.

It didn't take long for a rush of tributes and eulogies to pour forth from admirers and friends, from the man in the street to the man in the White House.

President Hoover said that Rockne's passing was "a national disaster." He told Bonnie Rockne that "every American grieves with you." Notre Dame's president, Father O'Donnell, accurately echoed the feeling on campus when he said that "Nothing has ever happened at Notre Dame that has so shocked the faculty and students." Rockne's longtime assistant Hunk Anderson had a hard time expressing his feelings. "I just can't believe it," he said. "He was part of Notre Dame; it can never be the same without him."

King Haakon VII of Norway sent a message of condolences to the Rockne family. From Yankee Stadium, where so much of Rockne's history was written, messages came from Babe Ruth and Lou Gehrig. Jack Dempsey wired Bonnie Rockne that he was trying to share her sorrow with her. From Washington, D.C., came eulogies from Secretary of War Patrick J. Hurley and from the chief of staff, Major General Douglas MacArthur, the man who had once thought of hiring Rockne to coach at West Point. Former president Calvin Coolidge talked about how Rockne taught the game of football. "No bluff would answer," said Coolidge. "Fifty percent would not do. His passing mark was 100 percent. He required perfection.

That was why men honored and loved him. That was the source of his power."

Will Rogers, who shared Rockne's passion for flying (and who would himself die in an air crash in Alaska four years later), wrote in his popular syndicated column that Rockne was a true national hero. What Rogers always had emphasized about Rockne was his humility and his genuine connection to people.

Major Ralph I. Sasse, whose Army team had fought the Irish on the gridiron, said that Rockne was undoubtedly the football genius of the twentieth century. "His code was simple," remarked Sasse. "Modest in victory, stout in defeat, generous to an opponent, and always fair. In my opinion his 1930 team was the greatest of all time."

The captain of the Four Horseman team, Adam Walsh, spoke for the legions who had played for Rockne: "His deep understanding of human nature caused his great spirit to be radiated to thousands that never knew him or even saw the man. To the boys who knew him well, he was an even greater man. His courage, infectious spirit of camaraderie, and sparkling humor, coupled with modesty, made him the man that we loved. Yes, we loved him as a father," said Walsh, who had become head line coach at Yale.

Elmer Layden, that wisp of a Horseman, could say only that he couldn't believe his friend and coach was gone. Lou Little, now at Columbia, where Rockne had once been wooed, had always regarded Knute as a close friend. He felt that "our leader has been taken away." Little recalled that "A coach's relationship with the player does not end with the final game of the year. Men who played football for Rockne constantly came to talk to him and get his advice, about life after football and their business chances. He always had time for them."

Many members of the press, including Grantland Rice, sent wires to Bonnie Rockne expressing their sadness. Rice was also moved to write his typical doggerel: "Yes, other teams upon remembered fields will hold their sway; but will they bring the same far-lasting dreams to span the sunset of an older day?" Joe Vila of the *New York Sun*, considered one of the top sports editors of his time, wrote that Rockne's place in the football world was no less outstanding than that of John McGraw in baseball. John Kieran of the *New York Times* had a wit as sharp as Rockne's, but when the occasion demanded it he could be serious. He quoted Shelley in paying a final tribute to the coach: "The soul of Adonais, like a star,

Beacons from the abode where the Eternal are." The editorial writer of the *Cleveland Press* said that Rockne was "The Buffalo Bill" of his generation, while the popular newspaper poet Edgar Guest said, "Boys down through the future will remember Rockne and be brave; they will remember him and be clean."

Newspaper editorials, generally reserved for pompous phrases about high and low finance and the peccadilloes of politicians, practically promoted Rockne into secular sainthood, a role that Rockne would have shunned. This was not a time to undercut the public perception of the man, although one New York editorial emphasized that Rockne was mainly a promoter belonging in the world of those hippodroming geniuses Tex Rickard of the boxing milieu and the circus impresario Phineas T. Barnum.

Ordinary folks of all backgrounds, religious persuasions, and occupations, drawn to the immigrant experience of the departed coach, flooded the Rockne family with telegrams, letters, and condolence cards. In the hours preceding the funeral in Holy Week, an entire country seemed to be mourning this stocky little man, for a while ignoring their own empty stomachs and wallets. "The Star-Spangled Banner," adopted as the national anthem in 1931, had momentarily been replaced by the Notre Dame Victory March.

Some, such as Pegler, who had been outspokenly caustic about Rockne's overcommercialization of the sport, now softened their messages. *De mortuis nihil nisi bonum.* In truth, Pegler had admired Rockne, even if he had been sardonic about Rockne's physical appearance and manner. "The youth of America had an idol in Rockne," Pegler acknowledged.

Avowed enemies of Rockne such as Stagg and Yost, appeared to be humbled by his death. Stagg said that he'd always been impressed by Rockne's "human qualities and unselfish personality," while Yost, who had tangled with Rockne on any number of occasions, admitted that Rockne was "football's most colorful figure."

In recapitulating the events of Rockne's career, the mythologists were already diligently rewriting the final moments of his life. The fact that he had died on the way to work on a motion picture, to be called *The Spirit of Notre Dame,* was not considered an ideal scenario for the eulogists. So a substitute story was contrived, suggesting that Rockne had gone to California to fulfill a promise to a friend. He was, according to this version, supposed to make a speech and then return immediately to South Bend. Rockne himself probably would have laughed at such bowdlerizing, for he was never shy about his extracurricular activities. Christy Walsh, so instrumental in carving out the images of other icons such as Babe Ruth, Christy Mathewson, and Lou Gehrig, continued to spread the word that Rockne had died while trying to help others.

Although he was hardly maladroit in the art of self-promotion, Rockne had never meant to be canonized. That he would have wanted his biographers to present him in a worshipful perspective was assuredly not the case, for he would have been the first to confess that he possessed any number of warts and flaws. But many at Notre Dame, a school eager for acceptance and still battling residual prejudice, were not going to go out of their way to diminish the life of Knute Rockne. Notre Dame needed its heroes; the sports world needed its heroes. And so did the country, floundering in the dismal Depression. It was not a time for knocking an icon off his pedestal.

A grieving Jesse Harper accompanied his old friend's body back to South Bend, in preparation for the funeral. As Rockne's blue-and-gold-draped casket arrived in Chicago, more than fifteen thousand people congregated at the railroad station. Heading for the funeral, Rockne's sons reluctantly posed for newspaper photographers, at a moment when they would have preferred their privacy.

On April 4, the day of the funeral, everything in South Bend seemed to come to a halt. All flags were at half mast, and businesses shut down. But even outside of the cloistered world of Notre Dame, Rockne's memory was honored. Many chose to close their shops for the day, further proof of the hold that this man had on many of America's 125 million citizens. People around the country mourned for the football coach, just as the young men in Notre Dame's dormitories spoke about him in whispers, their heads bowed.

King Haakon of Norway was represented at the funeral by six of his countrymen, including Norway's envoy in Chicago. Bonnie Rockne wanted all of the boys who had played for her husband to attend, if they could ("I want them near him to the last," she said). Most of them did come to the hushed Church of the Sacred Heart. As a light rain continued to fall on the worshipers the Four Horsemen, Gus Dorais, Jack Chevigny, Jack Cannon, Adam Walsh, Frank Carideo, Marchy Schwartz, Marty Brill, Ray Eichenlaub, Tommy Yarr, and so many others joined their onetime opponents from Northwestern, the University of Chicago and other local

At Rockne's funeral in South Bend several of his "boys," including Frank Carideo (left), served as pall bearers. Courtesy: UPI-Corbis-Bettmann.

schools, in the chapel. Because the chapel could accommodate, at most, fourteen hundred people, the overflow had to wait quietly in the churchyard. The mayors of Chicago and Philadelphia were there, and naturally so was Jimmy Walker, who brought along a wreath from the "sixty thousand unemployed in New York City," whom Rockne had helped in his last charity game. Fifty members of the press gathered, while CBS radio broadcast the services nationally.

Rockne's elderly mother was there, now a white-haired woman, who had instilled her own set of values into her son. Rockne's frenetic schedule, however, had hardly given him much time to visit often with her in his last years. His sisters, one of whom had urged her brother to attend Notre Dame, were there, too. Members of Rockne's last championship team of 1930 served as pallbearers, while several of his graduating class of 1914 stood by as honor guards. Then, to the strains of the "Miserere" and the "Subvenite," the casket was carried to the front of the church. As President Charles O'Donnell began his eulogy, several planes roared overhead, a dramatic reminder of how Rockne's life had been suddenly snuffed out.

O'Donnell's words were directed not only at his immediate, attentive audience but at that large group in the rest of the United States who were listening to the radio broadcast. "In this Holy Week of Christ's passion and death there has occurred a tragic event which accounts for our presence here today," President O'Donnell began. "Knute Rockne is dead. And who was he? *Ask* the president of the United States, who dispatched a personal message of tribute to his memory and comfort to his bereaved family. *Ask* the king of Norway, who sends a special delegation as his personal representatives to this solemn service. *Ask* the several state legislatures, now sitting, that have passed resolutions of sympathy and condolences. *Ask* the thousands of newspapermen whose labor of love in his memory has stirred a reading public of millions of Americans. *Ask* men and women from every walk of life, ask the children, ask the boys of America. *Ask* any and all of these, who was this man whose death has struck the nation with dismay and has everywhere bowed heads in grief?"

President O'Donnell reminded his listeners that "We are here only as a handful of his friends." Then he proceeded to answer his own questions. "I think, supremely, he loved his neighbor, his fellow man, with genuine, deep love. In an age that has stamped itself as the era of the 'go-getter,' he was a 'go-giver' . . . he was quite elementarily human and Christian, giving himself, spending himself—like water, not for himself, but for others. He has cast away to keep, he has lost his way to find it."

There were those who might have countered that the restless Rockne was, indeed, a "go-getter." After all, he wouldn't have been Rockne without his unleashed ambition and assertiveness. But there was no quibbling with President O'Donnell on that mournful day.

As the last of President O'Donnell's words echoed throughout the chapel, the casket was borne to Highland Cemetery, on Portage Avenue, some two miles from the center of the Notre Dame campus, which Rockne had helped to make famous throughout his adopted country. There, near an ancient tree named Council Oak, where Native Americans had once held council with their friends and enemies, Rockne was laid to rest.

Beyond the myths, the All-Americans, the coaches he tutored, and the many championship seasons he produced, Rockne has a legacy at Notre Dame—and elsewhere—that has been enduring. He made the Fighting Irish into a national institution, and the powers-that-be at Notre Dame were determined to maintain his winning tradition. There was inordinate pressure on Anderson, Rockne's successor, but in his three difficult years at the helm he was not able to do better than 16–9, with two ties, hardly comparable to Rockne's winning percentage. However, others who coached in the years after Anderson, principally Leahy, Ara Parseghian, and Lou Holtz, managed to survive the political wars at South Bend as they led the team to many remarkable seasons. In effect they followed in Rockne's footsteps even as they tried to evade the stomach-wrenching traumas that inevitably went with the Notre Dame coaching portfolio.

In time, Notre Dame became a constant Saturday afternoon attraction on television as well as a frequent competitor in a number of postseason Bowl games. Currently there is national television coverage of every Irish home game. For three decades Notre Dame games have been broadcast nationally on radio by the Mutual Broadcasting System, the type of saturation coverage that Rockne himself envisioned for his team. To this day the networks continue to battle over the rights to showcase Notre Dame each week, increasing the pressures on Irish coaches to keep winning.

The Rockne legend was further burnished with the release of the Warner Brothers film *Knute Rockne: All-American* in 1940. For some years after Rockne's death many at Notre Dame were eager to have a major motion picture produced that would forever preserve his heroic image for future generations of fans. Bonnie Rockne was determined that her husband be portrayed as something more than a football coach. She wanted the emphasis placed on his scholarly attainments and his intellect; the gridiron would play only a subsidiary role. The latter scenario was impossible to expect in such a biographical movie, and Bonnie knew that. However, she did ultimately exercise considerable control over the final script, which was essentially hagiographic.

The movie starred Pat O'Brien, one of Warner's most durable warhorses, as Rockne. Others, including James Cagney, Spencer Tracy of *Boy's Town* fame, and Paul Muni, whose range went from *Scarface* to *Émile Zola*, had also been considered for the part. Also featured in the film was Ronald Reagan, the sports-loving ex-lifeguard from Eureka, Illinois, who played the triple-threat ne'erdo-well Gipp. Years later, when he ran for president of the United States, Reagan was delighted to exploit his favorite movie role, and Republicans were equally happy to refer to their candidate as "The Gipper." Some of the scenes in the movie were shot on the South Bend campus, including the site of Rockne's funeral. As sports movies go (in those days all iconoclastic elements were carefully excised) it was a decent, sentimental production that certainly did little to dent Rockne's reputation. However, Reagan's Gipp emerged as the most memorable character in it.

Almost a half century after the release of the movie Rockne became the first football coach—or any athletic coach, for that matter—to be honored by a commemorative stamp. The U.S. Postal Service in 1988 issued such a stamp to dovetail with the hundredth anniversary of Rockne's birth, with the coach joining only seven other figures from the sports world (Babe Zaharias, Bobby Jones, Babe Ruth, Jim Thorpe, Jackie Robinson, Lou Gehrig, and Roberto Clemente) in such an anointment by stamp. The day that the stamp was issued President Reagan delivered a speech at Notre Dame before a capacity crowd of ten thousand at the Joyce Athletic and Convocation Center. It was evident that Rockne remained a truly imperishable figure, a man still much in the minds and hearts of a new legion of football fans.

Index

Printed in the United Kingdom
by Lightning Source UK Ltd.
129661UK00001B/1/A